FATHERING AND CHILD OUTCOMES

FATHERING AND CHILD OUTCOMES

Eirini Flouri

John Wiley & Sons, Ltd

Other Wiley Editorial Offices

John Wiley & Sons Inc., 111 River Street, Hoboken, NJ 07030, USA

Jossey-Bass, 989 Market Street, San Francisco, CA 94103-1741, USA

Wiley-VCH Verlag GmbH, Boschstr. 12, D-69469 Weinheim, Germany

John Wiley & Sons Australia Ltd, 33 Park Road, Milton, Queensland 4064, Australia

John Wiley & Sons (Asia) Pte Ltd, 2 Clementi Loop #02-01, Jin Xing Distripark,
Singapore 129809

John Wiley & Sons Canada Ltd, 22 Worcester Road, Etobicoke, Ontario, Canada
M9W 1L1

Wiley also publishes its books in a variety of electronic formats. Some content that appears
in print may not be available in electronic books.

Library of Congress Cataloging-in-Publication Data
Flouri, Eirini.
    Fathering and child outcomes / Eirini Flouri.
        p. cm.
    Includes bibliographical references and index.
    ISBN 0-470-86167-3 – ISBN 0-470-86168-1
    1. Fatherhood–Psychological aspects. 2. Child development. 3. Child psychology.
I. Title.
HQ756.F593 2005
306.874′2–dc22
                                                                        2004021920
British Library Cataloguing in Publication Data
A catalogue record for this book is available from the British Library
ISBN 0-470-86167-3 (hbk)
ISBN 0-470-86168-1 (pbk)

Typeset in 10/12pt Palatino by Dobbie Typesetting Limited, Tavistock, Devon
Printed and bound in Great Britain by TJ International Ltd, Padstow, Cornwall
This book is printed on acid-free paper responsibly manufactured from sustainable
forestry in which at least two trees are planted for each one used for paper production.

TABLE OF CONTENTS

ABOUT THE AUTHOR

Dr Eirini Flouri is Deputy Director of the Centre for Research into Parenting and Children, University of Oxford, and Lecturer in Statistics, St Hilda's College. Her main research area has been, broadly speaking, life-course development, and more specifically parenting (looking at fathering, in particular, since 2000) and child development in the long term. She has published in the area of economic psychology and especially economic socialisation and consumer values, children's resilience and recovery from emotional and behavioural problems, and children's outcomes associated with father involvement.

PREFACE

What is fathering, and why should we be concerned about its relation to child outcomes? Fathers were often assumed to be on the periphery of children's lives and so of little direct importance to children's development. Since the mid-1980s, however, the 'discovery' of the father, and the role of 'father involvement' in particular, has been one of the major themes in child developmental research and psychological research on fathering which, until then, had scarcely changed in focus from describing what fathers do to discussing what fathers should do with their children. This book summarises the research I carried out (mostly with Ann Buchanan) since 2000 on fathering and children's well-being with funding from the Joseph Rowntree Foundation and the UK Economic and Social Research Council. Children's well-being was mainly operationalised as objective outcomes of functional significance (school achievement, delinquency and employment), subjective assessments of states (happiness, life satisfaction, psychological distress, emotional and behavioural well-being, and academic motivation) and quality of interpersonal relationships (quality of relationships with partners, parents and peers).

Eirini Flouri

Oxford, August 2004

FOREWORD

By Ann Buchanan

As Eirini Flouri notes in Chapter 1, the 'discovery' of the father has been one of the major themes in child developmental research in the past 30 years, but it is only in the last 10 years that the topic has really gained significance. This book brings together the international literature, as well as reporting more than 20 studies by Eirini, using five different data sources spanning more than 40 years. For many years to come, it is likely to be an important reference book for academic researchers on fathering and all those interested in the policy implications of the research. Her meticulous, scholarly and objective approach to the subject, and her many academic papers and conference contributions, ensure that Eirini is now recognised as a world authority on fathering.

Eirini and I started our academic journey of investigation into fathering five years ago. From earlier research with JoAnn Ten Brinke using the National Child Development Study, and other smaller-scale studies, clues were emerging that the role of fathers may be underestimated. As a Centre for Research into Parenting and Children, research on fathering fell right into our remit. Rather than supporting any particular agenda, our interest was simply to learn more about the factors that promoted child well-being. Rather tentatively we put in a bid to the Economic and Social Research Council (ESRC) for research on fathering using the UK's National Child Development Study. This marvellous database, which covers all children born in one week in 1958 (some 17 000 children), has recorded events in children's lives for over 40 years. When the findings were published in 2001, showing strong associations between fathering and a wide range of child outcomes, there was a frenzied response from the world media. In 2001, Eirini was awarded her own ESRC three-year research Fellowship, won against competition from across the UK and the only one awarded on that round for that year. She has used this time to include research on fathering and child well-being from the BSC 70 – another of the UK's great longitudinal cohort studies that started in 1970. During this period, too, a third database came on line. One of the criticisms of the longitudinal cohort studies was that, by their very nature, they could be dated and because of the major changes that have taken place during this period in family life, they may be no longer relevant to modern-day fathering. The 2000 Family at the Millennium Study (FMS) was a cross-sectional study financed by the Joseph Rowntree Foundation (JRF). It offered an opportunity to test out whether things had changed. The JRF survey involved over 2000 teenagers in three secondary schools from different demographic areas, as well as more than 1000 of their parents. Linked to this were two other cross-sectional studies involving a further 2000 or more children. The particular interest of this book, therefore, is that it not only includes a summary of the world literature in each of the areas outlined in the chapters, but it also includes Eirini's own work based on five different data sources and gives clues on the centrality of some themes over time.

Eirini outlines these themes in the nine chapters of her book. Starting with an overview in Chapter 1, she explores fathers in the 'modern' family, cultural differences, the consequences of change, the controversies around family change and then the more focused research that seeks to define more precisely what fathers actually do in the modern family and how child well-being can be measured. Eirini's balanced and scholarly discussion of this highly controversial area sets the tone for the book.

Her second chapter looks at resident fathers' involvement with their school-age children and associated factors. This chapter, reporting findings from both the NCDS and the FMS, raises one of the central themes of the book: the close association between father involvement and mother involvement and the fact that child characteristics are related to the levels of involvement. Here the research raises a central dilemma: Which comes first? Do the characteristics of the child, such as easier behaviour and success in school, encourage more father involvement or is it the other way around? The answer – as Eirini repeatedly reminds us throughout the book – is that we cannot infer causation.

Chapter 3 is an important one, exploring as it does the relationship between father involvement and children's mental health. This chapter reports studies from three data sources: the FMS cross-sectional study, an earlier cross-sectional study of 1344 boys in Britain undertaken in 1999, and the NCDS. Although the evidence is stronger in the cross-sectional studies than the longitudinal, the studies suggest that there is a positive association between father involvement and children's mental health.

Chapter 4, on the relationship between father involvement and children's educational outcomes, describes another area that has attracted considerable attention, in particular from educationalists. The first study using the NCDS shows a strong relationship between fathers' involvement with children at age 7 and educational outcomes at age 20. The second and third studies, based on a cross-sectional study in Britain of 2722 adolescents in 1998/9, perhaps suggests how this may be operationalised. Both mother and father involvement contributed significantly and independently to positive *school attitudes* and, at the bivariate level, father involvement was significantly related to *'career maturity'* or the extent to which the young people had plans for their future working life, knew what they needed to do and the steps to get there. The final study in this section used the 1970 British Cohort Study. Here we see that although fathers' involvement did not predict later educational attainment in men, it did for women, but, in addition, which is perhaps more interesting, it showed that for both genders an internal locus of control was positively related to educational attainment. This may link to the ideas raised in recent research about the importance of young people's 'agency' in education. Young people achieve more where they believe that how hard they work will influence their futures (see Buchanan et al., in press).

Chapter 5 returns to a central concern of those responsible for public policy: aggressive behaviour delinquency in young people, the role of fathers and factors that might predict a reduction in antisocial behaviour. Using data from the NCDS, the first study, as might be predicted, found that for boys, being in trouble with the police was related to low IQ, low father involvement in childhood and parental criminality. The second study, based on cross-sectional data of 1147 adolescents between 14 and 18 in the UK in 2000, found that lack of father and mother involvement was associated with more bullying behaviour in the young person, while the final study based on the NCDS showed that there was some association between a cluster of protective factors, such as good parental relationships at age 16 and a decrease in antisocial behaviour.

In Chapter 6, Eirini suggests that, in addition to the hard outcomes such as mental health and education, there may also be a relationship between father involvements and less tangible outcomes such as relationships in adult life. Using data from the NCDS, Eirini shows that closeness to mothers and fathers in adolescence was related not only to good sibling relationships, but also to marital adjustment at age 33.

Chapter 7 takes the analyses one step further and considers whether, given concerns of welfare dependency, a lack of father involvement in childhood is associated with a greater risk of unemployment, homelessness, living on state benefits, or living in subsidised housing. Here it is helpful to report the negative findings. Although the findings are slightly different for men and women, welfare dependency, as defined, was more usually associated with the absence of a partner, mental health problems (particularly for men), coming from a large family, and low educational attainment rather than a lack of father involvement. The second half of the chapter goes some way towards explaining what may be happening. Financial difficulties in childhood were associated with a lack of materialistic values in later life.

Chapter 8, with the current debates surrounding contact and fathers' rights, also touches on highly topical issues. The question is: What is the relationship between non-resident fathers' involvement and children's psychological outcomes? The starting point was to use data from the FMS to find out the factors associated with non-resident fathers' involvement. Here we see two of the recurring themes throughout the book: fathers' involvement is closely linked to mothers' involvement, and there is likely to be less involvement where there is family conflict. Frequency of non-resident parents' contact was also likely to decline as the years pass following separation. When it comes to emotional well-being, we see the third major theme in the book: family conflict negatively impacts on children. Perhaps more controversially, however, while there was a significant relationship with mother involvement and child well-being there was no significant relationship with father involvement. How can this be? Cautions are attached to this finding because it may be related to the specific features of the data used. Further ideas, however, come from the qualitative element of the JRF study which relates to interviews with resident mothers, fathers and one of their children. This suggested that a central characteristic of the resident fathers is 'being there'. It is not so much what they do, but that they are around to help, advise and support when needed. If 'being there' is an essential attribute of modern-day fathering, it does make it more difficult to impact on child well-being if the father is non-resident. This suggests that non-resident fathers may need to learn a new way of being a 'dad'.

Eirini's final chapter epitomises her scholarly, meticulous and objective approach to her subject. She asks the question we all want to know: Does 'good' fathering promote 'good' children's outcomes? The answer, she says, is 'it depends...'.

> It depends on what we mean by fathering (and 'good' fathering in particular), what children's outcomes we have in mind and what groups of parents and children we look at... Father involvement was sometimes associated with 'good' outcomes. Certain aspects of fathers' involvement, in certain groups of fathers, was associated with certain outcomes, in certain groups of children.

Eirini's careful and well-balanced conclusion makes this book a mine of information. It is in the detail where the clues emerge on how to work with fathers to improve children's well-being.

Dr Ann Buchanan
August 2004

Reference

Buchanan, A., Bennett, F., Ritchie, S., Smith, T., Smith, G., Harker, L. and Vitali, S. (in press). *The impact of government policy on children age 0–13 and their families at risk of social exclusion*. London: SEU.

CHAPTER 1

FATHERING:
A CHANGING PERSPECTIVE

INTRODUCTION

During the last 10 years attention has focused on fathers more than at any time prior to the beginning of the twentieth century mainly because of the rapid pace of family change (i.e. the decline in the traditional household form of a single breadwinner and the growth of dual participant households). The consequences, especially for children, of these changes have long been the subject of research and debate. Subsequently, research on fathering has both expanded considerably and matured scientifically as it started to move away from exploring the consequences of 'father absence' for children to understanding possible mechanisms of influence of fathering in both father-present and father-absent families.

FATHERS AND THE 'MODERN' FAMILY:
THE CURRENT PICTURE

The role of fathers in developed countries has changed over time. In the USA, Demos (1988) discussed how, during the colonial period, fathers were the primary parent and had ultimate say in matters of the child; in the rare case of divorce, the law awarded custody to the father, as mothers were considered too emotional and too indulgent to raise children properly. The advent of industrialisation in the nineteenth century redefined the roles of mothers and fathers, with the role of fathers becoming predominantly that of 'provider', and mothers becoming the parent with primary responsibility for children, and the operation of the household (Demos, 1988). As 'homemakers' in the suburbs mothers became increasingly isolated from life outside the family, mainly because the contributions that they had previously made to the economic well-being of the family decreased. All European countries have also historically given patriarchal authority to the father, although the form that this has taken has varied. In the UK, for instance, equal guardianship rights were not secured by mothers over their children until 1973 (Lewis, 2001b). However, the rapid pace of family change over the past decade has meant that in Britain, for instance, in one generation the numbers marrying have halved, the numbers divorcing have trebled, and the proportion of children born outside of marriage has quadrupled (McRae, 2000). Britain is not alone in experiencing these changes. The most recent (2003) statistics show that all 15 European Union member states have recorded an increase in births outside marriage since the mid-1970s. There are some differences, however. Data for 2000 showed that of the 25 (as of 1 May 2004) European Union countries, Cyprus (2.3%) has the lowest rate followed by Greece (4.1%) and Italy (9.6%). At the end of the scale, the highest percentages are in Denmark (42.6%), France (42.6%), Latvia (43.1%), Sweden (55.5%) and Estonia (56.3%), where over half of all children are born outside marriage (*Eurostat Yearbook*, 2003). At around 40% the UK has a high percentage of live births outside marriage. Most of the increase in the number of births outside marriage has been to cohabiting couples (that is, parents living at the same address). In 2001 three-quarters of births outside marriage in England and Wales were jointly registered by both parents and, of these births, three in four were to parents living at the same address (Office for National Statistics, 2003). The growth in the proportion of births outside marriage, and divorce – in the UK the divorce rate has risen from 2.0 per 1000 married population in 1960 to 13.6 in 1995 (Office for National Statistics, 1998) – has resulted in an increase in lone-parent families. In Spring 2002 a fifth of dependent children in Britain lived in lone-parent families (2% lived in lone-father families, and 19% lived in lone-mother families), almost twice the proportion as in 1981. The current North American picture is not dissimilar, with the latter half of the twentieth century having witnessed a sharp rise in non-marital childbearing in the USA, as well. Although in 1940 only 4% of all births in the USA occurred outside marriage, in 1999 one-third of births were to unmarried mothers (Ventura & Bachrach, 2000). Currently, the proportion of children in the USA who lived with only one parent at some point during their childhood is expected to continue and exceed 50% (Cabrera, Tamis-LeMonda, Bradley, Hofferth & Lamb, 2000). Similarly, although in 1960 only 6% of families in the USA were headed by females in 1998, that proportion had risen to 24% (US Bureau of the Census, 1998). Generally, the percentage of female-headed households (usually, but not necessarily, with dependent children) is very high in some countries. The highest rates of female headship are reported in the African countries of Botswana (47%) and Swaziland (40%), and the Caribbean countries such as the US Virgin Islands (45%) and Haiti (39%). Some rates in the developed countries are at least equally high, ranging from 44% in Slovenia, 42% in Denmark and Finland, and 37% in New Zealand and Sweden (United Nations, 2000).

In addition, 1 in 8 children in the UK is expected to live at some stage before age 16 in a family in which their birth parent has either formed a new partnership or has remarried (Dunn, 2002), whereas in the USA it is estimated that about one-third of children will live with a step-parent, usually a stepfather, before reaching age 18 (Hofferth & Anderson, 2003). In 2000/01 in the UK stepfamilies accounted for 8% of families with dependent children whose head was under age 60. The majority (88%) of these consisted of a couple with one or more children from the previous relationship of the female partner only, as there is a tendency for children to stay with the mother following the break-up of a partnership. These demographic trends suggest that increasing numbers of children grow up in families that do not fit the traditional pattern of two parents with their biological children. This increase of father-absent and stepfather families should be considered alongside the increase of mothers in employment – one of the most dominant and persisting trends in European labour markets, which has also raised questions about the role of fathers. Recent results from the European Labour Force Survey in EU15 showed that among households with two people of working age those with both partners in the labour force were almost twice as numerous in 2000 as those with only one, averaging around 62% in total (Franco & Winqvist, 2002). The UK has experienced a steady increase in the proportion of married women engaged in wage labour, from a figure of 26% in 1951 to 71% in 1991 and, more recently, of married women with a preschool child from 27% in 1973 to 52% in 1994 (Walby, 1997). As a consequence, households supported by a single male earner are now a minority, comprising in 1991 34% of all two-adult households below retirement age, with the contribution of men to overall family income falling from nearly 73% in 1979–81 to 61% in 1989–91 and that of women rising from 15% to nearly 21% (Creighton, 1999). In the USA the proportion of married women engaged in wage labour with preschool children rose from 12% in 1950 to two-thirds in 1997 (Cabrera et al., 2000). Only about one-quarter of children in the USA live in two-parent families supported by a single male earner (Cabrera et al., 2000). Generally over the past two decades, women's economic activity rates increased in all United Nations regions except sub-Saharan Africa, the transition economies of eastern Europe and central Asia, and Oceania. The largest increase occurred in South America, where rates rose from 26% to 45% between 1980 and 1997. The lowest rates were found in northern Africa and western Asia, where less than one-third of women were economically active (United Nations, 2000).

However, recent evidence seems to suggest the relatively slow pace of change in men's contribution to domestic labour, and child care in particular, relative to women's increased participation in the workforce. Sandberg and Hofferth (2001) showed that in the USA children's mean weekly time with fathers increased only marginally between 1981 and 1997, although it increased significantly in families in which mothers were working, and that time with mothers in two-parent families generally increased over the period regardless of whether mothers were working. Sandberg and Hofferth's (2001) conclusion was that assertions that children spend less time with parents today than several decades ago because of changes in maternal labour market behaviour and in patterns of family formation and dissolution were largely unfounded. Yeung, Sandberg, Davis-Kean and Hofferth (2003) showed that on weekdays, fathers' earnings and work hours had a significant negative effect on their involvement with a child, but mothers' work hours or earnings did not have an effect on mothers' involvement, which suggests that despite women's increasing role in the labour market, most mothers remain the primary caregivers of young children on weekdays.

In fact, the very long work hours of women and men with children in some EU countries – for example, 1995 data showed that, of all the EU15 men and women with children under age 17, UK fathers and Greek mothers worked the longest hours at 46.9 and 39.5 hours per week on average, respectively, which mirrors the US averages of 50 and 41 hours (Polatnik, 2000) – added impetus to EU policies aimed to reconcile work and family, and reduce working hours. As two recent Equal Opportunities Commission reports suggest, policies such as parental leave, the promotion of 'family friendly' workplaces, and an attack on the long-hours culture are important as catalysts for an 'active fatherhood' debate and for changing expectations (Hatten, Vinter & Williams, 2002; O'Brien & Shemilt, 2003). The Council Directive 96/34/EC of 3 June 1996 on the framework agreement on parental leave guarantees men and women workers in the European Union the right to a minimum of three months' leave on the birth of a child or on the adoption of a child. Employees are protected against dismissal when applying for or taking parental leave. After the leave, they are entitled to return to the same job, or if that is not possible, to an equivalent or similar job. In addition, employees are entitled to time off for urgent family reasons. Although all EU15 countries offer at least 14 weeks' paid maternity leave, parental leave policies are poorly developed in most EU member states, reflecting little interest in fathers' care of young children, and therefore in bringing about equal employment opportunity for women. Furthermore, parental leave provisions differ widely between member states. Within the European Union Sweden has the oldest, most generous and flexible parental leave programme, aimed at both parents and designed to promote equal share of breadwinning and childcare responsibilities. Parents are entitled to share 450 days of paid leave at the birth or adoption of a child. Thirteen months of this leave are paid at 80% of salary up to a certain income level (circa $45 000) with the remaining three months paid at a low flat rate (circa $13 a day). Leave can be taken any time before the child completes the first year of school, and there are no restrictions on how often parents can take turns at taking leave. In 2001 the majority (74%) of all children aged 1 to 6 were in publicly subsidised childcare, and the majority (75%) of mothers with preschool-aged children were in the labour force (Haas, 2003). It is no coincidence that in the three EU15 states with the lowest (40%) women's overall labour force participation (Greece, Italy and Spain) fathers do not take leave in normal circumstances either because parental leave is unpaid (Spain), or not guaranteed in companies of less than 50 employees (Greece), or because it is not an individual non-transferable right (Italy). These three nations also score the lowest of all EU15 states on a composite index measuring women's equal employment opportunities (based on gender differences in employment rates, women's share of higher job positions, the gender wage gap, the proportion of women with low incomes, and the male–female gap in unpaid time spent on caring for children and other persons) (Haas, 2003). Yet, even in Sweden mothers take as much as 85% of all parental leave, with many fathers reluctant to use their 'papa months'. Furthermore, despite the fact that Sweden has one of the world's highest rates of female participation in the labour force, women's wages still lag behind men's, and only two out of 282 listed companies have female chief executives (*The Economist*, 2004). Other developed countries are far worse. By the average basic statutory paid leave for developed and developing nations of 16 weeks (Allen, 2003), the United States, New Zealand and Australia, for instance, stand out as having particularly minimal legislation. Until 1993, the United States was one of the few industrialised countries without any maternity leave legislation. The Family and Medical Leave Act (FMLA) that was passed in that year provided the right to a short (12-week) unpaid parental leave for workers who meet qualifying conditions (that is, those who work in companies of at least 50 employees and have worked at least 1250 hours in the prior year). Australia does not allow for any paid maternity or parental leave. New Zealand introduced paid maternity leave as recently as 2002, but still does not allow for any paid parental leave.

CROSS-CULTURAL DIFFERENCES: FATHERS ACROSS COUNTRIES

Despite these demographic changes and policy differences, however, fatherhood research has only recently integrated developmental, ethnographic and demographic approaches to fathering. In Britain, for instance, the first demographic analysis of fatherhood took place in the mid-1990s (Burghes, Clarke & Cronin, 1997) using evidence from the British

Household Panel Study (BHPS), the first nationally representative survey to ask men about fertility histories. Therefore, who fathers *are* (or, for the purposes of family policy-makers, who 'high-risk' fathers are) differs widely across Western countries. Recent demographic analyses comparing fatherhood between Britain and the United States have shown that young fatherhood was more common in the USA, especially among Black men, with 34% of men in Britain having their first child before age 25, compared to 41% of White fathers, 47% of Hispanic fathers and 61% of Black fathers in the USA, and with 54% of Black American fathers being co-resident with all their children compared to 76% of Hispanic Americans, 79% of White Americans and 85% of British fathers (see Clarke & O'Brien, 2004, for a review). In addition, what fathers *do* with their children is sometimes culturally prescribed and might not be in line with the empirical findings from the British, American or Australian studies with predominantly White middle-class samples in two-parent families which dominate the English literature. For example, although the father's role is recognised in all cultures, in Botswana the male kin who plays this role is the mother's brother (Townsend, 2002). Furthermore, although differences between paternal and maternal styles (with fathers being notably more playful than mothers) have been found in France, Italy, Switzerland, India, as well as in African-American and Hispanic-American households, Taiwanese, Aka, German and Swedish fathers, as well as men on Israeli kibbutzim, are not more playful than mothers (Lewis & Lamb, 2003). Significant cultural variability has also been documented in studies measuring the extent of the father–child interaction in Western countries even since infancy. Lamb (2002) summarised the evidence from earlier studies on father quantity of involvement in several countries. It seems that Swedish fathers in dual-earner families are probably most highly involved, spending an average of 10.5 hours per workday and 7.5 hours per non-workday with their infants, almost as much as the mothers do. Earlier studies showed that Israeli fathers spend 2.75 hours, British fathers spend less time with their infants than Israeli or Irish fathers, but German and Italian fathers spend a lot less than British, Israeli or Irish fathers. American fathers have been reported in some studies to spend around 3 hours per day interacting with their infants, and in others to spend around 15 to 20 minutes (Lamb, 2002). So far the highest degree of father involvement in any human society is found among the Aka pygmies, a hunter-gatherer people in the Central African Republic who were found to be present with an infant or child for 88% of the time, and to be holding an infant for 22% of the time (Hewlett, 1987). In the UK, Matheson and Summerfield (2001) showed that in households with children men reported spending around three-quarters of an hour a day caring for and playing with their children – just under half the amount reported by women. Using data collected in 1986 on the time that Japanese and American fathers spent with children aged 10 to 15, Ishii-Kuntz (1994) showed that American fathers were directly engaged for 1 hour on weekdays and 2 hours on Sundays with sons and for 0.5 hour on weekdays and 1.4 hours on Sundays with daughters. More recently Yeung et al. (2003) showed that biological fathers in the United States spend on average 1 hour and 13 minutes on a typical workday and 2 hours and 29 minutes on a weekend day in direct engagement with their children in intact families. The corresponding estimates were 5 hours and 21 minutes for children who live only with their biological mothers (with or without a stepfather), 1 hour 4 minutes and 1 hour 30 minutes for children who live only with their biological fathers (with or without stepmother), and 9 hours and 28 minutes for those who do not live with either biological parent. American studies consistently show, however, that most of the time men spend with their children is in the form of 'interactive activities', such as play or helping with homework (Yeung et al., 2003), with the division of labour in childcare responsibilities being far from egalitarian. Lee, Vernon-Feagans, Vazquez and Kolak (2003) argued that a reason for this might be simply that fathers underestimate mothers' involvement in caregiving tasks (in their study fathers' and mothers' estimates of fathers' involvement were almost identical, but fathers' ratings of mothers' involvement were significantly lower than mothers' ratings of their own involvement). Finally, what fathers *should do* with their children has resulted in significant differences in the family policy agendas between Western countries. For instance, the British family policy on fatherhood occupies an intermediate position between the American 'father involvement' agenda, criticised as an attempt to reinstate male dominance by restoring the dominance of the traditional nuclear family with its contrasting masculine and feminine gender roles (Silverstein & Auerbach, 1999), and the European 'gender equity' agenda (Clarke & O'Brien, 2004).

THE 'CONSEQUENCES' OF THE CHANGES

The psychological consequences (especially for children) of these demographic changes (i.e. the decline in the traditional household form of a single breadwinner and the growth of dual participant households) have long been the subject of research and debate. Recent attention has also been given to the consequences for fathers. A Swedish study (Ringbäck Weitoft, Burström & Rosén, in press), looking at premature mortality in lone fathers and childless men, for instance, showed that compared to long-term cohabiting fathers with a child in their household, lone non-custodial fathers and lone childless men faced the greatest increase in risks, especially from injury and addiction, and also from all-cause mortality and ischaemic heart disease. Being a lone custodial father also entailed increased risk, although generally to a much lesser extent, and not for all outcomes. The consequences for children, on the other hand (particularly in the short term), of parental 'deprivation' in one form or another – at one time, and also recently, maternal work outside the home, then father absence, and now parental separation – have been an increasing focus of attention (see Ni Bhrolchain, Chappell, Diamond & Jameson, 2000, for a review).

WHY (AND HOW) FAMILY STRUCTURE AFFECTS CHILD 'OUTCOMES'

Biblarz and Raftery (1999) usefully reviewed the main theories of the effects of family structure on children. Sociological theory, for instance, predicts that children from alternative families get fewer economic, social and cultural resources, which help to facilitate success. The sociological model also predicts less involvement by stepfathers and by partners who are not married to the mother because expectations are either, in the former, that they will be less involved with children or, in the latter, that social norms are not yet developed to guide unmarried partners in parenting their children (Hofferth & Anderson, 2003). Economic theory predicts that the two-parent family is among the best-functioning forms of modern capitalist society because it allows for the provision of household services by one partner and economic resources by the other, and as such it is an efficient system for maximising utility and the human capital of the children. Evolutionary approaches to understanding parenting behaviours in humans suggest that men invest more in their children when the indirect benefit they get is greater than the benefit they could get from using their time and energy to seek additional mates (see Josephson, 2002, for a discussion). Mothers invest more of their resources in their children than fathers because women's potential for having additional children is far lower than men's, and so more of the mother's than of the father's potential reproductive investment is tied up in any one child. Therefore, evolutionary psychology also predicts that children from two-biological-parent families will have an advantage over children from other forms of family but also, in contrast to economic theory's predictions, that children from alternative families will do better when raised by a single mother than by a single father, and that children from single-mother families will have advantages over those from stepfather families. Finally, the selection hypothesis suggests that the observed adverse outcomes of children of alternative family structures might represent selection effects. For instance, the adverse outcomes in children of divorce might be because people who divorce are less competent at family life and less 'child-centred' than those who do not divorce (Amato, 2000), or because of the high levels of interparental conflict which precede separation and the psychological distress from losing a parent (Hetherington & Stanley-Hagan, 1999). Similarly, the adverse outcomes of children in stepfather families might be because men who choose the step-parent relationship are negatively selected (lack of alternative opportunities, less attractive), and so are different from biological fathers in ways that lead to reduced investment and perhaps also more problems for children (Hofferth & Anderson, 2003).

CHILDREN OF LONE-PARENT FAMILIES: THE 'PATHOLOGY OF THE MATRIARCHY' VIEW

In general, empirical studies show lower attainments (McLanahan & Sandefur, 1994), earlier union formation, earlier entry into parenthood, more extra-marital fertility (Kiernan & Hobcraft, 1997), more partnership dissolution (Kiernan & Cherlin, 1999) and less psychological well-being (Amato & Sobolewski, 2001; Hetherington & Stanley-Hagan, 1999) in children of lone-parent families in comparison to children in two-parent intact families. This evidence has been used by many to support Moynihan's (1965) 'pathology of the matriarchy' hypothesis that the absence of a father is destructive to children, particularly boys, because it means that children will lack the economic resources, role models, discipline, structure and guidance that a father provides. However, recent studies have reported findings that cannot be neatly construed to fit with a 'pathology of matriarchy' view. For instance, in the USA, Biblarz and Raftery (1999) showed that, in line with an evolutionary view of parental investment, even with a significant socio-economic advantage, the sons from alternative male-headed households in their data (e.g. step-father and single-father families) did not have higher occupational achievements than those from single-mother families, and actually children from single-mother families had some advantages over children from other kinds of alternative families. Similarly, for Taiwan, Han, Huang and Garfinkel (2003) showed that although children in single-parent families had lower college attendance rates than children in two-parent families, when family income was taken into account, single-mother families were not significantly different from two-parent families on the outcome variables, and single-father families had significantly lower college attendance rates and educational expenditure. Earlier, Kiernan (1992) in the UK had shown that although bereaved children were no more likely than children brought up with both natural parents to make educational, occupational and demographic transitions at an early age, young men from stepfamilies were more likely to form partnerships and become fathers at an earlier age than their contemporaries from intact or lone-mother families. Kiernan also showed that for young women from both step- and lone-parent families the propensity to form unions in their teens, to have a child at an early age and to bear a child outside marriage was higher than for those who came from intact families, and that young people from step-families formed after death or divorce were most likely to leave home early, and for reasons of friction. Regarding children's psychological adjustment Amato and Keith's (1991) meta-analysis showed worse outcomes for children in stepfamilies than in single-mother families, and decreased well-being in girls (but increased well-being in boys) in stepfather families. Relatedly, studies looking at adolescent health outcomes associated with family structure show similar patterns. For example, Bjarnason and colleagues, who explored the role of family structure in alcohol use (Bjarnason et al., 2003a) and smoking (Bjarnason et al., 2003b) in adolescents from Cyprus, France, Hungary, Iceland, Ireland, Lithuania, Malta, the Slovak Republic, Slovenia, Sweden and the United Kingdom, showed that although adolescents living with both biological parents engaged less frequently in heavy alcohol use and smoked less than those living in any other arrangements, adolescents living with a single mother drank and smoked less than those living with a single father or with neither biological parent. Another recent study (Griesbach, Amos & Currie, 2003) comparing data from several European countries showed that although several risk factors were associated with higher smoking prevalence in all countries (Austria, Denmark, Finland, Germany, Norway, Scotland and Wales), even after risk factors were taken into account, there was an increased likelihood of smoking among adolescents in stepfamilies compared to adolescents in intact or in lone-parent families. Similarly, Demuth and Brown (2004) showed that although US adolescents in single-parent families were more delinquent than their counterparts residing with two biological parents, adolescents from single-father families were significantly more delinquent than those living in single-mother families. Hoffmann (2002), also in the USA, showed that adolescents who resided in single-parent or step-parent families were at heightened risk of drug use, with adolescents living in single-father families being at risk of both higher levels of use and increasing use over time. Patten et al. (1997) showed that although family structure was not related to depressive symptoms in their US adolescents' sample, significantly higher rates of depressive symptoms were found among adolescents who resided with parent(s) not perceived as supportive than those who lived with supportive parent(s), with girls being particularly vulnerable if they lived in a non-supportive, single-father household. In Finland, Luoma et al. (1999) showed that living with a single father was associated with having more externalising, school-related problems, while living with a stepfather was associated with having more internalising, home-related problems in their sample of 8–9 year olds. Exploring the role of family structure on even younger children's outcomes, Clarke-Stewart, Vandell, McCartney, Owen and Booth (2000) showed that US 3-year-old children in two-parent families performed better than their counterparts in single-mother families on assessments of cognitive and social abilities, problem behaviour, attachment security and behaviour with mother, with the associations with separated–intact marital status becoming insignificant after controlling for mothers' education and family income. In England McMunn, Nazroo, Marmot, Boreham and Goodman (2001) showed that although the high prevalence of psychological morbidity among 4- to 15-year-old children of lone mothers was a consequence of socio-economic effects, disappearing when benefits receipt, housing tenure and maternal education were taken into account, socio-economic factors did not explain the higher proportion of psychological morbidity among children with step-parents. The consensus (but see Harris, 1998) is that the deterioration of economic conditions that usually results from family disruption is the major explanation for children's lower ability and achievement, although not necessarily the emotional and behavioural problems (Duncan, Brooks-Gunn, Yeung & Smith, 1998). According to studies adopting a life-course adversity mode, a possible explanation for the weak link between a father's absence and a child's psychological adjustment might be that it is not the father's absence *per se* that is harmful for children, but rather that the stress associated with divorce or separation, family conflict, loss of a second parent, erosion of parental monitoring, or drop in family income may account for the relation between the father's absence and the child's outcomes (McLanahan, 1999). Another explanation (usually offered in genetically informative studies) is that, through genetic transmission, mothers and fathers who have a history of mental health problems both tend to form unstable relationships (Emery, Waldron, Kitzmann & Aaron, 1999) and have children who are at a greater risk for emotional and behavioural difficulties (Rhee & Waldman, 2002).

DIVORCE AS 'A BREAKDOWN OF THE MORAL ORDER'

However, although voices have been raised on both sides of the Atlantic (Coltrane & Adams, 2003; Walker, 2003) warning that claims that divorce reflects a breakdown of the moral order, and the portrayal of children as victims of divorce, legitimate the political objectives of specific interest groups and mask underlying issues of gender inequality, the rhetoric surrounding recent UK and US family policies is often dominated by idealised notions of the family of old (Lewis, 2001a) and looks to 'possibly disorienting and little-understood family change as a simple and persuasive explanation for contemporary social problems' (Ni Bhrolchain et al., 2000, p. 68). In linking poor child outcomes to family structure some researchers have pointed to the causal role of absent and uninvolved fathers in the development of children's behavioural and academic problems (Blankenhorn, 1995; Popenoe, 1996), leading some policy-makers to conclude that parents should be offered incentives to get married and remain married (Horn, 2001).

However, this has been criticised by many for various reasons, primarily because it offers more ideology than practical measures. For instance, Silverstein and Auerbach (1999) showed that it is not the decline of marriage that is discouraging responsible fathering. Rather, various social conditions inhibit involved parenting by unmarried and divorced men (unmarried teen fathers typically have low levels of education and job training, and so cannot easily contribute to the economic well-being of their children, and divorced fathers cannot sustain a positive emotional connection to their children after the legal system redefines their role from 'parenting' to 'visitation' or 'contact'). Henwood and Procter (2003) suggested that awareness of the various conflicting perspectives of the 'new fatherhood' model makes it possible to appreciate the different values and agendas that are playing out in contemporary discussion of men and family life. They described four such perspectives. The first offers the modest view of a father whose concern with sustaining relationships, rather than meeting expectations for male performance, provides children with the experience of being wanted by both parents. The second attempts to reinstate traditional family values by asserting men's 'rights' to retain their position as head of households over and above any competing claims about women's autonomy and children's needs for protection. The third questions the value society conventionally attaches to men being able to eschew their emotions and remain detached from relationships, but at the same time it adopts fixed and polarised views of what male and female parents can provide. Finally, the fourth reproduces hegemonic masculinity by portraying the image of the new (middle-class) man who is devoted and nurturing at home and successful outside it (thus enjoying the best of both worlds at little cost and much convenience). Empirical psychological research has also recently demonstrated that a narrow focus on family structure without a parallel focus on the quality of care that parents can provide may do some children more harm than good. Jaffee, Moffitt, Caspi and Taylor (2003) showed that when fathers engaged in high levels of antisocial behaviour, the more time they lived with their children the more conduct problems their children had, and Foley et al. (2004) found that in two-parent families boys who lived with an alcoholic stepfather had fewer conduct disorder symptoms than boys who lived with an alcoholic biological father, although girls who lived with an alcoholic stepfather had more conduct disorder symptoms than girls who lived with an alcoholic biological father. Bos, van Balen and van den Boom (2004) recently reviewed evidence showing that, compared to children in two-parent heterosexual families, children in planned lesbian families (two-mother families in which the child was born to the lesbian relationship) show no differences in outcomes such as social competence, behavioural adjustment and gender identity. In fact, studies on parenting behaviour showed that non-biological mothers in planned lesbian families have a superior quality of parent–child interaction than do fathers in heterosexual families (Flaks, Ficher, Masterpasqua & Joseph, 1995; Golombok, Tasker & Murray, 1997). On the other hand, concerns have been raised that hailing fathers' presence in families 'at all costs' could increase both domestic violence and child abuse rates. (A significant public health concern worldwide with WHO figures has shown that in every country where reliable, large-scale studies have been conducted, between 10% and 50% of women report that they have been physically abused by an intimate partner in their lifetime (World Health Organisation, 2000).)

Second, because the largely causal conclusions drawn in the literature examining the link between parental divorce and child adjustment are not justified, as the (overwhelmingly correlational) evidence is insufficient to allow the inference that divorce causes long-term adverse effects to the children (Ni Bhrolchain, 2001). Although most researchers now increasingly recognise and discuss the difficulties of establishing causal effects from cross-sectional or longitudinal data, there are still some problems with the usual interpretation of the empirical findings on the links between fathers' involvement or fathers' presence and children's 'outcomes', and with the proposed strategies to decrease fathers' absence or fathers' withdrawal in order to increase children's well-being. A problem with this kind of reasoning is that one assumes that father absence or father low involvement *causes* low well-being in children – a thesis not based on evidence. The research shows that fathers' low involvement or absence may be a 'correlate' (a measure somehow associated with the outcome) of low well-being in children, a 'sign' and 'symptom', 'concomitant' or 'consequence' of low well-being, and at best a 'risk factor' (a correlate shown to precede the outcome) for low well-being, but not a 'causal risk factor' (a risk factor that, when changed, is shown to change the outcome) for low well-being. Although terminological imprecision is increasingly avoided, researchers sometimes still seem to expect that 'bad fathering' is a causal risk factor for low well-being. However, causal effects should not be inferred from variations between individuals but should instead be inferred from changes within individuals (Kraemer, Stice, Kazdin, Offord & Kupfer, 2001), and so the term *causation* should only be reserved for variables that may change. Borrowing Loeber and Farrington's (1994) example, a study may demonstrate that even after controlling for other factors, male participants were more likely than female participants to be delinquents, which might lead some researchers to conclude that gender is a cause of delinquency.

With all this in mind, the following chapters explore links between fathering and child well-being (or 'good' children's outcomes), and between fathering and its antecedents in Britain. Before this, however, a brief description of what exactly is meant by 'fathering' and 'child well-being' is shown below.

WHAT IS FATHERING?

It is generally accepted that fathering is multifaceted and multidetermined, and more sensitive to contextual factors than mothering (Doherty, Kouneski & Erickson, 1998; Gerson, 1993). In the psychological literature, fathering is usually translated into father's presence status, and father's involvement. The empirical research on father absence and child outcomes largely overlaps with that on family structure/parental separation and child outcomes. In father-absent families the fathering dimensions that are usually explored in relation to child outcomes are non-resident fathers' economic support for their children, with US studies starting to also include the regularity of the child support payments, as well as other contributions that do not include the exchange of money, such as the purchase of clothes, presents, medical insurance and dental care. Other non-resident fathers' involvement indices typically include frequency (but also sometimes regularity) of contact (such as visits, phone calls, letters, e-mail, etc.) and, less often, quality of contact. Researchers have also recently stressed the importance of non-resident fathers' quality of parenting, or 'involvement' (Amato & Gilbreth, 1999). Recently, measures that assess non-resident fathers' involvement often use the same measures applied to resident fathers in intact families (Pasley & Brave, 2004).

In defining involvement, social scientists usually incorporate some of the following paternal functions that are common in many cultures, although the relative importance of each varies by culture. These are: *endowment*, acknowledging the child as one's own; *protection*, protecting the child from sources of potential danger and contributing to decisions that affect the child's welfare; *provision*, ensuring that the child's material needs are met; *formation*, socialisation activities, such as discipline and teaching; and *caregiving* (Gavin et al., 2002).

In many studies in English-speaking countries, father involvement is now usually taken to mean Lamb, Pleck, Charnov & Levine's (1985, 1987) influential 'content-free' construction of *engagement* (direct interaction with the child in the form of caretaking, play or leisure); *accessibility or availability* to the child (for example, cooking while the child plays), and *responsibility* for the child's welfare and care, which may involve no direct or indirect contact with the child (for example, making a dental appointment). Involvement has been measured both quantitatively and qualitatively. Before this formulation the paternal characteristics and behaviours studied in father-present families were largely qualitative such as warmth, responsiveness, power or playfulness (Pleck & Stueve, 2001). Early father involvement measures did not consider endowment and financial support and tended to assume that the fathers were resident (Radin, 1982). In Lamb et al.'s (1985, 1987) formulation involvement is a content-free construct, concerning only the quantity of fathers' behaviour, time, or responsibility with their children. Although in general the assessment of behavioural, cognitive and emotional involvement of resident fathers has been done differently in different studies, behavioural involvement (reflecting the constructs of engagement, availability and responsibility) is usually measured with the frequency of the father's participation in caregiving activities (such as making meals, taking the child to the doctor/dentist/school, etc.), cognitive involvement is measured with reasoning, planning and monitoring, and emotional involvement is measured with warmth, affection and feelings of closeness. Recently researchers have pointed out that frequently studies using these indices, however, do not take into account the developmental stage of the children, and do not capture variations in father involvement across socio-economic and ethnic groups (Cabrera et al., 2004). In addition, numerous scholars criticised Lamb et al.'s formulation of the involvement construct as limited especially because of its narrow focus on time (e.g. Marsiglio, Amato, Day & Lamb, 2000) and the exclusion of breadwinning or economic providing (Christiansen & Palkovitz, 2001), especially since father's presence or father's income presence is not always associated with providing for the child (i.e. the father does not contribute to household expenses or his consumption of resources drains the family budget, especially if he spends the family's funds for personal items or services), and subsequently improved child status. In Guatemala, Kenya and Malawi, for instance, children in female-headed households are better nourished than children living with both their biological parents, and in Botswana children in female-headed households receive better education than children in male-headed households (Engle & Breaux, 1998). Although current measurements of father involvement in studies looking at paternal involvement and child outcomes are looking at the qualitative aspects of father–child relations, such as closeness or quality of parenting (Leinonen, Solantaus & Punamäki, 2003a), or father's competence in the father's role (Hawkins et al., 2002), they still tend to exclude breadwinning.

Recently, organised attempts have been made to develop fathering indicators that might be applicable to different populations of fathers (such as married fathers living with their biological children, stepfathers, unmarried co-resident fathers, biological non-resident fathers, non-resident social fathers etc.). The National Center on Fathers and Families (NCOFF) Working Group on Fathering Indicators, for instance, identified six fathering indicators. These were: *father presence* (defined as father engagement, availability, and responsibility in relation to the child), *caregiving* (i.e. providing nurturance and performing routine tasks necessary to maintain the child's emotional well-being, physical health and appearance), *children's social competence and academic achievement, co-operative parenting* (i.e. establishing a supportive, co-operative and interdependent relationship with the child's other caregiver(s)), *father's healthy living* (providing a role model through healthy lifestyle and appropriate social behaviours that teach work and personal ethics as well as social norms), and *material and financial contribution* (Gadsden, Fagan, Ray & Davis, 2004).

Most of the remainder of the book will explore the role of fathering, and father involvement in particular, in outcomes for *children*. However, some related research has focused on father involvement and outcomes for *fathers* and *mothers*, and it is worth mentioning some of its main findings here. With regards to fathers' outcomes, evidence is limited but some of the findings of the longitudinal studies are very interesting. For instance, Snarey (1993) showed how involvement predicted later generativity in men. Earlier, Hawkins and Belsky (1989) had linked greater father involvement to decreased self-esteem, and lesser father involvement to increased self-esteem (which in their study was measured prenatally and when children were 15 months old). One possible interpretation of their findings was that as fathers were more involved with sons than daughters, and as boys were more difficult to care for than girls, the difficulties that fathers experienced caring for their sons led to decreases in their self-esteem. An alternative explanation was that higher levels of father involvement foster non-traditional development for men (i.e. men decline in masculinity, which is positively related to self-esteem). Regarding mothers' outcomes, low father involvement has been positively associated with mothers' stress levels (Milkie, Bianchi, Mattingly & Robinson, 2002), and anger (Ross & van Willigen, 1996), and negatively related to mothers' satisfaction with fathers' help (Simmerman, Blacher & Baker, 2001), quality of the interparental relationship (Olrick, Pianta & Marvin, 2002; Schoppe-Sullivan, Mangelsdorf, Frosch & McHale, 2004), as well as (in the case of paternal loss through death or separation) mothers' reduced care (Kitamura, Sugawara, Toda & Shima, 1998). Fathers' acceptance (which is related although it is not equivalent to involvement) has been found to buffer against postpartum depression when infants were highly reactive and when mothers were aggressive, and to reduce the impact of postpartum depression on mothers' sensitivity (Crockenberg & Leerkes, 2003).

WHAT IS 'CHILD WELL-BEING'?

It is increasingly being accepted that well-being is not merely the absence of disease or infirmity. The World Health Organisation measures the burden of disease by its consequences on well-being, which, therefore, commits WHO to the view that health and disease matter insofar as they affect well-being. Regarding child well-being, in particular, according to the Department of Child and Adolescent Health and Development of WHO, to promote well-being in children is to reduce death, illness and disability, and to promote improved growth and development. However, there is little agreement on how to measure child well-being (Pollard & Lee, 2003). Objective measures include mortality rates, educational assessments, suicide attempts and delinquency rates, and drug offence rates. Subjective measures of child well-being usually assess single indicators of well-being, such as psychological functioning (to tap well-being in the psychological domain), family and peer relationships (to tap well-being in the social domain), academic motivation (to tap well-being in the cognitive domain), economic hardship (to tap well-being in the economic domain) and physical health measures (to tap well-being in the physical domain) (Pollard & Lee, 2003). In this book, the aspects of child well-being that I looked at in relation to fathering included: objective outcomes of functional significance, such as school achievement, delinquency and employment (Chapters 4, 5 and 7, respectively); subjective assessments of states, such as happiness, life satisfaction, psychological distress, and strengths and difficulties (Chapter 3); academic motivation (Chapter 4); quality of interpersonal relationships, such as quality of relationships with partners and parents (Chapter 6), and relationships with peers (Chapter 5); and parent-reported assessments of emotional and behavioural problems (Chapter 3).

WHY FATHERING AND CHILD WELL-BEING?

Although aspects of parenting are significantly related to child development (Maccoby, 2000), fathering has received limited attention in research compared to mothering (Cabrera et al., 2000). For many years research on children's development and well-being focused on the dynamics between mothers and their children (Bowlby, 1982). Fathers were often assumed to be on the periphery of children's lives and therefore of little direct importance to children's development (Lamb, 1997). However, there are several reasons why one should expect fathers, especially within the nuclear family model of the Western societies, to be particularly significant in children's outcomes. In fact, the positive role of 'responsible fathering' for children's outcomes has also been recognised in extended matrifocal family systems in which the impression given is that fathers are either marginally present or completely absent from the family scene (Brunod & Cook-Darzens, 2002). Although these studies have stressed that more flexible concepts of 'fatherhood' than those dictated by the nuclear family model of Western societies should be applied in fathering research, they also acknowledge the benefits for children raised with more than one responsible caretaking adult (who usually is the child's father in Western nuclear families). First, a father's engagement with his child will likely exert influences on child development in the same way that a mother's engagement does (Lamb, 1997), and paternal accessibility might similarly offer the child a sense of emotional support (Cabrera et al., 2000). Second, fathers' relationships with their children are distinct from mother–child relations, with fathers encouraging their children to be competitive and independent and spending more time than mothers in playful and physically stimulating interactions with their children (DeKlyen, Speltz & Greenberg, 1998). Therefore, fathers may be particularly influential in the development of certain aspects of child behaviour. Fathers can also indirectly impact on their children's well-being. Fathers' continuing financial support of their children, in particular, can affect child outcomes by influencing the economic structure of the household (Crockett, Eggebeen & Hawkins, 1993). As discussed earlier, father involvement also influences maternal role satisfaction and maternal psychological health (via the effect the involved father has in emotionally supporting the mother) which are related to positive child outcomes (Downey & Coyne, 1990).

In this book, father involvement is explored in relation to children's mental health outcomes (Chapter 3), educational outcomes (Chapter 4), aggressive behaviour – including delinquency – (Chapter 5), family relationships (Chapter 6) and social and economic outcomes (Chapter 7). Chapter 2 explores factors associated with father involvement in two-parent families, and Chapter 8 investigates both the determinants of non-resident fathers' parenting and the children's mental health outcomes associated with non-resident fathers' parenting. Chapter 9 summarises the research and points to new research directions.

SUMMARY AND CONCLUSIONS

This chapter discussed how the 'discovery' of the father has been one of the major themes in child developmental research in the past 30 years, and provided an overview of the existing international research on fathering. It described how macrolevel, social, demographic, economic and technological changes have impacted on the meaning of fatherhood for men and their families, as well as how these changes are altering the nature of father involvement and, in turn, affecting children's developmental trajectories.

Family change in the Western world has been considerable in the past 30 years. For instance, all 15 European Union (EU15) member states have recorded an increase in births outside marriage since the mid-1970s, and current rates of female headship in several developed countries are high – ranging from 44% in Slovenia, 42% in Denmark and Finland, and 37% in New Zealand and Sweden (United Nations, 2000). Furthermore, in 2000 in EU15 among households with two people of working age, those with both partners in the labour force were almost twice as numerous as those with only one, and in the USA only about one-quarter of children lived in two-parent families supported by a single male earner. Although empirical studies show lower attainments, earlier union formation, earlier entry into parenthood and more extramarital fertility, more partnership dissolution, and less psychological well-being in children of lone-parent families in comparison to children in two-parent intact families, such evidence cannot easily support the 'pathology of the matriarchy' hypothesis, or the view that divorce reflects a breakdown of the moral order. First, because the evidence linking family structure and children's adjustment is largely correlational, causality cannot be established. Second, because it might not be father absence *per se* that is harmful for children, but rather the stress associated with divorce or separation, family conflict, loss of a second parent, erosion of parental monitoring, or drop in family income that may account for the relation between father absence and child 'adverse outcomes'. Subsequently, this chapter (as well as the book as a whole) took the view that a narrow focus on family structure without a parallel focus on the quality of care fathers or father figures can provide (always in the context of the social and economic circumstances of each family) could not promote a further understanding of fathering or enhance our knowledge of the relationship between fathering and child well-being. Child well-being was mainly operationalised as objective outcomes of functional significance (school achievement, delinquency and employment), subjective assessments of states (happiness, life satisfaction, psychological distress, strengths and difficulties, and academic motivation), and quality of interpersonal relationships (quality of relationships with partners, parents and peers).

CHAPTER 2

FACTORS ASSOCIATED WITH FATHER INVOLVEMENT IN TWO-PARENT FAMILIES

INTRODUCTION

Process models of parenting applied to fathers usually present a systemic framework that highlights the interacting influences of five different groups of influences on father involvement: contextual factors, father's factors, mother's factors, quality of the co-parental relationship, and child's factors. Father involvement (not tantamount to fathering, but still a part of it) with school-aged children and adolescents can be influenced by factors other than those that influence father involvement with younger children and infants. Furthermore, father involvement in two-parent families is predicted from factors that are different from those associated with father involvement in lone-mother families. This chapter presents two empirical studies, one longitudinal and one cross-sectional, carried out to explore the role of these groups of influences in fathers' involvement with their school-aged children in two-parent families.

MODELS OF FATHER INVOLVEMENT

As shown in Chapter 1, father involvement in Lamb et al.'s (1985, 1987) model is usually taken to mean *engagement, accessibility* or *availability to the child, and responsibility* for the child's welfare and care. In proposing the construct of 'paternal involvement', Lamb et al. (1985, 1987) suggested that four factors influence the level of father involvement: motivation, social support, skills and self-confidence, and institutional practices. Since then, several models of determinants of fathering have been proposed (Pleck & Stueve, 2001), and although their results varied (partly because of the different operationalisation of father involvement across studies), most of them have looked at the role of four major components: *contextual factors, the father's characteristics, the mother's characteristics*, and *co-parental relations*. In addition to these four major components, research has explored the role of another source of influence of parental involvement, which was not included in Lamb et al.'s (1985, 1987) original model but has proved a promising line of research, *the child's characteristics* (see Karras, Van Deventer & Braungart-Rieker, 2003; McBride, Schoppe & Rane, 2002; Pleck, 1997).

Although, as explained in Chapter 1, father involvement is not tantamount to fathering (even though it is a part of it), the theoretical treatments of the determinants of parenting may be useful in providing specific hypotheses of the determinants of father involvement. Most such treatments acknowledge the need to consider development and life-course risks as well as current social and interpersonal stresses (Belsky, 1984), and empirical studies usually focus on concurrent psychosocial risks, such as economic adversity, marital strain, family stress, and mental health problems (Doherty et al., 1998). Perhaps a more elegant parenting model was recently proposed by Bonney, Kelley and Levant (1999) who employed social psychology theory and, in particular, role theory (which suggests that social roles are shared norms and expectations about how an individual should behave in certain situations) to account for fathers' involvement with their preschool-aged children. According to role theory, because fathering can be considered a voluntary activity (Cabrera et al., 2000), standards and expectations for fathering are more variable than those for mothering (Doherty et al., 1998). As a consequence, fathers' behaviour is strongly influenced by the meanings and expectations of fathers themselves, as well as mothers, children, extended family, and broader cultures and institutions.

Despite the impressive findings from animal studies, however, psychological research on fathering has not demonstrated comparable concern for biological factors associated with fathering behaviours, perhaps with the exception of arguments advanced from sociobiological approaches and from behavioural genetics studies. Sociobiologists, for example, have long argued for the significance of 'ownness' (Daly & Wilson, 1998) although it is usually unclear if this is because parents and children who have similar characteristics become more involved and attached, or because most biological parent–child dyads have enjoyed a shared relationship from early infancy (Dunn, 2002, p. 157). In a similar vein, evolutionary approaches to understanding fathering in humans suggest that men invest more in their children when the indirect benefit they get is greater than the benefit they could get from using their time and energy to seek additional mates (see Josephson, 2002 for a discussion). Theoretical treatments (in behavioural genetics studies) of children's characteristics as setting the stage for the kind of bi-directional processes that emerge between them and their fathers also echo evolutionary approaches (Bell & Harper, 1977). The tendency for a child's behaviour to evoke a particular reaction from parents (called a reactive or an evocative effect) is an example of a gene–environment correlation – a correlation between a genetically influenced characteristic, such as a pleasing disposition, and a particular environmental variable, such as parental involvement (see Plomin & Bergeman, 1991, for a review).

This chapter describes and discusses two studies (one cross-sectional, one longitudinal) that the author carried out with Ann Buchanan (Flouri, 2004; Flouri & Buchanan, 2003d) to explore factors associated with fathers' involvement with their children. The approach of both studies was guided by Belsky's (1984) process model of parenting, and Doherty et al.'s (1998) model of fathering. Both models present a systemic framework that highlights the interacting influences of contextual factors, the father's factors, the mother's factors, the quality of co-parental relationship, and the child's factors on the parent–child relationship. Both models include children's psychological characteristics as a determinant of parenting but Doherty et al. (1998) offer no hypothesis as to how they are likely to affect fathering, whereas Belsky's (1984) model describes their role in determining parent–infant rather than parent–adolescent interactive behaviour. Below is an overview of the role of the five groups of influence (contextual factors, the father's factors, the mother's factors, co-parental relations, and the child's factors) in parental involvement. Because single-parent and two-parent families differ in many respects that can affect how parents spend their time, both studies looked at the determinants of fathers' parenting in two-parent families only. As fathers' involvement with school-aged children and adolescents can be influenced by different factors that influence fathers' involvement with younger children and infants, below is a discussion of factors associated with resident fathers' involvement with their children, with an emphasis on determinants of fathers' involvement with their school-aged children.

THE 'PROCESS MODEL OF FATHERING': PREDICTORS OF FATHER INVOLVEMENT

Contextual factors

With regard to contextual factors, biological relatedness and family type affect young children's feelings of closeness to their fathers, but not mothers (Sturgess, Dunn & Davies, 2001), with children in middle childhood and adolescents finding relationships with stepfathers particularly troubling (Dunn, 2002). Fathers are also less involved with residential children if they financially support non-residential children, with stepfathers who do not provide support to other children actually rating themselves as warmer than biological fathers (Hofferth & Anderson, 2003). Even so, however, children in stepfather families are monitored a lot less than children in stepmother and two-parent biological families (Fisher, Leve, O'Leary & Leve, 2003). Recently Macdonald and DeMaris (2002) showed that the quality of the stepfather–stepchild relationship depends on the biological father's involvement (a finding not supported, however, by Hofferth & Anderson, 2003): stepchildren whose biological fathers interact with them and have a great deal of parenting input are most likely to have poor relationships with their stepfathers when the stepfather demands conformity, whereas a stepfather's demand for conformity is likely to have the most positive effect on stepfather–stepchild relationship quality when the biological father's parenting input is great but his interaction with the child is minimal.

Other contextual influences of father involvement are family size and economic stress. Family size is negatively related to father involvement (Pleck, 1997) perhaps because, according to the resource dilution model, the availability of parental resources decreases as the number of siblings increases (Downey, 1995), and economic stress affects fathering more than it affects mothering perhaps because the provider role tends to be more central to fathering than it is to mothering (Harris & Marmer, 1996).

Leinonen, Solantaus and Punamäki (2002), who studied specific mediating paths between economic hardship and fathering, showed that in their Finnish fathers' sample economic hardship was associated with symptoms of anxiety which were related both directly and indirectly (via hostile marital interaction) to punitive and non-involved fathering. More recently, Uhlendorff (2004), who compared East and West German fathers' parenting attitudes, suggested that his finding that East German fathers raise their children in a more traditional and authoritarian manner was explained by the closer cohesion of the immediate family and the lower level of social support provided by the extrafamilial environment in the former East Germany.

Father and mother characteristics

Recent studies document increased involvement if the father had attended the child's delivery (Moore & Kotelchuck, 2004), which lends support to the finding that previous father involvement is a strong predictor of subsequent father involvement (Hwang & Lamb, 1997; Roberts, Block & Block, 1984), and indicates continuity through time in fathers' relationships with their children. Note, however, that others cautioned against the pressure for men to be present at childbirth as fathers' stress following childbirth may impact on the subsequent father–child relationships (Johnson, 2002). Some recent studies with fathers are looking at prebirth involvement (Lis, Zennaro, Mazzeschi & Pinto, 2004), and prebirth (Van Egeren, 2003) and at-birth predictors of subsequent father involvement (Johnson, 2002). Lis et al. (2004) described the prospective father involvement during pregnancy as 'expressive', 'instrumental' or 'observer', and Van Egeren (2001) showed that the father's co-parenting in infancy was predicted from the father's high occupational status, maternal ego development, co-parenting in the father's family of origin, and both parents' motivation to raise children measured at prebirth.

Although not consistently, studies have also identified links between father involvement and the father's socioeconomic characteristics: unemployed fathers, for instance, spend more time with their children (Pleck, 1997); more educated fathers are more involved with their children (Nord, Brimhall & West, 1997); and fathers who work for many hours are less involved with their children than fathers who work fewer hours (Coltrane, 1996). There is also some evidence that the father's age is either insignificantly or inversely related to father involvement (Pleck, 1997), although adolescent fathers are generally not as involved with their children as older fathers (Jaffee, Caspi, Moffitt, Taylor & Dickson, 2001; Rhein et al., 1997). The father's psychological characteristics have also been suggested to influence father involvement. Those few studies that have looked at the role of self-esteem and related concepts such as ego-resiliency in parenting behaviour, for instance, have shown strong relationships (e.g. Mondell & Tyler, 1981). In addition, research with fathers and their infants has shown that co-parenting in the family of origin predicted the father's co-parenting experiences (Van Egeren, 2003). Recent studies have started to examine ethnic differences in father involvement only to conclude that perhaps contextual factors contribute to any ethnic differences observed in the first place. Hofferth (2003), for example, showed in her American two-parent families' sample that Black fathers were more authoritarian with less warmth and greater control, whereas Hispanic fathers were more permissive with less control than White fathers, who overall exhibited less responsibility for childrearing than the two ethnic minority groups. However, she stressed that economic circumstances contributed to differences in paternal engagement and control (for example, Black fathers have larger families and are less likely to be the biological father, both of which result in more control and less warmth), and neighbourhood factors contributed to the differences observed in responsibility (Black and Hispanic fathers live in less desirable neighbourhoods, and living in such neighbourhoods is associated with more responsibility).

Evolutionary theory has also been applied to explain not only the father's absence (see Waynforth, 2002, for a review) but also the father's involvement, or 'variations in the father's parenting efforts' (Gray, Kahlenberg, Barrett, Lipson & Ellison, 2002), whereas economic models of the family have been applied to explain the relative contributions of fathers to childcare and involvement. According to a family economic bargaining model, for instance, domestic labour is undesirable and thus performed by the partner with less power (i.e. earnings). Therefore, husbands can use their earnings to 'buy out' sharing in household tasks, and wives can use their earnings to 'buy' increased participation by their husbands. Yeung et al. (2003) recently lent some support for this by showing that it was only when mothers contribute half or more of the total family income that father involvement increased (by 10 minutes on weekdays and 48 minutes on weekends). Related to this, studies have also shown that fathers are more likely to be involved with their children when mothers have more education, are older (Pleck, 1997), are employed for more hours (Coltrane, Parke & Adams, 2004), and when fathers have positive views of the mothers' employment (Peterson & Gerson, 1992). Finally, fathers are more likely to be involved when they are religious (King, 2003), and are more likely to be involved (Deutsch, 2001; Sanderson & Thompson, 2002) and also satisfied with their involvement (Renk et al., 2003) if they have egalitarian attitudes about gender roles. Recent research showed that gender roles might be related not only to levels of father involvement but also to fathers' parenting style. Sabattini and Leaper (2004) showed that in families where the division of childcare was egalitarian, fathers' parenting style was authoritative, whereas in families where the division of childcare was traditional, fathers' parenting was disengaged. Finally, fathers' perceptions of mothers' confidence in their own parenting, as well as mothers' emotional appraisal of fathers' parenting and their shared 'parenting philosophy', were significant predictors of father involvement in childrearing activities (McBride & Rane, 1998).

Co-parental relations

American research summarising the findings on the close associations between marriage and fathering suggest that the father–child relationship is a system with less internal regulation and thus depends on the marital system for buffering (Parke & Beitel, 1988). As Doherty et al. (1998) note, standards and expectations for fathering are more variable than those for mothering, and so fathers' behaviour is strongly influenced by the meanings and expectations of fathers, mothers, children, extended family, and broader cultures and institutions. Whereas the mother–child relationship is biologically based, the father–child relationship may be less evolutionarily programmed and therefore requires a supportive marriage and actual involvement to emerge (Feldman, 2000), as evolutionary theory would predict. Or, in line with role theory, because fathering lacks a clear 'job description' fathers' behaviour is strongly influenced by the meanings and expectations of both the family actors and broader cultures and institutions. Recently, Gartstein and Fagot (2003) showed that marital/family adjustment contributed to preschool children's externalising behaviours for fathers, but not for mothers, which is in line with research indicating that fathers' parenting and attitudes may be more sensitive to the effects of marital functioning (Coiro & Emery, 1998). Gartstein and Fagot (2003) suggested that fathers who perceive their marriages as unsatisfying and conflictual are also likely to express negativity in their approach to their children, and perceive their children as experiencing higher levels of behaviour problems. European (including British) research tends to treat cohabiting partners with children as married partners with children, and so the focus has become the quality of the relationship between two parents, rather than that between husband and wife. In any case, it seems that interparental conflict is associated with men's withdrawal from both their partners and their children (Howes & Markman, 1989; NICHD Early Care Research Network, 2000), with the impact of interparental conflict on fathers' parenting being especially detrimental for daughters (Kerig, Cowan & Cowan, 1993).

Children's characteristics

Of all the children's characteristics that have been explored as possible determinants of father involvement, gender has by far been most extensively researched. Some research has shown that a child's age might also be related to father involvement, and recent findings suggest that fathers, and especially stepfathers, are also more involved with younger children (Hofferth & Anderson, 2003). As noted earlier, a lot less is known about the role of the child's behaviour on the father's parenting. Below is a discussion of the evidence linking father involvement with (i) child's gender and (ii) child's behaviour.

(i) Child's gender

Although not consistently (Amato, 1994; Russell & Saebel, 1997), fathers are shown to be more involved with their sons than with their daughters (Barnett, Marshall & Pleck, 1992; Cabrera et al., 2000; Manlove & Vernon-Feagans, 2002; Updegraff, McHale, Crouter & Kupanoff, 2001), which is in line with research showing that a child's gender can influence various aspects of family dynamics. For example, Blair, Wenk and Hardesty (1994) found that paternal involvement, as indicated by time spent with children, increased as the number of sons present in the home increased. Recent US evidence has shown that girls are significantly more likely than boys to be in regular, non-relative care when they are between 3 and 6 years old (Hiedeman, Joesch & Rose, 2004), and that, compared to the birth of a daughter, the birth of a son speeds the mother's transition into marriage when the child is born before the mother's first marriage (Lundberg & Rose, 2003) and increases the father's labour supply and wage rate (Lundberg & Rose, 2002). Furthermore, there is evidence (Morgan, Lye & Condran, 1988) that families with a daughter have a higher divorce risk than families with a son (but see Diekmann & Schmidheiny, 2004). Earlier, Harris and Morgan (1991) had shown that although sons received more attention than daughters from their fathers, daughters with brothers received more attention than daughters who did not have brothers, suggesting that the presence of sons caused fathers to become more active parents, which, in turn, affected their involvement with daughters. Even when fathers are involved with both sons and daughters, fathers' parenting differs depending on the gender of the child, with fathers being likely to reward daughters for positive, compliant behaviours, and sons for assertive actions (Kerig et al., 1993), or to reward girls and punish boys for expressing sadness and fear (Garside & Klimes-Dougan, 2002). In fact, Cowan, Cowan and Kerig (1993) argued that the differential socialisation of daughters and sons occurs primarily with fathers.

(ii) Child's behaviour

Given that many men believe that involvement in children is a voluntary activity (Cabrera et al., 2000; Hosley & Montemayor, 1997), positive children's attributes (associated with increased parental inputs, in general (Eccles & Harold, 1996; Grolnick, Benjet, Kurowski & Apostoleris, 1997)) might be expected to lead fathers to invest more in their children. A recent study by Gadeyne, Ghesquiere and Onghena (2004) showed that young children's externalising and attention problem behaviour predicted high levels of control in mothers and low levels of support in fathers. Sheeber, Hops, Andrews, Alpert and Davis (1998) also showed that, in response to their adolescent's depressive behaviour, mothers tended to increase their facilitative behaviour whereas fathers tended to lower their involvement, a pattern of reactions consistent with the evolutionary approaches to determinants of men's and women's parenting effort. Under this perspective one should expect child factors to affect father involvement more than mother involvement, and social father involvement more than biological father involvement: stepfathers may be found to increase their involvement with those stepchildren that can be seen as good 'investments' (Josephson, 2002) or simply pleasant to be with (Hofferth, Pleck, Stueve, Bianchi & Sayer, 2002). Recently Dunn, Cheng, O'Connor and Bridges (2004) showed that conflict in children's relationships with their non-resident fathers was significantly correlated with conflict in child–stepfather relationships, which suggests that perhaps the characteristics of 'difficult' children contribute to negative relationships with both 'fathers' by eliciting similar responses from different people. Taking a role theory perspective, such a pattern of results would indicate that children who are confident and well-adjusted elicit high father involvement levels because they expect, and so encourage, their fathers to be involved. Indeed, recent studies have shown that high adolescent self-esteem promoted perceived parental acceptance over six months (Ohannessian, Lerner, Lerner & von Eye, 1998) and favourable parenting characteristics over one year (Shek, 1999). Under this perspective, because the stepfather's role is even less clearly defined than that of the biological father, stepfathers might be even more dependent than biological fathers on the expectations and support from the other family actors, and so well-adjusted and confident children might be more successful than withdrawn or difficult children in encouraging or eliciting high levels of involvement from their stepfathers.

STUDY I: LONGITUDINAL STUDY OF PREDICTORS OF RESIDENT FATHERS' INVOLVEMENT WITH THEIR CHILDREN IN CONTINUOUSLY INTACT TWO-PARENT BIOLOGICAL FAMILIES

This study (Flouri & Buchanan, 2003d) used longitudinal data from the National Child Development Study (NCDS) to explore the five major sources of influence on father involvement discussed above, and to propose a mediating model testing the relationship between child's temperament, marital relationship, and father involvement. The study was part of a larger project that Ann Buchanan and I carried out with research funding from the UK Economic and Social Research Council in 2000–01 to investigate father involvement and child outcomes as well as determinants of father involvement using the NCDS dataset. Several of the studies described in this book were the result of this larger project.

The National Child Development Study (NCDS)

The NCDS is a continuing longitudinal study of 17 000 children born between 3 and 9 March 1958 in England, Scotland and Wales. The aim of the study was to improve understanding of the factors affecting human development over the lifespan. The NCDS has its origins in the Perinatal Mortality Survey, which was sponsored by the National Birthday Trust and was designed to examine the social and obstetric factors associated with stillbirth and death in early infancy among the 17 000 children born in England, Scotland and Wales in that one week.

To date six follow-ups have been made. These were carried out in 1965 (when the cohort members were aged 7), in 1969 (aged 11), in 1974 (aged 16), in 1981 (aged 23), in 1991 (aged 33), and in 2000 (aged 42). In addition, records of examination attainments at school-leaving were obtained from schools and education authorities in 1978, when the cohort members were aged 20. Overall, the representative nature of the study has been generally maintained (Shepherd, 1993). Refusals have been low. However, a major problem with the NCDS is the possibility of bias in the responding sample. Analysis of non-response bias has indicated that there were particularly high losses of participants in some more disadvantaged groups. It is possible that those who could not be traced may be more disadvantaged than those who have been traced. Despite these limitations, the NCDS is one of the best datasets available to investigate the long-term effects of parental background.

These studies used data from the first three NCDS sweeps. In the third sweep in 1974 (when cohort members were aged 16) the child's parent or primary caregiver was asked if the child had lived continuously with his/her own parents. Of the 11 691 cohort members who were traced in 1974, 7802 had lived continuously until age 16 with both parents. This was our initial sample. For the majority of these cases the parent or primary caregiver answering the questions about the child was the child's mother. In particular, the informant was the mother for 98.7% of the cases at age 7, for 96.6% at age 11 and for 92.4% at age 16.

Measures

Father involvement and mother involvement at age 7, 11 and 16 in the NCDS

In the NCDS there were four 3-point scales pertaining to father involvement and three 3-point scales pertaining to mother involvement at age 7. The items on father involvement were 'outings with father', 'father reads to the child', 'father manages the child' (parental reports) and 'father is interested in the child's education' (teacher's report). Responses were 'most weeks', 'occasionally' and 'hardly ever' for the first two items, 'equal role', 'left to mother' and 'mother does more' for the third item, and 'very interested/over-concerned', 'some interest' and 'little interest' for the fourth item. The items on mother involvement (similarly anchored) were 'outings with mother' and 'mother reads to the child' (parental reports), and 'mother is interested in the child's education' (teacher's report). At age 11 the items on father involvement were 'outings with father' and 'father manages the child' (parental reports), and 'father is interested in the child's education' (teacher's report). The items on mother involvement were 'outings with mother' (parental report) and 'mother is interested in the child's education' (teacher's report). At age 16 only the teacher's assessment of the father's and mother's

Table 2.1 Father involvement in intact families in the NCDS ($N = 7802$)

Items	Age 7 (% of valid cases)	Age 11 (% of valid cases)	Age 16 (% of valid cases)
1. *Father reads to the child* 'Most weeks' (vs 'occasionally' and 'hardly ever')	37.4%	N/A	N/A
2. *Father takes outings with the child* 'Most weeks' (vs 'occasionally' and 'hardly ever')	72.7%	53.3%	N/A
3. *Father manages the child* 'Equal/big role' (vs 'mother does more' and 'left to mother')	60.0%	67.1%	N/A
4. *Father is interested in the child's education* 'Very interested/over-concerned' (vs 'some' and 'little interest')	43.6%	43.9%	46.9%

Source: Adapted from Flouri, E. & Buchanan, A. (2003d). What predicts fathers' involvement with their children? A prospective study of intact families. *British Journal of Developmental Psychology*, 21, 81–97.

interest in the child's education measured father and mother involvement. Because of the very small occurrence of low involvement responses in both mothers and fathers (e.g. only 4.6% of the fathers and only 1.3% of the mothers were reported to have never taken outings with the child at age 7), the low/middle involvement responses were combined (see Table 2.1).

Father's and mother's characteristics in the NCDS

The father's and mother's characteristics in the NCDS that were included in the study were age of mother and father at the time of the child's birth, age they left full-time education, and employment status at each childhood sweep (i.e. when the cohort child was aged 7, 11 and 16). The father's employment status at all childhood sweeps was measured with a dichotomous parental report indicating whether the father was employed or sick, disabled or retired. Mother's employment status at child's age 7 was measured by asking the parent if the mother had, or had not, worked full- or part-time since the child had been at school. At age 11, mother's employment status was 'employed' if the mother had had paid work since the last sweep (4 years ago), and at age 16

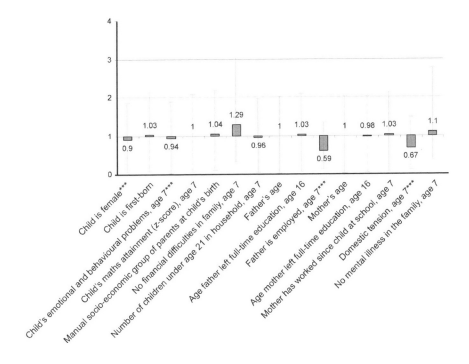

Figure 2.1 Multiple logistic regression's OR (with 95% confidence intervals) showing predictors of whether the father takes a role 'equal to mother's' in managing the child at age 7 in the NCDS ($N = 5432$)
Note: ***$p<0.001$

mother's employment status was measured with one dichotomous item asking whether the mother was in paid employment or not.

Co-parental relations and contextual factors in the NCDS

Two items were used to tap co-parental relations and three items measured contextual factors in the NCDS. Co-parental relations were measured with the Health Visitor's assessment at age 7 of evidence of domestic tension and mental illness in the family (both 1-item measures). The contextual factors were socio-economic status of parents at child's birth ('non-manual' vs 'manual'), sibship size (number of children under age 21 in the household) and evidence of financial difficulties. Financial difficulties were measured with receipt of free school meals at age 11 and 16, and, in absence of this measure at age 7, with the Health Visitor's 1-item assessment of evidence of

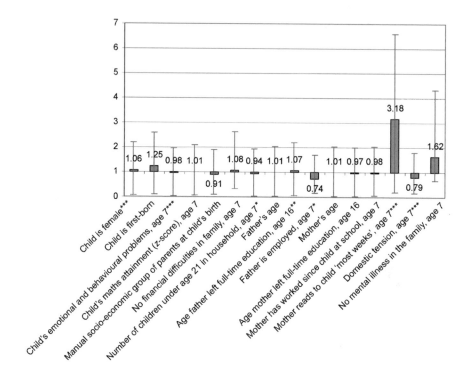

Figure 2.2 Multiple logistic regression's OR (with 95% confidence intervals) showing predictors of whether the father reads to the child 'most weeks' at age 7 in the NCDS (N = 5368)
Notes: *p < 0.05;   **p < .01;   ***p < .001

financial difficulties in the family at age 7. Of the 7802 cohort children who were the initial sample for this study, 6655 (85.3%) were assessed not to be in families characterised by financial difficulties at age 7, 7160 (91.8%) did not receive free school meals at age 11, and 7246 (92.9%) did not receive free school meals at age 16. For 1084 (13.9%) of the 7802 cases, the parents' socio-economic status at child's birth was manual, and for 238 (3.1%) there was evidence of domestic tension at age 7. For 7048 (90.3%) cases the Health Visitor reported no evidence of mental illness in the families of the cohort children when they were age 7.

Child's characteristics in the NCDS

The child's characteristics that were included in this study were gender, birth order (first-born child or not), emotional and behavioural problems,

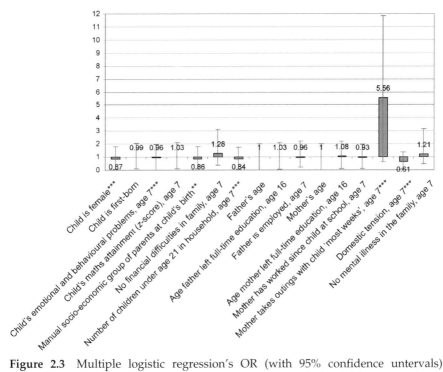

Figure 2.3 Multiple logistic regression's OR (with 95% confidence untervals) showing predictors of whether the father takes outing with the child 'most weeks' at age 7 in the NCDS ($N = 5423$)
Notes: $*p < 0.05$; $**p < 0.01$; $***p < 0.001$

and educational attainment at each age (7, 11 and 16 years). Of the 7802 NCDS children of the study, 3811 (48.8%) were female and 3006 (38.5%) were first-born. In the NCDS, emotional and behavioural problems in childhood and adolescence were assessed with the Rutter 'A' Health and Behaviour Checklist (Rutter, Tizard & Whitmore, 1970), which has been widely used to measure emotional and behavioural well-being both in the United Kingdom and elsewhere. In the NCDS the full Rutter 'A' Health and Behaviour Checklist (31 items) was completed by the parent or primary caregiver at age 16, whereas for ages 7 and 11 a shortened version (23 items) was used. Elliott and Richards (1991) used 14 of the Rutter 'A' items to assess the child's behaviour at ages 7 and 11. These 14 parental reports were: the child is disobedient at home, fights with other children, is irritable and quick to fly off the handle, destroys own or others' belongings, is squirmy or fidgety, has difficulty settling to anything, worries about many things, is upset by new situations, is bullied by other children, is miserable or tearful, has twitches or mannerisms, sucks thumb or finger, bites nails,

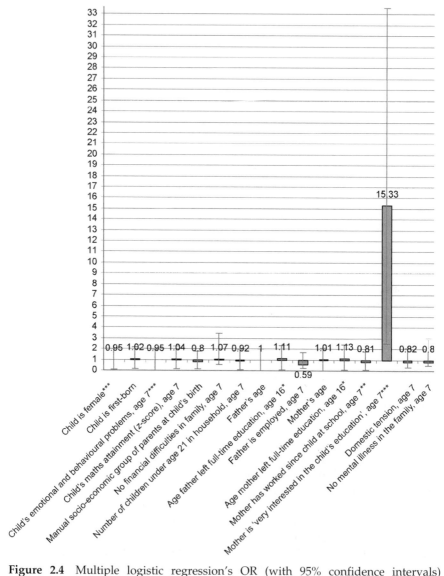

Figure 2.4 Multiple logistic regression's OR (with 95% confidence intervals) showing predictors of whether the father is 'very interested in the child's education' at age 7 in the NCDS ($N = 3592$)
Notes: *$p < 0.05$; **$p < 0.01$; ***$p < 0.001$

and prefers to do things alone. At all three times (ages 7, 11 and 16) the parent was asked whether the description of the behaviour applies to the child 'never' (coded '0'), 'sometimes' (coded '1') or 'frequently' (coded '2'). The mean Rutter 'A' score (ranging from 0 to 24) at ages 7 and 11 was 6.18

(SD = 3.51) and 6.24 (SD = 3.47), respectively. At age 16 the mean 'full' Rutter 'A' score (ranging from 0 to 35) was 5.34 (SD = 4.39). Attainment in childhood and adolescence was measured with mathematics tests designed by the National Foundation for Educational Research (NFER); in particular, with a 10-item problem arithmetic test at age 7, a 40-item mathematics test at age 11, and a 31-item mathematics comprehension test at age 16.

Results

We carried out separate logistic regression analyses to predict each aspect of father involvement at each childhood sweep. As can be seen in Figures 2.1 to 2.4, a father was more likely to take an active role in managing his child at age 7 if he was not employed, if the child was male and if the child was psychologically adjusted, and if the co-parental relationship was good. A father was more likely to read to his child at age 7 if he was more educated and not employed, if the child was first-born and if the child was psychologically adjusted, if the family was smaller and its socio-economic status not manual, and if the mother also read to the child. A father was more likely to take outings with his child if the child was male and if the child was psychologically adjusted, if the family was smaller and its socio-economic status not manual, if the mother was more educated and took outings herself with the child and if the co-parental relationship was good. Finally, a father was more likely to be 'very interested' in his child's education if the child was psychologically adjusted, if the family's socio-economic status was not manual, if both he and the child's mother were more educated, if the mother had not worked since the child started school, and if the mother herself was 'very interested' in the child's education.

A father was more likely to have an active role in managing his child at age 11 if he had managed the child at age 7, if the child was male and if the child was psychologically adjusted, if the family was smaller, and if there had been no mental health difficulties in the family when the child was aged 7. A father was more likely to take outings with his child at age 11 if the father was younger and had taken outings with the child when the child was aged 7, if the child was male and did well at his maths exams, if the mother took outings with the child at age 11, and if the co-parental relationship when the child was aged 7 was good. Finally, a father was more likely to be interested in his child's education when the child was aged 11 if the father was interested in the child's education when the child was aged 7 and if the father was more educated, if the child did well in his or her maths exams, if the family was smaller, and if the mother had not worked since the child was aged 7, and was also interested in the child's education at age 11. Finally, a father was more likely to be interested in his child's education at age 16 if the father was more educated, if the child did well at school, if the

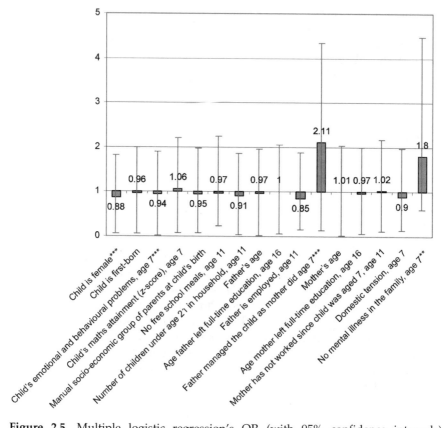

Figure 2.5 Multiple logistic regression's OR (with 95% confidence intervals) showing predictors of whether the father takes a role 'equal to mother's' in managing the child at age 11 in the NCDS (N = 5756)
Notes: **p < 0.01; ***p < 0.001

family was smaller, and if the mother was also interested in the child's education at age 16. Figures 2.5 to 2.8 show graphically the results of the logistic regressions carried out to explore predictors of these aspects of father involvement.

Child's academic attainment and psychological adjustment: Causes or results of father involvement?

Because it was not clear from the results above if child's concurrent psychological adjustment and child's good academic attainment were the 'causes' or the 'effects' of high father involvement (especially because, as I discuss in Chapters 3 and 4, both child's adjustment and child's attainment

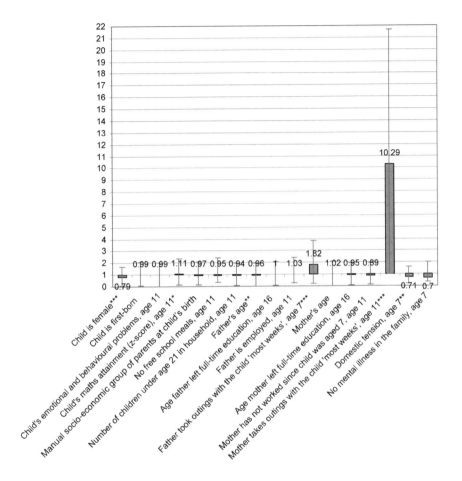

Figure 2.6 Multiple logistic regression's OR (with 95% confidence intervals) showing predictors of whether the father takes outing with the child 'most weeks' at age 11 in the NCDS ($N = 5720$)

Notes: **$p < 0.01$; ***$p < 0.001$

are seen as 'effects' of father involvement), we looked at the relationship between aspects of father involvement and earlier child's psychological adjustment and academic attainment. When we substituted child's emotional and behavioural problems at age 11 with child's emotional and behavioural problems at age 7 we found that emotional and behavioural problems at age 7 predicted father's role in managing the child at age 11 even after controlling for father's role in managing the child at age 7 (OR = 0.97, 95% CI = 0.96, 0.99, $p < 0.01$, chi-square = 713.75, df 16, $p < 0.001$) and all the other factors in the model. Child's emotional and behavioural problems at age 7, however, did not predict outings with father at age 11 (OR = 0.99, 95% CI = 0.97, 1.02, $p > 0.05$) or father's interest in child's education at either age 11 (OR = 0.99, 95% CI = 0.95, 1.02, $p > 0.05$) or age 16 (OR = 0.98, 95% CI = 0.93, 1.04, $p > 0.05$). Father's interest in the child's education at age 16 was not predicted from the child's emotional and behavioural problems at age 11 either (OR = 1.00, 95% CI = 0.95, 1.06, $p > 0.05$).

Unfortunately in the NCDS there is no information on the child's behaviour before age 7 so we could not see if father involvement at age 7 could be predicted from the child's emotional and behavioural problems earlier in life. Similarly, the child's maths attainment at age 7 could not predict the father's role in managing the child at age 11 (OR = 1.01, 95% CI = 0.95, 1.07, $p > 0.05$), outings with the father at age 11 (OR = 1.05, 95% CI = .96, 1.15, $p > 0.05$), or the father's interest in the child's education at age 16 (OR = 1.14, 95% CI = 0.94, 1.39, $p > 0.05$), although it predicted the father's interest in the child's education at age 11 (OR = 1.30, 95% CI = 1.14, 1.48, $p < 0.001$). Attainment at age 11 also failed to predict the father's interest in the child's education at age 16 (OR = 1.23, 95% CI = .99, 1.53, $p > 0.05$).

Does domestic tension mediate the relationship between the child's behaviour and father involvement?

In attempting to shed some light on how the relationship between the child's emotional and behavioural well-being and father involvement might work we followed Leve, Scaramella and Fagot (2001) who suggested that children's emotional and behavioural problems might affect the quality of the co-parental relationship which then may impact on the level of father involvement. In particular, Leve et al. (2001), based on evidence showing that a temperamentally difficult child may strain both the parent–child relationship (Stocker, 1995) and the marital relationship (Sheeber & Johnson, 1992), showed that for fathers, but not for mothers, a temperamentally difficult child puts stress on the marital relationship, which then decreases the father's pleasure in parenting.

However, in this study there was no evidence that domestic tension at age 7 mediated the relationship between the child's emotional and behavioural problems at age 7 and any of the four indicators of father involvement at age 7. There was similarly no evidence that domestic tension mediated the relationship between the child's emotional and behavioural problems at age 7 and any of the indicators of father involvement at age 11 and 16 (for full results, see Flouri & Buchanan, 2003d).

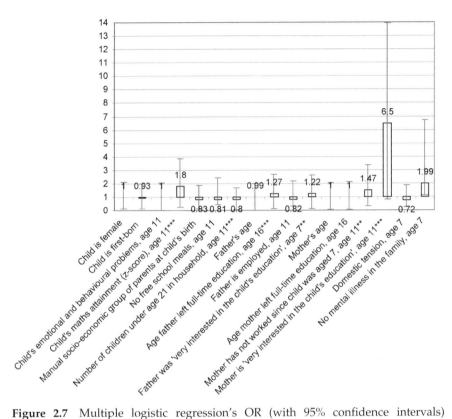

Figure 2.7 Multiple logistic regression's OR (with 95% confidence intervals) showing predictors of whether the father is 'very interested in the child's education' at age 11 in the NCDS ($N = 2860$)

Notes: **$p < 0.01$; ***$p < 0.001$

Discussion

This study explored predictors from five different groups of influence (the child's characteristics, contextual factors, the father's characteristics, the mother's characteristics, and the co-parental relationship) of fathers' involvement with their children in intact families at three different developmental stages: at age 7, 11 and 16. Father involvement was predicted by different factors at different children's ages but generally it was continuous and multidimensional, and strongly associated with mother involvement. Low parental socio-economic status and the child's behavioural problems were negatively related to father involvement at age 7. With older children father involvement was inversely related to family size and poor school performance. Financial difficulties in the family were not related to father involvement at any age. Domestic tension was

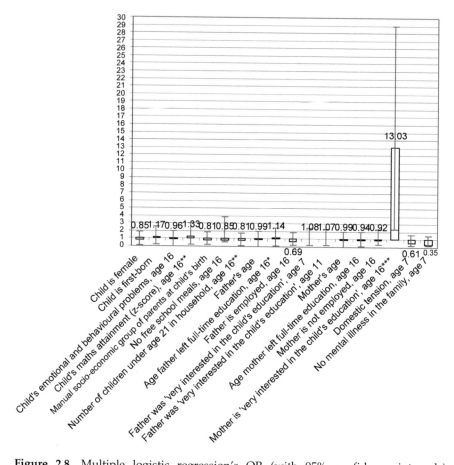

Figure 2.8 Multiple logistic regression's OR (with 95% confidence intervals) showing predictors of whether the father is 'very interested in the child's education' at age 16 in the NCDS ($N = 1937$)
Notes: *$p < 0.05$; **$p < 0.01$; ***$p < 0.001$

negatively related to certain aspects of father involvement with younger children, whereas the father's education was positively related to father involvement.

Caution should be exercised in interpreting these findings, however. First, there remain the limitations of any longitudinal study, in particular attrition, and the limitations of using data from the National Child Development Study which may be dated. It is possible that fathering and mothering in Britain of 1965–74 may be very different from fathering and mothering in today's families. Our sample was growing up in the 1960s, when fathers' involvement with their children was less active and 'intact' families with mothers outside of the labour force were more common than today. Second, since we know that the losses to the NCDS were greatest among the more disadvantaged children, it is possible that this study underestimates the long-term impact of disadvantage. Related to this, issues emerge from using what are largely middle-class indices of father involvement. Further, for the majority of the cases the mother assessed both father and mother involvement and so, in essence, this study explored the predictors of mothers' perceived father involvement. Finally, only father involvement in continuously intact families was explored in this study. As is discussed below (as well as in Chapter 8), father involvement is influenced by different factors in different family settings. Even so, these results show that father involvement is continuous, is strongly related to mother involvement and is multidimensional, and suggest the importance of children's behaviour for both researchers and practitioners as they address issues related to father involvement.

STUDY II: CROSS-SECTIONAL STUDY OF PREDICTORS OF RESIDENT FATHERS' INVOLVEMENT WITH THEIR CHILDREN IN BIOLOGICAL AND RESTRUCTURED TWO-PARENT FAMILIES

This study was carried out in order to address some of the limitations of the longitudinal study described above. Whereas the aim was still to explore predictors of father involvement, this study differed from the previous one in the following respects. First, it was cross-sectional and so, despite making inferences of causality particularly difficult, it reflected fathering in modern British families, something for which the NCDS has been particularly criticised. Second, the study looked at both social and biological fathers. Third, it explored relationships in both restructured and intact families. Fourth, it explored predictors of both father-reported father involvement and child-reported father involvement, thus bringing on board the potentially different perspectives of the different family actors.

The Families in the Millennium Study (FMS)

The data for this study came from a research project we carried out in 2001–02 (Welsh, Buchanan, Flouri & Lewis, 2004) to explore fathers' involvement with their secondary school-age children in modern Britain. Pupils (aged 11–18 years) at three comprehensive British schools (one in an inner city, one in the suburbs, and one in a rural area) – selected to have an average

Ofsted[1] result and around 1000 pupils each – took part in the study. Children were asked to fill out a questionnaire in class and take questionnaires for their parents or parent figures to fill out at home. In all, 989 girls and 1212 boys (17 children did not state their gender) and 1091 parents (635 mothers of whom 618 were biological, and 452 fathers of whom 408 were biological – 4 parents did not state their gender) took part in the study. The mean age of mothers was 41.1 (SD = 5.6) years and the mean age of fathers was 44.8 (SD = 6.9) years. In all, 20.4% of the mothers and 10.3% of the fathers reported that they did not work, and 19.6% of the mothers and 22.4% of the fathers reported that their highest educational qualification was a university degree or higher. Of the 1091 parents, 624 were members of family groups. Therefore, a total of 312 couples took part in the study. For 265 of those, the child's responses to the questionnaire were also obtained, and so for 265 families perceptions and responses from three family members (mother figure, father figure and child) could be combined. In all, data from 158 (60.5%) boys and 103 (39.5% girls) were available (4 children did not state their gender). The mean age of the children was 13.39 (SD = 1.66) years. Of the 265 families, in 233 both parent figures lived together. Of the 233 children, 203 reported that they lived with both their natural parents, 22 with their natural mother and stepfather, 3 with their natural father and stepmother, 2 with their foster parents, 2 with their grandparents, and 1 lived in some 'other' family structure. Because the aim of the study was to explore parental involvement in biological and restructured families, only the children who lived with their natural parents and those who lived in restructured families were included in the study. The three restructured families in which the mother figure was a stepmother were dropped from the analysis due to the small sample size.[2] Therefore 225 families were included in the study. This was the initial sample size.[2] The majority of the families were White and a sizeable proportion was University educated: 77.2% of the fathers and 78.7% of the mothers were 'White British', and 19.4% of the fathers and 18.6% of the mothers had a university degree or higher. Eight (3.6%) of the 225 families reported to have children receiving free school meals.

Measures

Father involvement and mother involvement in the FMS

Father involvement was measured with the Modified Inventory of Father Involvement (Hawkins et al., 2002). Fathers were asked to think of their

---

[1]Ofsted (Office for Standards in Education) is a non-ministerial UK government department, set up on 1 September 1992, whose main aim is to help to improve the quality and standards of education and childcare through independent inspection and regulation, and provide advice to the Secretary of State.
[2]Although in the results section some illustrative findings from the 'full' children's sample (N = 2218) are also reported.

experiences as parents over the past 12 months and rate in a 26-item 5-point scale how good a job (ranging from 'very poor' to 'excellent') they did in bringing up the study child. Sample items were: 'Disciplining him/her' and 'Praising him/her for being good or doing the right thing'. Mothers filled out the same questionnaire adapted to assess their own experiences as parents. Cronbach's alphas were 0.93 for mothers and 0.95 for fathers. Children were also asked to complete the same questionnaire to assess their mothers' and fathers' involvement. In all, Hawkins et al.'s (2002) measure of father involvement was composed of nine subscales capturing the different dimensions of father involvement. These were: discipline, school encouragement, mother support, providing, talking together, praise, developing talents, reading support and attentiveness.

Father's and mother's characteristics in FMS

These included age of mother and father, self-reported educational attainment (ranging from (0) 'no qualifications' to (4) 'university degree') and employment status. For mothers, employment status was assessed as 'working full-time', 'working part-time', or 'no work'. For fathers the item was 'employed' (full- or part-time) or 'no work' (as only six fathers worked part-time). Wiggins and Bynner's (1993) 8-item 5-point Gender Equality Scale, completed by both mothers and fathers, was also used. Sample items were: 'When both partners work full-time the man should take an equal share of the domestic chores' and 'Women should have the same chances as men to get some training or have a career'. Cronbach's alphas were 0.81 in the fathers' sample and 0.71 in the mothers' sample. In addition, parents assessed their own father involvement and mother involvement. These were 5-point scales (of 5 and 4 questions, respectively) using the items from the first sweep of the National Child Development Study described in Study I above as well as a single item asking parents if their own father/ mother 'was involved with them'. Fathers' paternal and maternal involvement scales had Cronbach's alphas of 0.88 and 0.84, respectively. Mothers' paternal and maternal involvement scales had Cronbach's alphas of 0.88 and 0.83, respectively. Parents also filled out the 12-item version of the General Health Questionnaire (GHQ-12) which measures aspects of poor psychological functioning (Goldberg, 1978; Goldberg & Williams, 1988) with items such as 'lost much sleep over worry', and seven 5-point items from Rosenberg's (1965) Self-Esteem Scale. In the fathers' sample, Cronbach's alphas were 0.91 and 0.88, respectively. In the mothers' sample, Cronbach's alphas were 0.90 and 0.87, respectively.

Contextual factors and quality of the co-parental relationship in the FMS

The contextual factors were socio-economic status of parents (assessed with receipt of free school meals), number of children under age 21 in the household, and family structure (assessed as living with both biological parents versus living in stepfather families). Co-parental relations were measured with nine items (measured in 5-point scales) from the Parenting Alliance Inventory (Abidin & Brunner, 1995) measuring inter-parental conflict, completed by mothers and fathers. Cronbach's alphas were 0.80 in the fathers' sample and 0.86 in the mothers' sample. Children assessed interparental conflict by completing nine items (measured in 3-point scales) from Grych, Seid and Fincham's (1992) Children's Perception of Inter-parental Conflict Scale. Cronbach's alpha was 0.85.

Child's characteristics in FMS

The child's characteristics that were included in this study were gender, age and emotional and behavioural problems as assessed by the 25-item Strengths and Difficulties Questionnaire (Goodman, 1994, 1997), which was filled out by fathers, mothers and children (Cronbach's alphas were 0.82 in both the fathers' and the mothers' sample and 0.81 in the children's sample). The Strengths and Difficulties Questionnaire (SDQ) measures four difficulties (hyperactivity, emotional symptoms, conduct problems, and peer problems), as well as prosocial behaviour. Children also filled out the same seven items from Rosenberg's (1965) Self-Esteem Scale that their parents completed, and stated their educational attainment by reporting the highest exam they had taken (on a 6-point scale ranging from 'none' to 'AS level').

Results

For 1475 of the 2218 children of the study there was information regarding father's biological relatedness to the child, father's residency status, and father's involvement. The father figure was 'resident and biological' for 1081 of those children, 'social' for 130, and 'non-resident and biological' for 264. Resident biological fathers were perceived by the children as the most involved and social fathers as the least involved ($F(2, 1472) = 133.123$, $p < 0.001$). Boys did not give higher overall father involvement scores than girls ($F(1, 1497) = 1.846$, $p < 0.05$), but compared to girls they reported their father to talk to them more ($F(1, 1983) = 9.189$, $p < 0.01$). Figure 2.9 shows the mean scores for each dimension of child-reported father involvement for the three groups of fathers in the whole children's sample, and Figures 2.10 and 2.11 show the results by child's gender.

Biological resident fathers were scored as significantly the most involved in all nine aspects of father involvement by their children although there was

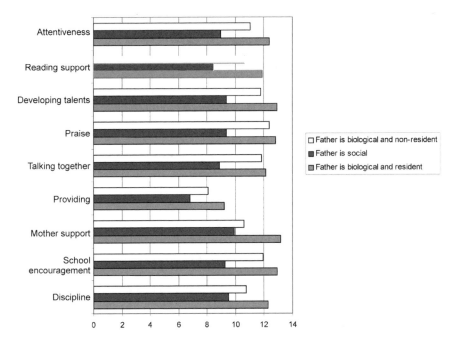

Figure 2.9 Mean father involvement scores in the whole children's sample

no statistically significant difference in the mean score given to 'talking together' between the biological resident and biological non-resident fathers. Social fathers were perceived as the least involved of both the resident and the non-resident biological fathers in all nine father involvement dimensions. There was no difference between social fathers and non-resident biological fathers in mother support, however. To explore any gender differences in father involvement scores across these nine dimensions, Figures 2.10 and 2.11 show the mean scores given separately by daughters and sons.

As with the whole sample, daughters gave the highest levels of involvement to their resident biological fathers, and the lowest to their social fathers. There was no difference in 'praise' and 'talking together' between the non-resident and the resident biological fathers.

As with the whole sample, sons gave the highest levels of involvement to their resident biological fathers, and the lowest to their social fathers. There was no difference in 'praise' and 'talking together' between the non-resident and the resident biological fathers, and there was no difference in

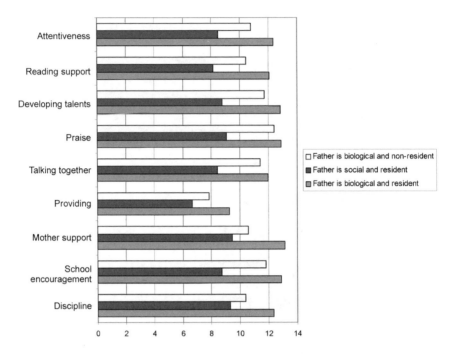

Figure 2.10   Mean father involvement scores given by daughters in the children's sample

mother support between the non-resident biological fathers and the social fathers.

Coming back to the matched family sample ($N = 233$), it was found that although father-reported father involvement and child-reported father involvement were interrelated ($r = 0.405$, $p < 0.001$), perhaps not surprisingly fathers and mothers reported lower levels of involvement than those ascribed to them by their children (see Figure 2.12). In line with previous research, father involvement was related to mother involvement ($r = 0.424$, $p < 0.001$). Child-reported father involvement was strongly related to child-reported mother involvement ($r = 0.816$, $p < 0.001$). Figure 2.13 shows the results from the multiple linear regression predicting father-reported father involvement from fathers' and mothers' self-reports, whereas Figure 2.14 shows the results from the multiple linear regression analysis carried out to predict child-reported father involvement.

As can be seen in these two figures, the strongest predictor of father involvement was mother involvement. Child-reported mother involvement predicted child-reported father involvement, and mother-reported mother

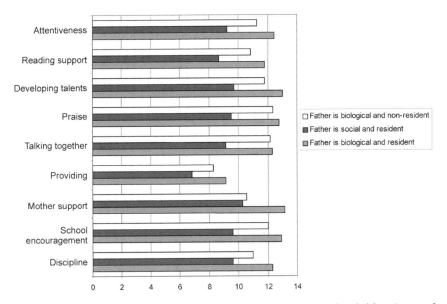

Figure 2.11   Mean father involvement scores given by sons in the children's sample

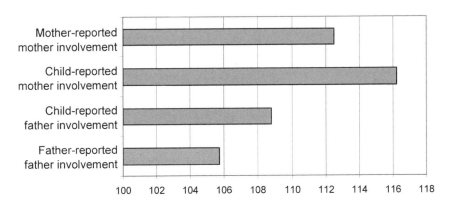

Figure 2.12   Mean involvement scores as reported by the different family actors ($N = 233$)

involvement predicted father-reported father involvement. In fact, mother involvement was the sole predictor of father involvement, as assessed by fathers. Child-reported father involvement, on the other hand, was positively associated with the child's self-esteem, and was higher for adolescents in biological than in restructured two-parent families.

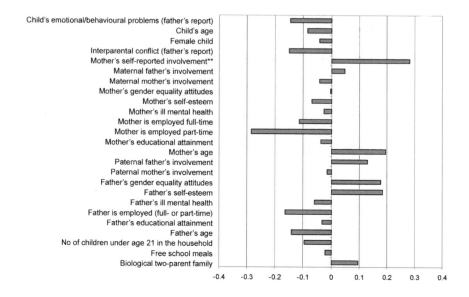

Figure 2.13 Standardised regression coefficients (β) predicting father-reported father involvement ($N = 115$)
Note: **$p < 0.01$

Discussion

Apart from the problems with the design and execution of this study, there are a further two limitations that I must acknowledge. First, the study investigated resident mothers' and fathers' involvement with their adolescent children in two-parent families and so the findings may not be applicable to different children's and parents' ages, to single-parent families, or non-resident parents. Second, involvement in this study was assessed by the parent's self-reported perception of his/her competency in the parental role, and by the child's perception of his/her parents' competency in that role, and so social desirability and self-presentation bias cannot be ruled out.

However, despite any cautionary notes, both studies described above were useful in pointing to promising directions for fathering research. Both underlined the importance of mother involvement, and the potential usefulness in exploring the role of the child's characteristics in father involvement. Although it is not clear if the child's self-esteem was the cause or the result of father involvement in the cross-sectional study, the

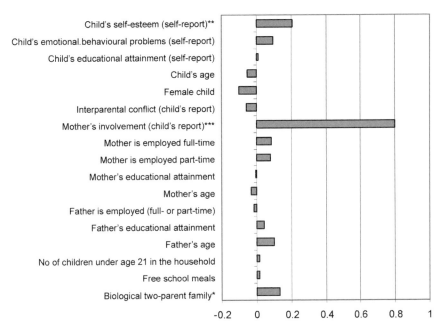

Figure 2.14 Standardised regression coefficients (β) predicting child-reported father involvement ($N = 92$)
Notes: $*p < 0.05$; $**p < 0.01$; $***p < 0.001$

longitudinal study showed that the child's emotional and behavioural problems in early childhood predicted low father participation in the management of the child in middle childhood, and the child's poor academic attainment in early childhood predicted a low father interest in the child's education in adolescence. It is quite likely that causation runs in both directions, with fathers more likely to be involved when their children are doing well in school and have fewer emotional and behavioural difficulties, and children doing better both academically and psychosocially when their fathers are involved. Further, both studies suggest that the generalisation of fathers' great involvement with their sons requires some further specification. In fact, the cross-sectional study found no evidence to support any gender differences in father involvement. Child-reported father involvement was not higher for boys than for girls, and fathers were as likely to be involved with their daughters as they were with their sons, at least in adolescence. Although the longitudinal study showed that in early and middle childhood fathers were more likely to manage and take outings with their sons than with their daughters, there was no gender difference, however, in the frequency with which the father read to the child or in the level of the father's interest in the child's education at any developmental stage.

SUMMARY AND CONCLUSIONS

According to Lamb et al. (1985, 1987) four factors influence the level of father involvement (usually taken to mean engagement, accessibility or availability to the child, and responsibility for the child's welfare and care): motivation, social support, skills and self-confidence, and institutional practices. According to role theory, because fathering can be considered a voluntary activity, fathers' behaviour is strongly influenced by the meanings and expectations of fathers themselves, as well as mothers, children, extended family, and broader cultures and institutions (Bonney et al., 1999). Evolutionary approaches to understanding fathering in humans suggest that men invest more in their children when the indirect benefit they get is greater than the benefit they could get from using their time and energy to seek additional mates (see Josephson, 2002, for a discussion). Other models (e.g. Belsky's (1984) model of parenting, and Doherty et al.'s (1998) model of fathering) present a systemic framework that highlights the interacting influences of five different groups of influences on father involvement: contextual factors, father's factors, mother's factors, quality of co-parental relationship, and child's factors. This chapter presented two empirical studies (one longitudinal and one cross-sectional) carried out to explore the role of these groups of factors in fathers' involvement with their school-aged children in two-parent families.

The longitudinal study, using data from the National Child Development Study (NCDS), which traces all children (ca 17 000) born between 3 and 9 March 1958 in England, Scotland and Wales, explored fathers' involvement with their children in intact families at three different developmental stages: when children were aged 7, 11 and 16. Father involvement was measured with the items: 'father takes outings with the child', 'father reads to the child', 'father manages the child', and 'father is interested in the child's education'. Father involvement was predicted by different factors as children increased in age but generally it was continuous and multi-dimensional, and strongly associated with mother involvement. Low parental socio-economic status and child behaviour problems were negatively related to father involvement at age 7. With older children, father involvement was inversely related to family size and the child's poor school performance. Domestic tension was negatively related to certain aspects of fathers' involvement with younger children, whereas the father's education was positively related to father involvement. Although, of course, several of these factors are related to socio-economic disadvantage, financial difficulties *per se* were not related to father involvement at either age. With regards to gender differences, in early and middle childhood fathers were more likely to manage and take outings with their sons than with their daughters, although there was no difference in the frequency with which fathers read to their children or in the fathers' level of interest in their children's education at any developmental stage. Domestic tension did not mediate the relationship between the children's emotional and behavioural problems and father involvement, a finding contrasting previous research showing that children's emotional and behavioural problems affect the quality of the co-parental relationship, which then impacts on the level of father involvement.

The cross-sectional study used data from 2218 pupils (aged 11–18 years) of three comprehensive 'average' British schools (one in an inner city, one in a suburban area, and one in a rural area) and 1091 of their parents. Father involvement was measured with the Modified Inventory of Father Involvement (Hawkins et al., 2002), asking fathers to think of their experiences as parents over the past 12 months and to rate on a 26-item 5-point scale how good a job (ranging from 'very poor' to 'excellent') they did in bringing up the study child. The 26 items were further grouped into 9 subscales capturing the different dimensions of father involvement. These were: discipline, school encouragement, mother support, providing, talking together, praise, developing talents, reading support, and attentiveness. Mothers filled out the same questionnaire adapted to assess their own experiences as parents. Children were also asked to complete the same questionnaire to assess their mothers' and fathers' involvement. For 1475 of the 2218 children of the study, there was information regarding father's biological relatedness to the child, father's residency status, and father's involvement. The father figure was 'resident and biological' for 1081 of those children, 'social' for 130, and 'non-resident and biological' for 264. Resident biological fathers were perceived by both sons and daughters as the most involved, and social fathers as the least involved. Children reported their mothers to be more involved than their fathers and, similarly, compared to mothers, fathers reported lower involvement with their children. However, compared to daughters, sons did not report higher father involvement scores, and fathers did not report higher involvement with sons than with daughters. In this study, when controlling for other factors, the only predictor of father-reported father involvement was mother involvement. Mother involvement was also positively related to child-reported father involvement, which was also associated with the child's self-esteem, and was higher for adolescents in biological than in restructured two-parent families.

In summary, the findings from both these studies suggest that mother involvement and father involvement are strongly interrelated and that it seems that fathers are more likely to be involved when their children are doing well in school and have fewer emotional and behavioural difficulties, whereas children are more likely to do well both academically and psychosocially when their fathers are involved. The longitudinal study showed that fathers were more likely to both manage and 'be seen' with their sons than with their daughters (at least when the children were aged 7), a finding that was not replicated in the cross-sectional study, which explored fathers' involvement with adolescent children in today's Britain. Furthermore, the cross-sectional study showed that boys did not give higher overall father involvement scores than girls. Taken together, these findings could suggest that perhaps today's fathers hold more egalitarian gender attitudes. Alternatively, these findings could suggest that father involvement in adolescence is less gender-specific. What the two studies presented here could not show, however, was whether, even when fathers were involved with both sons and daughters, fathers' parenting differed depending on the gender of the child. Other studies have shown, for example, that even when fathers are involved with both sons and daughters, they are more likely to reward daughters for positive, compliant behaviours, and sons for assertive actions, or to reward girls and punish boys for expressing sadness and fear. Finally, both studies showed that financial difficulties in the family were not related to father involvement at either age. This finding contrasts previous research, showing that economic stress affects fathering because the provider role still tends to be central to fathering. Leinonen et al. (2002), for example, showed that economic hardship was associated with symptoms of anxiety which were related both directly and indirectly (via hostile marital interaction) to punitive and non-involved fathering. An explanation of the finding that, in both the studies presented here, financial difficulties were not related to father involvement might have to do with the way financial difficulties were operationalised. In particular, rather than assessing specific economic hardships, the longitudinal study measured financial difficulties with receipt of free school meals at age 11 and 16, and, in the absence of this measure at age 7, with the Health Visitor's 1-item assessment of evidence of financial difficulties in the family when the cohort child was aged 7. The cross-sectional study, in turn, measured financial difficulties with receipt of free school meals. Arguably, these measures might not tap specific economic hardships. What is more, in both studies the percentage of children living in families characterised by financial difficulties (as operationalised in these studies) was small. In particular, only 8 (3.6%) of the 225 children of the cross-sectional study received free school meals. In the longitudinal study the Health Visitor assessed 6655 (85.3%) of the 7802 cohort children as living (at age 7) in families not characterised by financial difficulties, and only 8.2% of the 7802 cohort children at age 11 and 7.1% of the 7802 cohort children at age 16 received free school meals.

CHAPTER 3

FATHER INVOLVEMENT AND CHILDREN'S MENTAL HEALTH OUTCOMES

INTRODUCTION

Several (usually cross-sectional) studies have shown that father involvement is related to positive mental health outcomes for children even after controlling for mother involvement. Some studies have found no additive effect of father involvement in broad indices of children's mental health outcomes, and relatively few studies have shown adverse mental health in children of families where the father was reported to have been more affectionate than the mother. Extensive research has been carried out to explore the role of father absence (rather than involvement) in children's mental health. This chapter presents the findings from six empirical studies exploring the role of father involvement in children's mental health in Britain. All six studies adopted Bronfenbrenner's (1979) paradigm which locates factors associated with psychological outcomes in several 'ecological' domains, i.e. factors within the person, and factors that are related to family, school and the social environment.

EVIDENCE SHOWING POSITIVE ASSOCIATIONS BETWEEN FATHER INVOLVEMENT AND CHILDREN'S MENTAL HEALTH

Studies that have separated mothering from fathering showed that this might be a useful way of exploring parenting in relation to children's mental health outcomes. Barnett et al. (1992), for instance, showed that sons who reported a positive relationship with their mother or father had relatively low levels of psychological distress. In fact, when measures of both the mother–child relationship and the father–child relationship were entered simultaneously into a regression equation, only the father–child relationship was significantly related to a son's distress. More recently,

Dubowitz et al. (2001) showed that in their sample of 6 year olds child-perceived father support was associated with fewer depressive symptoms and greater sense of social competence, and Stocker, Richmond, Low, Alexander and Elias (2003) showed that, even after controlling for maternal negativity, paternal negativity predicted both internalising and externalising behaviour problems in school-age children. Earlier, Harris, Furstenberg and Marmer (1998) had shown that high involvement and increasing closeness between fathers and adolescents in intact families protected adolescents from engaging in delinquent behaviour and experiencing psychological distress, and Amato (1994) showed that closeness to fathers during childhood was positively related to adult daughters' and sons' educational and occupational mobility, psychological adjustment and well-being. Relatedly, Australian studies have shown that low maternal and paternal care are each associated with a two- to three-fold higher rate of depressive disorder in adolescents (Patton, Coffey, Posterino, Carlin & Wolfe, 2001), and that fathers' physical parenting style increased adolescent sons' (but decreased adolescent daughters') self-reported delinquency scores, whereas fathers' low warmth was positively related to adolescents' depressed mood, especially among daughters (Heaven, Newbury & Mak, 2004). Pedersen (1994) reported that among Norwegian adolescents, perceptions of bonding and caring on the part of one's father strongly predicted anxiety and depression. In Britain, research using data of children born in 1958 from the National Child Development Study has shown that children with involved fathers tended to engage in less antisocial behaviour (Flouri & Buchanan, 2002a) and to have more successful intimate relationships (Flouri & Buchanan, 2002b). At the same time, studies also suggest that father absence is a factor contributing to the lower well-being of children in mother-only families (Dornbusch et al., 1985), although other research suggests that father absence has few consequences for children once economic factors are controlled for (Crockett et al., 1993). More recently, De Leo et al. (2002) showed that death of the father in childhood increased the odds of a repeated suicide attempt in their elderly European suicide attempters' sample. Dubowitz, Black, Kerr, Starr and Harrington (2000) showed, in their study of inner-city 5 year olds in the USA, that although father absence was not associated with child neglect, in families with an identified and interviewed father, father's duration of involvement, sense of parenting efficacy, and involvement with household tasks were negatively associated with neglect.

Recent studies have also started to expand the domain of the father's role to include paternal influences other than strictly 'involvement'. A dimension of fathering that has received some attention, in relation to daughters' mental health outcomes in particular, is paternal over-protection. For example, Mori (1999) showed that fathers' overprotection predicted low self-esteem in younger adolescents, but had no effect in older adolescents' self-esteem, and Kitamura, Sugawara, Shima and Toda (1999) showed that paternal low care and paternal overprotection predicted antenatal depression. More recently, Dixon, Gill and Adair (2003) showed that fathers who believed strongly in the importance of attractiveness and careful control of food intake by women were significantly more likely to have adolescent daughters who induced vomiting to lose weight.

EVIDENCE SHOWING NEGATIVE OR NO ASSOCIATIONS BETWEEN FATHER INVOLVEMENT AND CHILDREN'S MENTAL HEALTH

However, although studies are generally salutary of the positive effects of father involvement (Black, Dubowitz & Starr, 1999) there are exceptions. Jorm, Dear, Rodgers and Christensen (2003), for instance, who explored retrospective reports of parental affection in anxiety and depression in mid-adulthood, showed that although retrospective reporting of greater affection from both fathers and mothers was generally associated with fewer anxiety and depression symptoms and lower neuroticism, there was also a significant interaction effect, such that mental health was worse in families where the father's level of affection was higher than the mother's. The authors suggested that family problems (such as higher rates of emotional problems in the parents, conflict in the home, parental separation or divorce, and parental mistreatment) accounted for much of the interaction observed, concluding that where the father was reported to have been more affectionate (but not more 'involved') than the mother, there tended to be increased family problems and increased risk for the offsprings' mental health problems. Coley's (2003) study of daughter–father relationships in low-income African American families also showed that although daughters' perceptions of anger and alienation from fathers was related to greater emotional and behavioural problems in adolescence, perceptions of trust and communication with fathers were not predictive of youth outcomes.

This chapter describes six studies I carried out with Ann Buchanan since 2000 to explore the role of the father figure's involvement in British children's mental health outcomes. The children's mental health outcomes explored were emotional and behavioural well-being, as assessed with Goodman's Strengths and Difficulties Questionnaire (Study I), psycho-logical distress, as assessed with the 12-item version of the General Health Questionnaire (Study II), emotional and behavioural well-being, as assessed with the Rutter 'A' Health and Behaviour Checklist (Study III), psychological distress, as assessed with the Malaise Inventory (Studies III and IV), life satisfaction (Study V), and happiness (Study VI). Mother involvement was controlled for in all studies apart from Studies I and V. In Study I, father involvement was measured with Hawkins et al.'s (2002) Modified Inventory of Father Involvement (see Study II of Chapter 2), and in Studies II and III with the 4 items assessing father involvement in NCDS (see Study I of Chapter 2), namely 'father takes outings with the child', 'father reads to the child', 'father manages the child', and 'father is interested in the child's education'. Father involvement was measured with 1 item asking whether the father read to the child at age 7 (Study IV), with a 5-item 3-point scale asking whether the father 'spends time with the child', 'hugs the child', 'shows an interest in the child's school work', 'talks through the child's worries with the child', and 'talks to the child about relationships' (Study V), and with a 4-item 3-point scale asking whether the father 'spends time with the child', 'talks through the child's worries with the child', 'takes an interest in the child's school work', and 'helps with the child's plans for the future' (Study VI).

STUDY I: FATHER INVOLVEMENT AND ADOLESCENTS' MENTAL HEALTH

Using the data from the Families in the Millennium Study (see Chapter 2) I recently (Flouri, under review – a) explored the role of father involvement in children's mental health outcomes after adjusting for concurrent confounding factors in the sample of the fathers of the 11- to 18-year-old British adolescents who took part in the study (see Study II of Chapter 2). Of the 452 fathers who took part in the study 408 were biological fathers, 42 were social fathers (of whom 32 were stepfathers, 6 adoptive fathers, 2 grandfathers, 1 foster father, and 1 'other'), and 2 father figures had missing data on their relationship to the study child. Of the biological fathers 369 were biological and resident and 34 were biological and non-resident (for 5 biological fathers there was no information on whether they lived with their child). The first set of analyses I describe below is on the data from the 408 biological fathers' sample, and the second on the data from the 445 biological and resident, biological and non-resident, and social fathers' sample. The reason I cut the fathers' sample in different ways was because biological-parent and social-parent families differ in many respects that can affect both parental involvement with the child (Lamb et al., 1985) and the child's mental health (McMunn et al., 2001), although not consistently (Dubowitz et al., 2000; Silverstein & Auerbach, 1999).

Of the 445 fathers, 9.7% reported that they did not work, 22.9% that their highest educational qualification was a university degree or above, 6.9% that their children did not receive free school meals, and 77.3% that they owned their house. Their mean age (ranging from 28 to 74) was 44.56 (SD = 7.34) years. In all, 337 (76.1%) were 'White British', 6 were 'White Irish', 3 'White and Black Caribbean', 1 'White and Black African', 11 'any other White', 5 'African', 6 'Caribbean', 2 'any other Black', 41 'Indian', 4 'Pakistani', 6 'Bangladeshi', 4 'Chinese', 7 'any other Asian', 3 'any other mixed', and 7 'any other ethnic group'. There were no 'White and Asian' fathers in the sample, and 2 fathers had missing data on ethnic group membership. One hundred and seventy-four (40.4%) fathers sent their children to the suburban school of the study, 37.4% to the rural school, and 22.3% to the inner-city school.

Control factors included interparental conflict (as there is considerable evidence that it affects children's mental health (Buchanan, Ten Brinke & Flouri, 2000) and disrupts fathering more than mothering (Coiro & Emery, 1998)), and parents' psychological distress (as there is evidence that maternal depression (Weissman & Jensen, 2002) and paternal depression (Downey & Coyne, 1990; Foley et al., 2001) are related to child maladjustment). The study also checked for moderator effects. Because it has been suggested that a child's gender and family structure (Amato, 1994) may moderate the relationship between father involvement and the child's mental health, this study also considered whether the association between father involvement and the child's mental health is stronger for sons or daughters, and for children who lived in intact or non-intact families.

Measures

The contextual and structural factors that were included in the study were the child's gender and age as well as the father's report of free school meals receipt, number of children under age 21 living in the household, and the father's educational attainment, which was assessed with a 5-point scale ranging from 'no qualifications' to 'university degree'. Family structure in the biological fathers' sample ($N = 408$) was 'intact' if both parent figures lived together, 'restructured' if the father lived with another partner, and 'alone' if the father lived alone. As in Study II of Chapter 2, father involvement was measured with the Modified Inventory of Father Involvement (Hawkins et al., 2002), the father's mental health with the GHQ-12, interparental conflict with nine 5-point items from the Parenting Alliance Inventory, and the child's emotional and behavioural problems with the Strengths and Difficulties Questionnaire (SDQ). In this study SDQ was completed by fathers. As mentioned in Study II of Chapter 2, SDQ is a 25-item 3-point (ranging from 0–2) scale measuring four difficulties

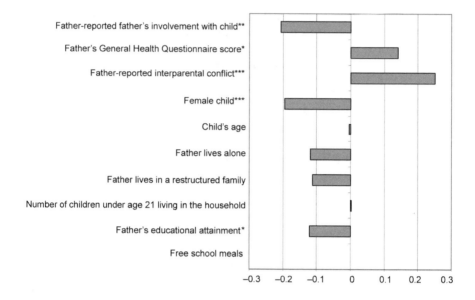

Figure 3.1 Standardised regression coefficients (β) predicting father-reported child's emotional and behavioural problems in the biological fathers' sample ($N = 258$)
Notes: $^*p < 0.05$; $^{**}p < 0.01$; $^{***}p < 0.001$

(hyperactivity, emotional symptoms, conduct problems, and peer problems), as well as prosocial behaviour.

I. The biological fathers' sample ($N = 408$)

Multiple linear regression analysis was carried out to explore the role of father involvement (controlling for other factors) in children's mental health. It was found that father-reported father involvement was negatively related to father-reported child emotional and behavioural problems, as measured by the SDQ, even after controlling for confounding variables. As can be seen in Figure 3.1, interparental conflict and the father's ill mental health were positively related, whereas the father's educational attainment was negatively related, to the child's psychological maladjustment. Fathers perceived sons to be more difficult than daughters. The amount of variance in the child's emotional and behavioural problems explained by these variables was 16%, and the regression model was significant ($F(10, 247) = 5.958$, $p < 0.001$). The association between father involvement and

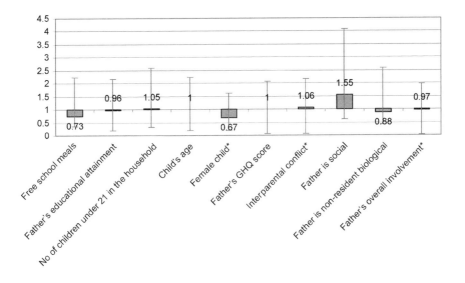

Figure 3.2 Multiple logistic regression's OR (with 95% confidence intervals) showing predictors of children's severe prosocial behaviour problems in the fathers' sample ($N = 445$)
Note: $*p < 0.05$

the child's adjustment was not stronger for sons than for daughters or for children in intact families than for children in non-intact families.

II. The biological resident, the biological non-resident, and the social fathers' sample (N = 445)

In this set of analyses the father's relationship to the child was explored in more detail as, apart from biological relatedness, co-residence was also assessed. In addition, in order to shed more light as to which aspects of the child's psychological adjustment the father figure's involvement might affect more, father involvement was also explored in relation to the five SDQ subscales (hyperactivity, emotional symptoms, conduct problems, peer problems, and prosocial behaviour). Each subscale had five items such as 'constantly fidgeting or squirming' (hyperactivity), 'many worries, often seems worried' (emotional symptoms), 'steals from home, school or elsewhere' (conduct problems), 'rather solitary, tends to play alone' (peer problems) and 'helpful if someone is hurt, upset or feeling ill' (prosocial behaviour). All five scales were reliable (Cronbach's alphas were 0.74, 0.70,

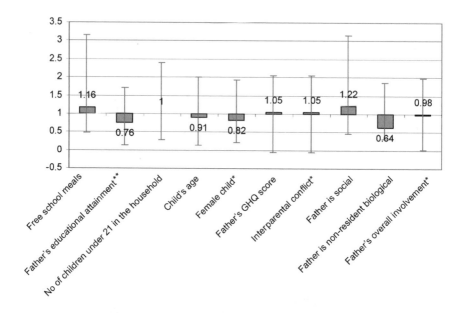

Figure 3.3 Multiple logistic regression's OR (with 95% confidence intervals) showing predictors of children's severe total difficulties in the fathers' sample (N = 445)

Notes: *p < 0.05; **p < 0.01

0.63, 0.59 and 0.74, respectively). The total difficulties scale (computed by summing the scores for hyperactivity, emotional symptoms, conduct problems, and peer problems) was also reliable (Cronbach's alpha was 0.84). With a theoretical range of 0–40 for total difficulties and 0–10 for prosocial behaviour, the fathers in the sample gave scores ranging from 0 to 29 and 0 to 10, respectively. Cut-off scores for the borderline/abnormal range were 14+ for total difficulties, 4+ for emotional symptoms, 3+ for conduct problems, 6+ for hyperactivity, 3+ for peer problems, whereas the borderline/abnormal range for prosocial behaviour was 0–5. With these cut-off scores roughly 20% of children in community samples are borderline/abnormal (Goodman, 1997). In all, in this study 17% were in the borderline/abnormal range for prosocial behaviour, 21.8% for emotional symptoms, 24.6% for conduct problems, 20% for hyperactivity and 25% for peer problems. Figures 3.2 to 3.7 present the logistic regression analyses results showing the risk of being in the borderline/abnormal range for each type of problem.

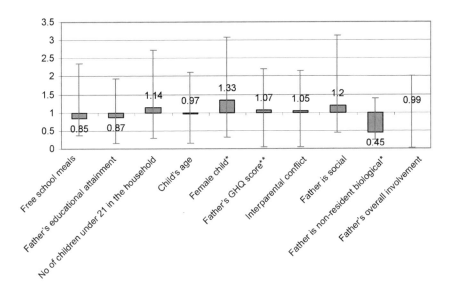

Figure 3.4 Multiple logistic regression's OR (with 95% confidence intervals) showing predictors of children's severe emotional symptoms in the fathers' sample ($N = 445$)
Note: $^*p < 0.05$; $^{**}p < 0.01$

Results

This study showed that, in general, the father figure's involvement was negatively associated with the children's severe prosocial behaviour problems, conduct disorder, and hyperactivity disorder. It also showed the father figure's relationship to the child to be of particular significance. Generally speaking, compared to resident biological fathers, social fathers were more than twice as likely to report hyperactivity disorder in their children. In contrast, compared to resident biological fathers, non-resident biological fathers were half as likely to report severe emotional symptoms in their children. Whether this reflects stepfathers' low tolerance of 'difficult' behaviour in their stepchildren as sociobiologists would argue, or, conversely, complacency on the part of resident biological fathers, or whether this is further evidence for the higher risk for child maladjustment in restructured families (Dunn, 2002, for a review) is unclear, however. It is equally unclear if, compared to resident biological fathers, non-resident biological fathers are less likely to detect or acknowledge depression and anxiety symptoms in their children (perhaps because of the limited time spent interacting with them), or if this is another piece of evidence for the higher prevalence of children's internalising behaviour problems in

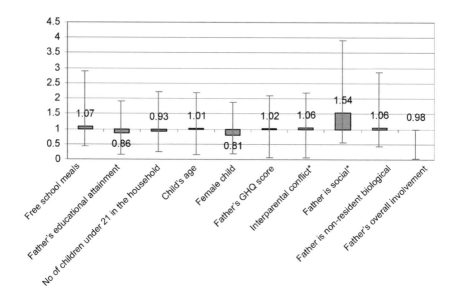

Figure 3.5 Multiple logistic regression's OR (with 95% confidence intervals) showing predictors of children's conduct disorder in the fathers' sample ($N = 445$)
Note: $*p < 0.05$

single-parent families relative to two-parent biological families (O'Connor, Dunn, Jenkins, Pickering & Rasbash, 2001).

This study pointed to useful directions but suffered from two important limitations. First, all measures, including the child's emotional and behavioural problems, were father-reported which makes the validity of such assessments questionable, especially in children with very infrequent contact with their non-resident fathers. Secondly, mother involvement was not controlled for. Therefore, it was not clear in this study if fathers make an independent contribution to children's outcomes above and beyond that of mothers, as it is likely that families in which fathers are highly involved are also those in which mothers are involved and competent, caring, and encouraging of fathers' participation in childcare. As such, the extra attention of fathers may be largely 'redundant, once one takes into account the mother's involvement' (Amato, 1994). The study I describe below addresses these two issues and extends these findings by exploring the role of the father figure's involvement in depression and anxiety symptoms (the link between father's involvement and externalising problems is discussed in detail in Chapter 5) later in life in a particularly vulnerable population: women.

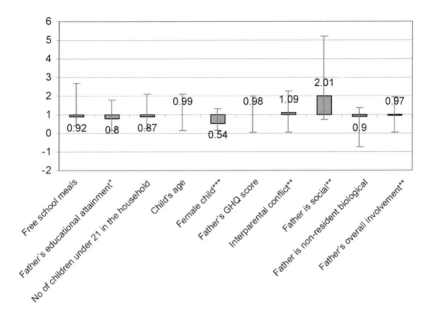

Figure 3.6 Multiple logistic regression's OR (with 95% confidence intervals) showing predictors of children's hyperactivity disorder in the fathers' sample ($N = 445$)
Notes: $*p < 0.05$; $**p < 0.01$; $***p < 0.001$

STUDY II: RETROSPECTIVE FATHER INVOLVEMENT AND WOMEN'S PSYCHOLOGICAL DISTRESS IN MID-CHILDHOOD

Women suffer more than men from depression and anxiety disorders throughout the reproductive years (Bebbington et al., 1998). Women with dependent children (Meltzer, Gill, Petticrew & Hinds, 1995) and lone mothers (Benzeval, 1998) have a greater risk of psychological distress than women without children, with mental health symptom levels varying with the number and ages of children (Rodgers, 1991). Explaining why has generated an enormous debate and mixed evidence (see Kuh, Hardy, Rodgers & Wadsworth, 2002, for a review) although the consensus is that elucidating the link between psychological functioning and both structural and process risk factors associated with the early environment is a promising line of research (Sadowski, Ugarte, Kolvin, Kaplan & Barnes, 1999). This study explored the effect of paternal involvement in the mothers

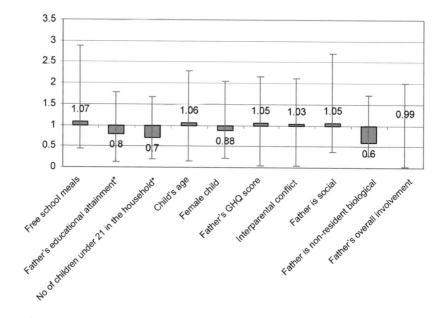

Figure 3.7 Multiple logistic regression's OR (with 95% confidence intervals) showing predictors of children's severe peer problems in the fathers' sample (N = 445)
Note: *p < 0.05

of the children who took part in the Family in the Millennium Study (see Chapter 2) after controlling for the effect of maternal involvement and known confounding variables. These were labour force participation, partner status, socio-economic status, education, age, and number of children. Being employed and being partnered provide both psychological and social benefits that are related to adaptive psychological functioning. Being partnered generates well-being through its role as a buffer in difficult times, and through the emotional and economic support it provides, whereas work provides an optimal level of stimulation, positive social relationships and a sense of identity (Diener, Suh, Lucas & Smith, 1999). In contrast, persisting and accumulating experiences of socio-economic disadvantage is one of the most important risk factors of adverse adult outcomes (Schoon et al., 2002). Educational attainment is usually protective against adverse psychological outcomes in high-risk individuals (Resnick et al., 1998) mainly because it is associated with stable career lines, and interesting and well-paid employment (Pulkkinen, Nygren & Kokko, 2002), although it has also been argued that because education raises aspirations it may interfere with psychological well-being if it leads to expectations that cannot be met, especially in rich nations (Hartog & Oosterbeek, 1998). Of the 635 mothers who took part in the Family in the Millennium Study, 621 stated their age. Of those, 4 were aged 60 or above, and so (as the study explored psychological distress in mid-adulthood) were excluded from the analysis. Their mean age was 41.15 years (SD = 5.70). In all, 257 (41.7%) were aged 28–39, 308 (49.9%) were aged 40–49, and 52 (8.4%) were aged 50–59. These 617 women were the study sample.

Measures

Psychological distress was assessed with the GHQ-12. The reliability (Cronbach's alpha) of the scale using the 0–1–2–3 Likert scoring convention was 0.90. The range of the scores (MEAN = 11.73, SD = 5.68) was 0–35, with higher scores indicating higher psychological distress. For the purposes of presenting case level, the 0–0–1–1 scoring system was adopted. Using this scoring system a GHQ-12 score of 4 or more is taken as an indicator of possible psychiatric morbidity. In this study 23.7% of the sample had scored above the cut-off point (in England, around 19% of women aged 16 and over in the general population report a score of 4 or more in GHQ-12 (Colhoun & Prescott-Clarke, 1996)). In total, 85.1% described themselves as White. Overall, 41.1% had children attending the suburban school, 23.3% the inner-city school, and 35.6% the school in the rural area. The average number of children under age 21 in the household (ranging from 0 to 6) was 2.20 (SD = 0.91), and the average educational attainment (measured on a 5-point scale ranging from (0) 'no qualifications' to (4) 'university degree') was 1.98 (SD = 1.31). Free school meals receipt was used to tap socio-economic status. In all, 12.2% of the sample had children who received free school meals. Of the 617 women who took part in the study, 611 provided information on their parental family structure which was assessed as 'intact' if participants stated that they lived 'most of the time' with both their biological parents (84.6% of the sample). In all, 19.6% of the participants did not work and 21.4% lived alone. Own father's and mother's involvement were assessed with a 5-item and a 4-item scale, respectively, using items from the first sweep of the National Child Development Study (see Study I of Chapter 2). In particular, the father involvement items were: 'How interested was your father figure in your education?', 'How involved was your father figure with you?', 'How often did your father figure read to you?', 'How often did your father figure take outings with you?' and 'What part did your father figure take in managing you?' The mother involvement items were: 'How interested was your mother figure in your education?', 'How involved was your mother figure

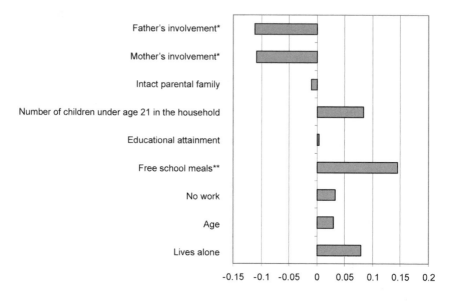

Figure 3.8 Standardised regression coefficients (β) predicting women's GHQ-12 score ($N = 525$)
Notes: $*p < 0.05$; $**p < 0.01$

with you?', 'How often did your mother figure read to you?' and 'How often did your mother figure take outings with you?' Cronbach's alphas were 0.88 and 0.83, respectively. The average father involvement score (ranging from 5 to 25) was 14.96 (SD = 5.62), and the average mother involvement score (ranging from 4 to 20) was 14.56 (SD = 3.83) with higher scores indicating higher parent involvement. Figure 3.8 shows the regression analysis results predicting GHQ-12 score in women.

Results

As can be seen in Figure 3.8, although parental family structure was not related to psychological functioning in women after controlling for known socio-demographic confounds, mother and father involvement were negatively (and similarly) related to psychological distress. Low socio-economic status was positively related to psychological distress. A major problem with this study, however, is that father involvement was assessed retrospectively, which suggests that current circumstances may colour the assessment of experiences. In addition, the study findings may not be generalisable to women who are not middle-aged, to middle-aged women without children, or to middle-aged women with children who are not secondary school-aged. Furthermore, as a higher than expected proportion of women in this study had scored above the cut-off point for psychiatric morbidity, these findings may not be easily generalised to women in the general population in the UK or in other western countries. Perhaps, however, the greatest limitation of both these two studies is their cross-sectional design. Our third study (Flouri & Buchanan, 2003a), using longitudinal data from NCDS to explore the long-term effect of both biological and social father involvement in children's mental health outcomes, tackled these problems (although, as will be shown below, it also introduced others). Its aim was to explore the role of father's involvement at age 7 in mental health outcomes at age 16, and the role of father's involvement at age 16 in mental health outcomes at age 33 after controlling (in both cases) for the role of mother involvement and confounding factors. In addition to checking for any interactions between father involvement and the child's gender, and between father involvement and family structure, that study also explored if father involvement is more important to children's later mental health when mother involvement is low rather than high (Amato, 1994).

STUDY III: FATHER INVOLVEMENT AND CHILDREN'S LATER MENTAL HEALTH

As mentioned above the study used data from sweeps of the NCDS (for a description see Study I of Chapter 2). Because the aim of this study was to explore the role of father involvement in mental health outcomes in adolescence (age 16) and adult life (age 33) the initial study sample was those individuals ($N = 8441$) with complete mental health data at both age 16 and age 33. For 7563 of those 8441 cohort members there was information on their relation to the informant when they were aged 7. In particular, the informant was the mother or the mother figure for 97.9% of the cases, 'other' for 1.5% of the cases, 'from records' for 35 cases (0.5%), and 'adoption study' for 7 (0.1%) cases. At age 16 there was information on the relationship of the informant to the child for 8362 cases. Of those, the informant was the mother or mother figure for 90% of the cases, the father or father figure for 5.9% of the cases, 'other' for 1.8% of the cases, and both parents for 2.3% of the cases.

Measures

Mental health outcomes in childhood and in adult life (age 33) were assessed with the Rutter 'A' Health and Behaviour Checklist (see Study I of Chapter 2 for a description) and the Malaise Inventory, respectively. As in Study I of Chapter 2, when cohort members were 7 years old 14 of the 31 items that compose the full Rutter 'A' Health and Behaviour Checklist were used. The Malaise Inventory is a 24-item list of symptoms from the Cornell Medical Index, developed by the Institute of Psychiatry, and is a measure of psychological distress. The 24 Malaise symptoms are positive responses to items such as 'feels miserable and depressed', 'gets annoyed by people', and 'has had a nervous breakdown'. Test scores ranged from 0 to 24 for the 14-item Rutter 'A' at age 7, from 0 to 39 for the 31-item Rutter 'A' at age 16, and from 0 to 22 for the Malaise Inventory at age 33. The average Rutter 'A' score at age 7 was 6.18 (SD = 3.51), the average Rutter 'A' score at age 16 was 5.38 (SD = 4.42), and the average Malaise score at age 33 was 2.45 (SD = 3.01).

Father involvement and mother involvement were assessed at ages 7 and 16 (see Study I of Chapter 2). Because of the very small occurrence of low-involvement responses in both mothers and fathers the low/middle-involvement responses were combined (see Table 2.1 in Chapter 2) and two scales measuring father involvement and mother involvement were computed from the sum of the four and the three dichotomous items, respectively. Thus, the father involvement scale ranged from 0 to 4 and the mother involvement scale from 0 to 3. The average father involvement score was 2.16 (SD = 1.19), and average mother involvement score was 1.82 (SD = 0.90). At age 16 there was only one item pertaining to father involvement and one item pertaining to mother involvement (the teacher's assessment of the parent's interest in child's education). To compare father and mother involvement at age 7 with father and mother involvement at age 16, parents in the low/middle group were compared with parents in the high-involvement group, and so 46.3% of fathers and 47.2% of mothers were 'highly involved' with their children at age 16 whereas 53.7% of fathers and 52.8% of mothers were in the 'middle/low-involvement' group.

The study also controlled for general ability (assessed at age 11 with an 80-item general ability test – ranging from 0 to 80 – designed by the National Foundation for Educational Research) and low academic motivation, assessed with an 8-item self-report scale (ranging from 8 to 40) at age 16. The 8-item 5-point self-reports were anchored with 'not true at all' and 'very true' and were as follows: 'I feel school is largely a waste of time', 'I am quiet in the classroom and get on with my work' (inversely coded), 'I think homework is a bore', 'I find it difficult to keep my mind on my work', 'I don't like school', 'I think there is no point in planning for the future – you should get things as they come', and 'I am always willing to help the teacher' (inversely coded). Cronbach's alpha of the low academic motivation scale was 0.75, and the mean score was 19.15 (SD = 5.98). The mean general ability score was 44.70 (SD = 15.43).

Educational attainment by age 20 was operationalised as in Maughan, Collishaw and Pickles (1998): When cohort members were aged 20, results in public examinations were collected from school and educational authorities. The examination system in operation at the time included both the Certificate of Secondary Education (CSE) and the General Certificate of Education (GCE) for England and Wales, and the Scottish Certificate of Education (SCE) for Scotland. Data were collected on all examinations taken up to the time each cohort member left school. Passes in each type and level of examination were combined to form a 4-item scale of the highest qualification achieved, which was as follows: (0) none, (1) less than O-level equivalent grades, (2) one or more O-level equivalent grades, (3) one or more A-level equivalent grades. The mean educational attainment in this study was 1.60 (SD = 0.94). Other variables included socio-economic status of parents when the cohort member was born, and evidence of domestic tension and mental health problems in the family at age 7 (all assessed as in Study I of Chapter 2). For 1139 (13.5%) cohort members parental socio-economic status was 'manual'. At 33, cohort member's socio-economic status ('non-manual' vs 'manual'), parent status (has children or not) and partner status (is partnered or not) were also included in the analysis. In all, at age 33, of the 8441 participants, 2529 (30%) were in 'manual' occupations, 5830 (69.1%) were partnered, and 5877 (69.6%) had children. Father's status was 'biological' if the child's father figure was the child's natural father and 'non-biological' if the father figure was a social father. Regarding family structure at age 7, there was information regarding fathers and father figures for 7554 cohort members. For 94.2% of those children the father figure was their natural father, for 1.2% their stepfather, for 0.1% their foster father, for 1.2% their adoptive father, for 0.7% a grandfather, for 0.1% 'other person', for 0.1% 'other situation', and for 2.2% (169 cases) there was no father figure. At age 16, there was information regarding fathers and father figures for 8439 cohort members. For 87.7% of those children the father figure was their natural father, for 1.4% their adoptive father, for 2.6% their stepfather, for 0.1% their foster father, for 0.3% a grandfather, for 0.3% an elder brother, for 0.5% their mother's cohabitee, for 0.2% an uncle, for 0.1% a 'house-father', for 0.1% 'other', and for 6.6% (558 cases) there was no father figure. At age 16 there was information relating to mother figures for all 8441 participants of the study, and at age 7 for 7543 cohort members. The mother figure was the child's natural mother for 98% of the cases at age 7, and for 95.4% of the cases at age 16.

Results

Figures 3.9 and 3.10 show the standardised regression coefficients of the multiple linear regression analyses carried out to predict mental health outcomes from earlier father figure's involvement after adjusting for mother

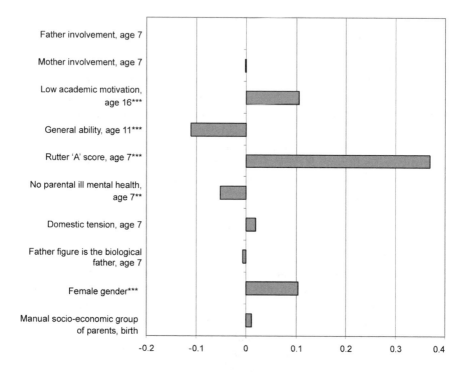

Figure 3.9 Standardised regression coefficients (β) predicting parent-reported child's emotional and behavioural problems at age 16 from parent- and teacher-reported father's involvement at age 7 and other factors ($N = 2686$)
Notes: $*p < 0.05$; $**p < 0.01$; $***p < 0.001$

figure's involvement and other confounding factors. As can be seen in Figure 3.9, compared to their counterparts, girls and children from families with mental health problems had higher Rutter 'A' scores at age 16. The father's biological status and parental socio-economic status were not related to child's later mental health. General ability test scores and academic motivation were negatively and emotional and behavioural problems at age 7 were positively related to emotional and behavioural problems in adolescence. Neither mother involvement nor father involvement at age 7 was related to Rutter 'A' scores at age 16. The amount of variance in psychological maladjustment at age 16 explained by the variables in the model ($F(10, 2675) = 62.055$, $p < 0.001$) was 19%. Figure 3.10 shows a similar pattern. Again, father involvement and mother involvement at age 16 were not associated with psychological distress at age 33. As expected, adult psychological distress was higher for women and was

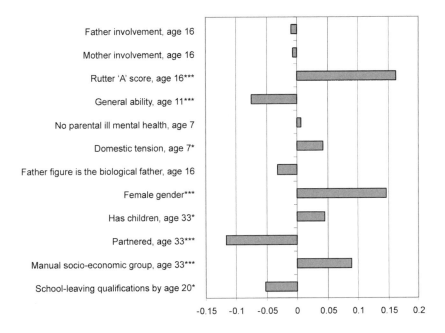

Figure 3.10 Standardised regression coefficients (β) predicting self-reported psychological distress at age 33 from teacher-reported father involvement at age 16 and other factors ($N = 2790$)
Notes: $*p < 0.05$; $***p < 0.001$

significantly predicted from emotional and behavioural problems at age 16. Compared to their counterparts, the partnered at age 33 had lower and those with children had higher Malaise scores. General ability and educational attainment were negatively related to psychological distress in adult life but domestic tension in the parental family when the cohort member was growing up and current manual socio-economic status were positively related to psychological distress at age 33. Father's biological status in adolescence or parental ill mental health in childhood were not related to adult psychological distress. The amount of variance in psychological distress at age 33 explained by the variables in the model ($F(12, 2777) = 28.180$, $p < 0.001$) was 11%.

There were interesting moderator effects, however. The interaction between father's biological status and father involvement at age 7 was significant in predicting psychological maladjustment at age 16 ($t = 2.258$, df 2674, $p < 0.05$), for instance. In particular, early father involvement had more impact on decreasing emotional and behavioural problems in adolescence when the father figure was not the child's biological father than when he was. In addition, the association between father involvement at age 16 and psychological distress at age 33 was stronger for daughters than for sons ($t = 2.308$, df 2776, $p < 0.05$). In order to compare this interaction effect with the insignificant one found in the cross-sectional field study described above, I selected only those cohort members whose father figure at age 16 was their biological father. However, the interaction effect between the biological father's involvement at age 16 and the cohort member's gender in psychological distress at age 33 was still significant ($t = 2.522$, df 2678, $p < 0.05$). Finally, the interaction term between father involvement at age 7 and mother involvement at age 7 in psychological distress at age 33 was significant ($t = 2.386$, df 2937, $p < 0.05$), which suggests that the relationship between father involvement at age 7 and psychological distress at age 33 was stronger when mother involvement at age 7 was low than when mother involvement at age 7 was high.

Discussion

The study's strengths (namely its longitudinal design) should be evaluated in the light of several of its limitations. First, apart from the usual limitations associated with the use of longitudinal data in general and the NCDS in particular (for a full discussion see Chapter 2), in order to compare psychological assessments at two time periods only the cohort members who had complete data on mental health at both age 16 and 33 were included in this study. Second, in order to assess the impact of father involvement some cohort members with no fathers or father figures at age 7 and 16 were excluded from the analyses even if they had complete mental health data. Third, the two father involvement measures (at age 7 and 16) as well as the two mental health assessments were very different. Father involvement at age 7 was a composite measure of being interested in the child's education, taking outings with the child, reading to the child, and having an active role in managing the child. At age 16 in NCDS the only item pertaining to father involvement was the father's interest in the child's education. Regarding the mental health measures, the Rutter 'A' (which was used at ages 7 and 16) is a parent-report assessment, while the Malaise Inventory (which was used at age 33) is self-reported. Ideally, mental health problems should be assessed from various sources. In this study that was not possible. However, parental reports of the child's mental health are generally very stable over time (Achenbach, 1995). On the other hand, it is possible that the Malaise Inventory, which is more focused on emotional/depressive symptoms, was rated up in women and down in men.

The individual aspects of father involvement in later mental health

Ann Buchanan, JoAnn Ten Brinke and I carried out another study using longitudinal data from sweeps of the National Child Development Study to explore the role of a specific dimension of father involvement and education-related non-economic paternal involvement in children's mental health outcomes. Education-related non-economic father involvement has been shown (as I will discuss in the next chapter) to be perhaps the most important non-economic dimension of father involvement in predicting children's scholastic achievement. The difference with most of the studies exploring its role in child outcomes is that the outcomes they assessed were educational rather than psychological. In NCDS there were two items measuring education-related non-economic paternal involvement. These were the parent-reported item of 'father reads to child' at age 7 and the teacher's report of whether 'father is interested in the child's education' assessed at ages 7, 11 and 16. Study IV explores the effect of the first in adult psychological distress.

STUDY IV: FATHER'S FREQUENCY OF READING TO THE CHILD IN EARLY CHILDHOOD AND PSYCHOLOGICAL DISTRESS IN MID-ADULTHOOD

Our fourth study (Buchanan, Flouri & Ten Brinke, 2002) explored the role of father's frequency of reading to the child at age 7 and other 'protective' factors at age 7 (outings with mother, good creative skills, and good numeric skills), controlling for mental health in childhood and other confounding variables, in the risk for psychological distress at age 33. The initial sample size was 6441 individuals for whom there were complete data on mental health in both childhood (7, 11 and 16 years) *and* adulthood (33 years) having excluded 860 cohort members who were mentally disabled or had chronic illness or disability.

Measures

Mental health was assessed with the Rutter 'A' Health and Behaviour Checklist in childhood and with the Malaise Inventory in adult life (see Study III of this chapter). A score of 8+ has been widely used to identify people at risk for psychological distress (Sloper, 1996), and was also adopted in this study. With regards to the Rutter 'A' Checklist two subscales were derived to identify children whose problems were internalised ('neurotic') and children whose problems were externalised ('antisocial'). As explained in Study I of Chapter 2, in 1974 when the cohort members were aged 16 the full Rutter 'A' (31 questions) was completed by the parent or primary caregiver. At ages 7 and 11 a shortened version of the Rutter 'A' (23 items) was used. The factor analysis carried out on the items of the shortened Rutter 'A' to examine its dimensionality in this sample confirmed that two sets of behaviour grouped together (see also Silberg et al., 1996). The 'internalising' subgroup was based on the total score for positive responses to *having headaches, stomach aches, sleep problems, worries, and being solitary, miserable and fearful.* The 'externalising' subgroup was based on the total score for positive responses *to being fidgety, destroying things, fighting, not being liked, and being irritable, disobedient and unsettled.* A third group appeared to relate to health problems. Children in the top 20% of the total score from the shortened Rutter 'A' at age 7 were designated as showing some disorder (N = 1416). Children with an 'internalising' score exceeding their 'externalising' score were designated as having an *'internalising'* problem (N = 806), while those with an 'externalising' score exceeding their 'internalising' score were designated as having an *'externalising'* problem (N = 466). In an attempt to explore independently the effects of internalising and externalising problems on adult mental health, children who had equal internalising and externalising scores, the *comorbid* group (N = 144), were omitted from the analysis.

In this study, the *demographic variables* used were gender of the cohort member and cohort members' parental socio-economic status at birth (assessed as in Study I of Chapter 2). *Parental mental health* when the cohort member was aged 7 (assessed as in Study I of Chapter 2), *family structure, experience of severe social disadvantage,* and *experience of care* were also included in the analysis. Family structure was 'birth' if children were brought up by birth parents until age 16, and if there was no experience of severe social disadvantage or care; 'step' if children lived at age 16 with step-parent(s), and if there was no experience of severe social disadvantage or care; 'widowed' if children lived with a widowed parent at age 16, and if there was no experience of severe social disadvantage or care; and 'lone' if children lived with a lone (not widowed) parent at age 16, and if there was no experience of severe social disadvantage or care. Severe social disadvantage (for children who lived with birth or step-parents at age 16 and had not experienced care) was defined by the presence of 4 of the following 5 factors at age 11: more than 4 children in the family; more than 1.5 people per room; privately rented or local authority accommodation; lack of sole use of at least two basic amenities (bathroom, indoor lavatory, hot water supply), and free school meals receipt. Experience of care (for children who had not experienced severe social disadvantage) was defined as having ever being looked after in public care.

The *cluster of risk factors*, present when the cohort members were aged 7 years, included the following variables (all assessed by the Health

Visitor when cohort children were aged 7): family involvement with the police/probation service, agency referral for difficulties at school, social services involvement, and domestic tension. The *cluster of protective factors*, present when the cohort members were aged 7 years, included the following variables: outings with mother (assessed by the parent), father reads to child (assessed by the parent), and child's good numeric and creative skills (both assessed by the teacher). Both clusters were the sum of their individual four dichotomous components, ranging from 0 to 4.

Results

The results at the multivariate level for the 2904 women and the 2687 men with valid data for the logistic regressions showed that although our grouping of risk factors did not predict malaise in adulthood, our grouping of the above protective factors at age 7 predicted that women were less likely to have high Malaise scores in adult life. There was no association between psychological distress in adulthood and internalising problems in childhood. People who had externalising problems in childhood, however, were nearly twice as likely as those without such problems to have high Malaise scores in adulthood.

The role of father involvement in aspects of subjective well-being

Related studies that Ann Buchanan and I carried out to assess the role of father involvement not in children's mental health as such but in other indicators of children's subjective well-being (SWB) seem to also provide evidence for the role of the father figure's involvement. Subjective well-being is a person's evaluation of his or her life. This evaluation can be in terms of cognitive states such as satisfaction with one's life, and in terms of ongoing affect (i.e. presence of positive and absence of negative affect) (Diener, Sapyta & Suh, 1998). In both studies described below we explored the role of father involvement in life satisfaction (Study V) and positive affect (Study VI), which, although not directly comparable to our previous mental health measures of psychological maladjustment and psychological distress, are two components of positive psychological health and are becoming central in a world where basic needs are met and greater respect is given to individuals (Diener et al., 1998).

STUDY V: FATHER INVOLVEMENT, PEER VICTIMISATION AND LIFE SATISFACTION IN ADOLESCENT BOYS

In this study (Buchanan & Flouri, 2002a) of 1344 adolescent boys aged 13–19 years in Britain we explored the role of father involvement in children's life satisfaction and peer victimisation. As research has shown that in secondary schools the bullying of boys tends to be more physical than that of girls (Björkqvist, Lagerspetz & Kaukiainen, 1992), and that boys are bullied more frequently (Olweus, 1993), we chose to look at only boys for this study. The data came from a confidential questionnaire (printed in the *Express* newspaper on 16 March 1998) researching the views and experiences of boys aged between 13 and 19 in the UK. To control for possible newspaper response bias, additional questionnaires were distributed in schools and youth clubs. Readership surveys of the *Express* indicate that 12% of the readership is aged between 15 and 24 compared to 15% of the population nationally (with readership divided equally between men and women). There is a slight class bias, however; only 16% of the readership belong to social classes D and E compared to 28% of the population. Life satisfaction was assessed with a 1-item measure asking participants to rate their satisfaction with life on a 5-point scale anchored with 'least happy and 'most happy'. Of the 1224 boys with complete data on life satisfaction, 25.7% reported that they are 'most happy' and only 3.3% said that they are 'least happy'. Peer victimisation in school was assessed with a scale composed of six dichotomous questions asking whether at school boys had been physically attacked, made to give up money, threatened with violence, called names, picked on by a group, and experienced racism. Cronbach's alpha was 0.68. To assess perceived father involvement, participants were asked to indicate on a 5-item 3-point scale how involved their father (or father figure) was with them. Items were: 'does your dad (or father figure) spend time with you?', 'hug you?', 'show an interest in your school work?', 'talk through your worries with you?', and 'talk to you about relationships?'. Cronbach's' alpha was 0.78. We also controlled for age and family structure (assessed as 'intact' if the participants stated that they lived with both their parents and 'non-intact' if they reported that they lived otherwise (i.e. lived with a parent and a step-parent, were cared for in a home, lived with another relative, lived on their own or lived with a friend)). Of the 1344 boys who completed the questionnaire 76.2% reported that they lived with their parents.

Results

Multiple regression analysis showed that low father involvement and peer victimisation contributed significantly and independently to low levels of life satisfaction in boys. Age was negatively related to life satisfaction, and family structure was not related to life satisfaction. The amount of variance explained in life satisfaction by all these variables was 18%. There was also evidence relating to a buffering effect of father involvement in that father involvement protected children from extreme victimisation, which suggests that perhaps the contribution of father involvement is greatest in cases where bullying is experienced most. It is acknowledged, however, that findings from this cross-sectional study do not allow us to establish which factors, if any, have a causal status. It is possible that low father involvement and peer victimisation lead to low life satisfaction. It is also possible, however, that a low level of mental health may elicit both low levels of father involvement and victimisation by others. Furthermore (as in Study I above), mother involvement was not controlled for.

STUDY VI: FATHER INVOLVEMENT AND HAPPINESS IN ADOLESCENTS

In this study (Flouri & Buchanan, 2003b) we explored the effect of father involvement after adjusting for the effect of mother involvement and other factors in both boys' and girls' self-reported happiness in adolescence. In addition, following Amato (1994), we explored if the association between father involvement and happiness is stronger for sons than for daughters, if family disruption weakens the association between father involvement and happiness, and if father involvement is more strongly related to offspring happiness when mother involvement is low rather than high. The data for this study came from a confidential questionnaire researching the views and experiences of 2722 British adolescents (1124 male and 1402 female, 196 did not state their gender) aged between 14 and 18 years. In all, 8500 anonymous questionnaires were distributed into schools and youth clubs where entire classes or groups undertook to complete them usually within the school day or youth club setting. Of the 2722 participants, 923 (33.9%) reported that the highest educational qualification achieved in their family was a university degree, and 167 adolescents (5.9%) reported that no one in their family worked, which is significantly lower than the average proportion of workless households in Britain (19%) (Office for National Statistics, 1998). However, 20.5% of participants reported that they had received free school meals at some point during their schooling, which compares well with the 19.8% of pupils known to be eligible for free meals in nursery and primary schools and the 17.5% of pupils known to be eligible for free meals in secondary schools in England (Statistics of Education, 1998).

Measures

Happiness was assessed with a 1-item measure asking participants to rate how often they feel 'happy and confident' about themselves on a 4-point scale anchored with 'never' and 'often'. Of the 2722 adolescents, 2.9% answered 'never', 6.8% 'hardly ever', 47.9% 'sometimes', and 42.4% 'often'. The 4-point scale was subsequently recoded into a dichotomous one with 'never', 'hardly ever' or 'sometimes' compared to 'often'. *Father involvement* was measured on a 4-item 3-point scale asking children to assess how involved their father (or father figure) was with them. In particular, children were asked to indicate the extent to which their father (or father figure) 'spends time with you', 'talks through your worries with you', 'takes an interest in your school work', and 'helps with your plans for the future'. Cronbach's alpha was 0.83. To assess perceived *mother involvement*, questions comparable to those asked about the father or father figure were used. Again, on a 4-item 3-point scale the participants had to indicate the extent to which their mother (or mother figure) 'spends time with you', 'talks through your worries with you', 'takes an interest in your school work', and 'helps with your plans for the future'. Cronbach's alpha was 0.81. We also controlled for *parental socio-economic status* (assessed with receipt of free school meals), *gender*, *age* (ranging from 14 to 18) and *family structure* (measured as 'intact' if the participants stated that they lived with both their parents and 'non-intact' if they reported that they lived otherwise (i.e. lived with a parent, with other relatives, on their own, were cared for in a home, etc.)). Other factors included self-efficacy, feelings of depression, and parental conflict. *Self-efficacy* (see also Study III of Chapter 4) was measured with five 5-point items (anchored with 'strongly disagree' and 'strongly agree') that were taken from the Measure of Guidance Impact (MGI), developed for the Department of Employment by the National Foundation for Educational Research (Christophers, Stoney, Whetton, Lines & Kendall, 1993). The items were: 'I have made a plan for my future working life', 'I know what I would need to get the education or training that interests me', 'I know what I would need to get the job that interests me', 'I can see the steps I must go through to make a decision' and 'I know myself well enough to know what kind of help I want'. Cronbach's alpha was 0.80. *Feelings of depression* were assessed with a 3-point measure asking participants if they 'ever feel depressed'. Answers were 'often', 'sometimes' or 'never'. *Parental conflict* was measured with a dichotomous item asking participants to indicate whether 'conflict at home' made them stressed or not.

Results

The logistic regression analysis carried out to explore the role of these factors in self-reported happiness showed that self-efficacy and age were positively related, and feelings of depression were negatively related to self-reported happiness. Boys were more likely than girls to report that they feel happy 'often'. It was also shown that even after controlling for mother involvement, father involvement was significantly related to self-reported happiness. Furthermore, the association between father involvement and happiness was not stronger for sons than for daughters. There was no evidence to suggest that family disruption weakens the association between father involvement and happiness, or that father involvement is more strongly related to offspring happiness when mother involvement is low rather than high.

SUMMARY AND CONCLUSIONS

This chapter reviewed the burgeoning literature on the role of father involvement on children's mental health outcomes and reported the results from six studies examining links between father involvement and children's mental health. Two of these studies (Studies III and IV) were longitudinal, using data from sweeps of the 1958 British birth cohort (NCDS). The rest were cross-sectional. The children's mental health outcomes that were explored (assessed differently in each study) were emotional and behavioural well-being (Studies I and III), psychological distress (Studies II, III and IV), life satisfaction (Study V), and happiness (Study VI). Mother involvement was controlled for in all studies apart from Studies I and V. In Study I, father involvement was measured with Hawkins et al.'s (2002) Modified Inventory of Father Involvement (see Study II of Chapter 2), and in Studies II and III with the four items assessing father involvement in the NCDS (see Study I of Chapter 2). Father involvement was measured with one item asking whether the father read to the child at age 7 (Study IV), with a 5-item 3-point scale asking whether the father 'spends time with' and 'hugs' the child, 'shows an interest in the child's school work', 'talks through the child's worries with the child', and 'talks to the child about relationships' (Study V), and with a 4-item 3-point scale asking whether the father 'spends time with the child', 'talks through the child's worries with the child', 'takes an interest in the child's school work', and 'helps with the child's plans for the future' (Study VI). The fact that both the operationalisation of father involvement and the children's mental health outcomes, as well as the design of the six studies described above, are very different makes drawing any firm conclusions a difficult task. In addition, period effects should not be discounted: father involvement was measured in 1965 and in 1974 in the longitudinal studies, and in 1998–2001 in the cross-sectional ones.

It seems that the message from all these studies is that father involvement is negatively associated with children's mental health problems in certain circumstances. But father involvement was directly related to children's mental health outcomes only in our cross-sectional studies (although the father's frequency of reading to the child at age 7 as part of a broader cluster of 'protective' factors was negatively associated with psychological distress in women at age 33) which makes for a weak claim for its role in predicting psychological maladjustment in children (see also Chapter 2). At the same time, the methodological limitations of the cross-sectional studies described in this chapter, and in particular those of Studies V and VI, are especially serious. For example, in both Study V and Study VI the main dependent variables (self-reported life satisfaction and self-reported happiness, respectively), as well as two of the main predictor variables in Study VI (depression and parental conflict), were single-item proxies; in Study VI some of the respondents might have come from the same family and therefore it is possible that there is a degree of clustering within the data; in Study V we looked only at boys and we did not control for mother involvement, and, of course, none of the cross-sectional studies allow for any causality claims.

Furthermore, it should be noted that another reason why drawing firm conclusions from the studies presented in this chapter should be done with caution is because father involvement and the child's mental health were assessed not only with different measures and in different samples (with regards to gender, age, and time periods) across the studies, but also by different informants. In other words, reporter bias should not be discounted. Father involvement was parent-reported (usually by mother) in Studies III and IV. Child's mental health was child-reported in Study V and in the part of Study III looking at psychological distress at age 33, whereas it was parent-reported (usually by mother) in the part of Study III looking at emotional and behavioural problems at age 16. Father involvement and the child's mental health were child-reported in Studies II, V and VI, and father-reported in Study I. The finding of Study I, in particular, that father-reported father involvement was negatively associated with father-reported children's prosocial behaviour problems, hyperactivity and total difficulties should be seen in the light of research, for example, showing that in response to their adolescent's depressive behaviour mothers tend to increase their facilitative behaviour, whereas fathers tended to lower their involvement (Sheeber et al., 1998), and that compared to mothers, fathers tend to under-report emotional problems in their children (Luoma, Tamminen & Koivisto, 2004). Furthermore, the largely positive findings of the cross-sectional studies in which both father involvement and the child's mental health were child-reported should be accepted with caution. If we assume that children's ratings are intersubjectively valid (i.e. correlate with fathers' views, which is not always the case, as shown in Study II of Chapter 2) then we might conclude, of course, that involved fathering might facilitate children's well-being. If the ratings are not intersubjectively valid, this association might simply mean that believing that one's father is involved raises one's well-being regardless of what one's father actually does. A third and more problematic possibility with respect to this kind of data collection is that children's affect level colours their evaluations of their relationships, and therefore the association may reflect nothing more than a general response bias.

Study I also showed that the father figure's residency status and biological relatedness to the child are of particular importance. The study showed that, compared to resident biological fathers, social fathers were more than twice as likely to report hyperactivity disorder in their children, and that compared to resident biological fathers, non-resident biological fathers were half as likely to report severe emotional symptoms in their children. As mentioned earlier (see also Chapter 2), whether this reflects stepfathers' low tolerance of 'difficult' behaviour in their stepchildren, or whether this is further evidence for the higher risk for child's psychological maladjustment in restructured families, is unclear, however. It is equally unclear if compared to resident biological fathers non-resident biological fathers are less likely to detect or acknowledge depression and anxiety symptoms in their children (perhaps because of the limited time spent interacting with them), or if this is further evidence for the higher prevalence of children's internalising behaviour problems in single-parent families compared to two-parent biological families.

Despite the limitations of the study, this is perhaps a step in the right direction. Understanding *why* and *how* father involvement is related to the child's mental health is bound to be a much more difficult exercise than simply exploring linear effects, but it would help to make sense of the disparate findings from empirical studies.

To sum up, it seems that the studies presented here provide another piece of evidence for the positive role of father involvement in children's mental health. The studies presented in this chapter showed that, on the whole, father involvement did not have any direct effects on overall indices of psychological maladjustment, with the exception of its negative effect on psychological distress in women as assessed with the GHQ-12 in Study II. Even in the cross-sectional studies, father involvement tended to be related to *aspects* of mental health rather than *overall indices* of wellness or maladjustment. In particular, father involvement was positively related to life satisfaction (Study V) and happiness (Study VI), both of which tap aspects of subjective well-being, and was negatively related to risk for low prosocial behaviour, and risk for total difficulties and hyperactivity disorder (Study I), although it was not related to children's risk for severe emotional symptoms, as assessed with the Strengths and Difficulties

Questionnaire (SDQ). Similarly it was not related to emotional and behavioural problems, as assessed with the Rutter 'A' Health and Behaviour Checklist in Study III. Furthermore, one should treat the positive effects of father involvement in these three subscales of the SDQ in Study I, as well as the effects of father involvement in the GHQ-12 score in Study II, with even greater scepticism as mother involvement was not controlled for (Study I), and father involvement was assessed retrospectively (Study II), suggesting that self-presentation bias cannot be ruled out.

Of more interest are perhaps the moderator effects found in some of these studies providing evidence of the 'buffering' or 'protective' role of father involvement in certain situations. For example, Study II showed that early father involvement had more impact on decreasing emotional and behavioural problems in adolescence when the father figure was not the child's biological father than when he was. In addition, the association between father involvement at age 16 and psychological distress at age 33 was stronger for daughters than for sons, and the relationship between father involvement at age 7 and psychological distress at age 33 was stronger when mother involvement at age 7 was low than when it was high, which suggests that high father involvement compensates for low mother involvement. Study V showed that the contribution of father involvement in the life satisfaction of adolescent boys was greatest in cases where bullying was regularly experienced. Future research should perhaps begin to explore more systematically in which circumstances, for which 'at risk' groups, and for which mental health outcomes in children is the father figure's involvement effect likely to be of most significance.

CHAPTER 4

FATHER INVOLVEMENT AND CHILDREN'S EDUCATIONAL OUTCOMES

INTRODUCTION

Father involvement has been variously linked with children's educational outcomes, although the contribution of fathers to children's scholastic achievement over and above that of mothers is not yet well documented. However, studies in western industrialised countries show that although father's absence (which is related to father involvement) is not always related to mental health problems in children (see also Chapters 1 and 8) it is associated with a higher risk of low academic achievement. This chapter describes four studies (two longitudinal and two cross-sectional) which explored the role of father involvement, controlling for mother involvement, in children's academic outcomes. The first looks at educational attainment, and the fourth explores whether father involvement is linked to educational attainment via its impact on the child's self-esteem and locus of control. The second and third explore the role of father involvement in two correlates of educational attainment: academic motivation and career maturity.

EVIDENCE SHOWING POSITIVE ASSOCIATIONS BETWEEN FATHER INVOLVEMENT AND CHILDREN'S EDUCATIONAL OUTCOMES

There is substantial evidence that parental involvement is associated with children's academic performance (Bynner, 1998; Feinstein & Symons, 1999; Georgiou, 1999; Keith et al., 1998; Maughan et al., 1998; Miedel & Reynolds, 1999; Reynolds, 1992), yet relatively few studies have investigated the individual contributions that mothers and fathers make to their children's schooling. Even less research has looked at the role of father involvement in children's academic performance, which is unfortunate given that there are several reasons why father involvement should be expected to be positively associated with the child's educational outcomes. First, as discussed in Chapter 1, fathers who are involved support their children financially, which affects children's educational attainment by influencing the economic structure of the household (Crockett et al., 1993). Second, fathers who are involved with their children are likely to engage their children in physical play and parent–child play, especially the parent's ability to be responsive to the child's initiative; allowing for a nurturant give-and-take in their play is particularly important for the child's emotional and cognitive development (Biller & Lopez Kimpton, 1997). Third, in families where fathers are involved, mothers are also involved (Amato, 1994), and therefore children raised in such families benefit from having two highly involved parents with the consequent diversity of stimulation and increase in social capital (Coleman, 1988). Fourth, as discussed in Chapter 2, fathers are more likely to be involved when the co-parental relation is good (Coiro & Emery, 1998; NICHD Early Child Care Research Network, 2000), and therefore in families where the father is involved the overall family context in which children are raised is positive, which is an important factor contributing to positive child outcomes (Kelly, 2000). In addition, it is possible that father involvement might be indirectly related to educational outcomes, via its effect on other factors influencing attainment. For instance, father involvement is related to the child's positive mental health outcomes (see Chapter 3) which are associated with positive educational outcomes (Silbereisen, Robins & Rutter, 1995; Smith, 1995). Father involvement has also been shown to be related to personality variables such as self-esteem and locus of control, both of which are related to educational outcomes (Ross & Broh, 2000). For instance, Williams and Radin (1999) showed that greater father involvement contributed to a more internal locus of control, particularly in sons, and, more recently, Deutsch, Servis and Payne (2001) found that father's emotional-involvement was positively related to children's self-esteem.

In her review of the importance of fathers in children's lives, Radin (1981) concluded that there are several channels through which a father may influence his children's cognitive development, for example

> through his genetic background, through his manifest behavior with his offspring, through the attitudes he holds about himself and his children, through the behavior he models, through his position in the family system, through the material resources he is able to supply for his children, through the influence he exerts on his wife's behavior, through his ethnic heritage, and through the vision he holds for his children. (p. 419)

According to a report from the National Center for Educational Statistics (Nord et al., 1997), compared to their counterparts, children with involved fathers are more likely to have participated in educational activities with their parents (e.g. to have visited a museum or a historical site with their parents in the past month), and are also more likely to have access to multiple types of resources at home (as measured by the proportion of parents who belong to community or professional organisations, or regularly volunteer in the community). Further, because fathers who are involved with their children are also likely to be involved in their children's schools, it is possible that father involvement changes the children's school environments in ways that make the environments more conducive to learning, and influences teachers and administrators so that they intervene early when potential problems in the children's academic performance or behaviour are noted.

Indeed, although the contribution of fathers to children's scholastic achievement over and above that of mothers is not yet well documented (Parke, 2000), some of the first findings are impressive (Grolnick & Slowiaczek, 1994; Hwang & Lamb, 1997). Yongman, Kindlon and Earls (1995), for instance, showed that father involvement in their sample of Black families was associated with improved cognitive outcomes in pre-term infants, even after adjusting for family income, neonatal health, treatment group status and paternal age. Earlier Radin (1976) had similarly found that in her 4-year-old boys' sample father nurturance was associated with boys' intelligence scores both concurrently and at 1-year follow-up, and Fagan and Iglesias (1999) showed that involved fathering in their Head Start children was associated with higher mathematics readiness change scores. More recently, Kaplan, Dungan and Zinser (2004) showed that infants of chronically depressed mothers learn in response to fathers', but not mothers' or other women's, infant-directed speech. Rowe, Cocker and Pan (2004), who compared fathers' and mothers' talk with toddlers in low-income families, showed that compared to mothers fathers tended to pose more *wh*-questions to children and to ask them to clarify themselves. As both *wh*-questions and clarification requests anticipate a verbal response from the child, fathers' more frequent use of these pragmatic functions required children to assume more communicative responsibility in the interaction. Indeed, the authors showed that children talked more, used more diverse vocabulary, and produced longer utterances when interacting with their fathers. Rowe et al. (2004) concluded that their study provided further support for the 'bridge hypothesis', which suggests that fathers serve as a linguistic bridge to the outside world: fathers request clarifications more frequently than mothers when talking to their young children as they generally spend less time with their children and are so less able to understand children's marginally intelligible utterances. Therefore, in this role, fathers give children experience conversing with more challenging communicative partners with whom they share less background knowledge. Earlier studies with older children seem to confirm that the teaching strategies that fathers use place higher cognitive demands upon the child than the strategies used by mothers (Laakso, 1995). Father involvement also appears to be an important factor in the school-aged child's academic performance. Radin, Williams and Coggins (1994), for instance, found that the more Native American fathers were involved in childrearing, the more likely were their children to do well in school, both academically and socially, and, more recently, Updegraff, McHale and Crouter (1996) showed that in families where the father participated equally in child-oriented activities girls maintained a high level of achievement across the transition to the seventh grade, whereas girls from traditional families declined in maths and science performance. Similarly, Seginer and Mahajna (2004) more recently showed that fathers' perceived beliefs about traditional women's roles were negatively related to adolescent girls' academic achievement. Studies of adults also show supporting evidence. Amato (1994) showed that closeness to fathers during childhood (assessed retrospectively) was positively related to adult daughters' and sons' educational and occupational mobility. Harris et al. (1998), however, showed that although in their intact families sample closeness to fathers in adolescence was not related to. children's economic and educational attainment in adult life, father involvement remained a significant predictor.

EVIDENCE SHOWING NEGATIVE ASSOCIATIONS BETWEEN FATHER ABSENCE AND CHILDREN'S EDUCATIONAL OUTCOMES

Relatedly, the decrease in father involvement typically associated with divorce can have negative effects on both cognitive functioning and academic performance. Studies in western industrialised countries show that although father absence is not always related to mental health problems in children (see also Chapters 1 and 8) it is associated with a higher risk of low academic achievement. Studies in the USA (Pong & Ju, 2000), Britain (Kiernan, 1992), the Netherlands (Dronkers, 1994) and Sweden (Murray & Sandqvist, 1990), for instance, show that children in single-parent homes face a higher risk of low academic achievement and of dropping out of school than do children who live in two-parent families. Generally, children in mother-only families have been found to score lower than other children on measures of academic achievement and cognitive ability (Hetherington, Cox & Cox, 1982; Mulkey, Crain & Harrington, 1992) and to be more likely to drop out of school (Sandefur & Wells, 1999). On the other hand, research also suggests that father absence has few consequences for children once economic factors have been controlled for (Crockett et al., 1993; Furstenberg, Morgan & Allison, 1987). Other studies show, however, that even when economic factors are controlled for, father absence continues to be associated with an increased risk of child problems (Amato, 1994), suggesting that low socio-economic status may be an additional stressor but it does not transcend the risk of inadequate father involvement. More recently, however, Pong, Dronkers and Hampden-Thompson (2004) investigated the gap in maths and science achievement of third- and fourth-graders who live with a single parent versus those who live with two parents in 10 industrialised countries: the United States, Australia, Austria, Britain (England and Scotland), Canada, Ireland, Iceland, the Netherlands, New Zealand and Norway. They showed that the United States and New Zealand ranked last among the countries compared in terms of the equality of achievement between children from single-parent families and those from two-parent homes. Single parenthood was less detrimental when family policies equalised resources between single- and two-parent families, with the single- and two-parent achievement gap being greater in countries where single-parent families were more prevalent.

This chapter discusses four studies which explored the role of father involvement, controlling for mother involvement, in children's academic outcomes. These outcomes were: educational attainment (Studies I and IV), academic motivation (Study II), and career maturity (Study III). Study IV also explored whether father involvement is related to children's educational attainment through increasing children's self-esteem (see also Study II of Chapter 2) and locus of control. Self-esteem and locus of control are popular and important constructs in psychology and have also been explored extensively as correlates of achievement in students (Ross & Broh, 2000). A hypothetical construct self-esteem is the overall affective evaluation of one's worth, value or importance (Blascovich & Tomaka, 1991). The association between self-esteem and achievement has received considerable research attention during the past two decades, although recent studies have shown that empirical support for a causal relationship between self-esteem and school achievement is often weak and confounded (Midgett, Ryan, Adams & Corville-Smith, 2001). Like self-esteem, locus of control is also used primarily as a generalised trait, and, in particular, a generalised expectancy pertaining to the connection between personal characteristics and/or actions and experienced outcomes (Lefcourt, 1991). An internal locus of control, or the belief that outcomes are contingent upon actions, is associated with scholastic achievement (Mau, Domnick & Ellsworth, 1995). Although there is some research linking locus of control and self-esteem to father involvement (Deutsch et al., 2001; Williams & Radin, 1999), research looking at the relationships between these three variables, especially with respect to children's educational outcomes, is certainly very limited (McClun & Merrell, 1998). McClun and Merrell showed that adolescents who perceived their parents as having an authoritative parenting style had both a more internal focus of control and higher self-esteem than those who perceived their parents as having either an authoritarian or permissive parenting style.

Similarly, both academic motivation (Abu & Maher, 2000; Fortier, Vallerand & Guay, 1995; Wigfield & Eccles, 2000) and career maturity (Mau et al., 1995) are significant correlates of educational attainment. With regard to the determinants of career maturity in adolescents, the role of family as a fundamental influence in the career development of adolescents has been stressed by some classic theories of career development and choice (Santos & Coimbra, 2000). Parental involvement in particular has been negatively associated with career indecision (Murry & Mosidi, 1993), and positively with career exploration (Schmitt-Rodermund & Vondracek, 1999), and research has distinguished the effect of mothers from that of fathers. Guerra and Braungart-Rieker (1999), for instance, showed that career indecision was predicted by less maternal but not less paternal acceptance in their university students, which may be explained by the different perceptions the participants had of their mothers as opposed to fathers; although fathers were viewed as more encouraging of independence than mothers, support by the mother may be particularly salient in decision-making. Regarding the role of fathers, Chung, Baskin and Case (1999) showed that the financial support and role-modelling effects of a father or father figure strongly influenced the career development of some of their Black American young men.

STUDY I: FATHER INVOLVEMENT AT AGE 7 AND EDUCATIONAL ATTAINMENT AT AGE 20

In this study Ann Buchanan and I (Flouri & Buchanan, 2004b) used longitudinal data from the NCDS to explore the role of early father involvement in children's later educational attainment independently of the role of early mother involvement and other confounding factors. As in Studies III and VI of Chapter 3, we also investigated whether gender, family structure and mother involvement moderate the relationship between father involvement and the child's (in this study) educational attainment. Finally, we explored whether father involvement is indirectly related to educational outcomes through increasing academic motivation or through decreasing emotional and behavioural problems, both of which are related to educational outcomes.

Measures

Father involvement, mother involvement and educational attainment were assessed as in Study III of Chapter 3. In all, 7259 cohort members had valid data on mother involvement at age 7, father involvement at age 7 and school-leaving qualifications by age 20. Of those, 1212 (16.7%) had no qualifications by age 20, for 1996 (27.5%) the highest qualification obtained was lower than O-level, for 2644 (36.4%) O-level, and for 1407 (19.4%) A-level. These 7259 cohort members formed our initial sample. We also adjusted for child factors (emotional/behavioural problems, cognitive ability and academic motivation, all assessed as in Study III of Chapter 3). Structural factors were family structure, sibship size (both assessed as in Study I of Chapter 2) and residential mobility. Family structure was 'intact' if the child had lived with both natural parents since birth until the age of 16 or 'otherwise'. Sibship size was assessed as the number of children under 21 (including those living away) when the cohort member was aged 7, and residential mobility was measured with the number of family moves since the child's birth until the child was aged 7. Control factors were gender, parental socio-economic status (manual vs non-manual) at the child's birth (both assessed as in Study I of Chapter 2), normal birthweight (>2.5 kg), and age at which the father and mother (measured when the cohort child was aged 16) left full-time education.

Results

As can be seen in Figure 4.1, which shows the results of the multiple linear regression analysis carried out to explore the independent role of father involvement in children's educational attainment, even after controlling for mother involvement and other confounding factors, father involvement was significantly associated with educational attainment. Mother involvement, normal birthweight, intact family structure throughout childhood, maternal education, paternal education, academic motivation in adolescence and cognitive ability were also positively related to educational attainment at age 20. Family size and emotional and behavioural problems in childhood were negatively related to educational attainment. Men compared to women, and those born to parents of non-manual socio-economic status, compared to those born to parents of manual socio-economic status, had higher educational attainment. The model was significant ($F(13, 3289) = 277.918$, $p < 0.001$), with the amount of variance in educational attainment explained by these variables being 52%. Father involvement was not more important for educational attainment when mother involvement was low rather than high. Not growing up in an intact two-parent family did not weaken the association between father or mother involvement and

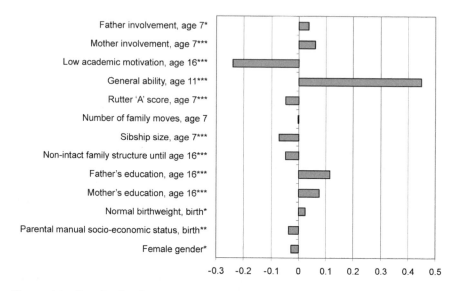

Figure 4.1   Standardised regression coefficients (βs) predicting educational attainment at age 20 from father and mother involvement at age 7 in NCDS ($N = 3303$)
Notes: $^*p < 0.05$; $^{**}p < 0.01$; $^{***}p < 0.001$

educational outcomes. Neither emotional and behavioural problems nor academic motivation mediated the relationship between father and mother involvement and later educational attainment (for full details see Flouri & Buchanan, 2004b).

STUDY II: FATHER INVOLVEMENT AND CHILDREN'S ACADEMIC MOTIVATION IN ADOLESCENCE

In this study (Flouri, Buchanan & Bream, 2002), we explored the role of father involvement in adolescents' academic motivation after adjusting for mother involvement and known confounds in a cross-sectional study of 2722 adolescents in Britain (for more about this study's methodology, see Study VI of Chapter 3).

Measures

Positive attitudes to school were measured with Flouri and Buchanan's (2002c) 10-item 3-point scale which included two of the items of the NCDS Academic Motivation Scale at age 16 ('I feel school is largely a waste of time' and 'I never take my work seriously') which taps pro-school attitudes and perfectionism (Accordino, Accordino & Slaney, 2000). The Cronbach's alpha of the scale was 0.65. Father involvement and mother involvement were measured as in Study VI in Chapter 3. We also controlled for socio-economic status (assessed by receipt of free school meals), age, gender and family structure (measured as 'intact' if the participants stated that they lived with both their parents and 'non-intact' if they reported that they lived otherwise).

Results —

The multiple linear regression carried out to predict positive attitudes to school showed that both father involvement and mother involvement contributed significantly and independently to positive school attitudes. Gender and socio-economic status were insignificantly related to positive attitudes to school. However, compared to their counterparts, older children and children from intact families had more positive attitudes to school. The amount of variance in school attitudes explained by these variables was modest (11%). Furthermore, the association between father involvement and school attitudes was the same for sons and daughters. We did not find evidence to support the notion that being in a non-intact family weakens the association between perceived father involvement and school attitudes, or that the impact of perceived father involvement on school attitudes depends on the level of perceived mother involvement.

The findings from this cross-sectional study, however, do not allow us to establish which factors, if any, have a causal status. It is possible that children who have negative attitudes to school may elicit low levels of father and mother involvement. Conversely, children may have negative attitudes to school because they lack parental support.

STUDY III: FATHER INVOLVEMENT AND CHILDREN'S CAREER MATURITY IN ADOLESCENCE

In this study we used the same dataset that we used in Study II above, but this time we explored the role of father involvement independently of mother involvement in career maturity (Flouri & Buchanan, 2002d).

Measures

Five items measured in 5-point scales anchored with 'strongly disagree' and 'strongly agree' were taken from the Measure of Guidance Impact (MGI), developed for the Department of Employment by the National Foundation for Educational Research (Christophers et al., 1993) to measure career maturity. The items were: 'I have made a plan for my future working life', 'I know what I would need to get into the education or training that interests me', 'I know what I would need to get into the job that interests me', 'I can see the steps I must go through to make a decision' and 'I know myself well enough to know what kind of help I want'. Cronbach's alpha was 0.80. We also controlled for socio-demographic characteristics (age, socio-economic status, gender, family structure, all assessed as in Study II above), personal characteristics (academic motivation, happiness, feelings of pressure), and work-related skills and career role models. Academic motivation was assessed as in Study II above. Happiness was assessed (as in Study VI of Chapter 3) with a 1-item 4-point scale anchored with 'never' and 'often' asking participants to state the extent to which 'they felt happy and confident about themselves'. Similarly, a 1-item dichotomous variable asked participants whether they are feeling pressurised about the choices they must make about their studies or work. Work-related skills (job skills, computing skills and work experience) and role models were also controlled for.

Results

The multiple linear regression carried out to explore the role of father involvement in carer maturity, controlling for the effect of mother involvement and confounding factors, showed that although father involvement was significantly related to career maturity at the bivariate level, its effect failed to reach significance in the multivariate model. Similarly, mother involvement, academic motivation, happiness and socio-demographics were not related to career maturity at the multivariate level. However, having work-related skills and having a career role model were positively (and having career pressure was negatively) associated with career maturity in the regression analysis. The amount of variance in career maturity explained by the variables in the model was modest at 7%.

STUDY IV: FATHER INVOLVEMENT, SELF-ESTEEM AND LOCUS OF CONTROL AT AGE 10, AND EDUCATIONAL ATTAINMENT AT AGE 26

This study, using the longitudinal study from the 1970 British Cohort Study, explored whether father involvement is associated with long-term educational attainment in a more recent than the 1958 birth cohort. The study also explored whether father involvement is linked to educational attainment via its impact on the child's self-esteem and locus of control (Flouri, under review – c).

The 1970 British Birth Cohort Study (BCS70)

The study used data from sweeps of the 1970 British Birth Cohort Study (BCS70). BCS70 is a continuing longitudinal study of all children born between 5 and 11 April 1970 in England, Scotland and Wales. Data sweeps took place when the cohort members were aged 5, 10, 16, 26 and 30 years. Information was collected by the midwife present at birth, and from clinical records. In 1975 and 1980 parents were interviewed by the Health Visitor, cohort members undertook ability tests, and the school health service gathered medical information on each cohort child. At ages 10 and 16 head and class teachers also completed questionnaires. The follow-up at age 26 was carried out by a postal survey, and at age 30 data were collected by interview with the cohort member. At age 26 information about the highest educational qualification obtained was collected from 8366 cohort members. Because the aim of this study was to explore the relationships between father involvement, mother involvement, and children's self-esteem, locus of control, and educational attainment, only those cohort members with valid data in all these five variables ($N = 4003$) were included in the study. The initial sample size consisted of 1737 men and 2033 women (for 233 participants no information about their sex was recorded at birth).

Measures

At age 26 the highest qualifications of cohort members were grouped into six major categories, roughly equivalent to NVQ/GNVQ levels. These were: No qualifications (0); Sub-GCSE/NVQ1 (1); GCSE grades A–C – 'O Level'/ NVQ2 (2); GCSE A Level/NVQ3 (3); Sub-degree Higher Education/NVQ4 (4); and Degree+/NVQ5/6 (5) (Bynner & Joshi, 2002). The mean educational attainment of the 4003 participants of the study was 2.775 (SD=1.524). Father and mother involvement at age 10 was assessed by the child's teacher who reported how interested the child's mother and father were in the child's education. In all, 55.5% of the fathers of all cohort members at age 10 were reported to be 'very interested', 32.7% were 'moderately interested', 6.5% showed 'little interest', and 5.2% were 'uninterested'. Of the mothers, 55% were 'very interested', 35.7% 'moderately interested', 6.2% showed 'little interest', and 3% were 'uninterested'. The 'no'/'little' and 'some' interest responses were subsequently combined to form dichotomous variables assessing father's and mother's interest as 'high' or 'otherwise', which were used instead. At age 10 a 12-item scale measuring self-esteem and a 16-item scale measuring internal locus of control (Butler, Despotidou & Shepherd, 1980) were completed by the cohort members. For both scales responses were anchored with 'yes' and 'no'. Items of the locus of control scale included 'wishing makes things happen' and 'nice things are only through luck' (both inversely coded). Cronbach's alpha for the whole BCS70 cohort was 0.63. Self-esteem items included 'feel foolish in front of peers' and 'feel foolish talking to parents' (both inversely coded). Cronbach's alpha for the whole BCS70 cohort was 0.73. The average score of the self-esteem scale (ranging from 13 to 24) was 20.736 (SD = 2.152), and the average score of the locus of control scale (ranging from 18 to 32) was 26.552 (SD = 2.219). Several family-related and individual factors were also included in this analysis. These were four factors tapping the family's socio-economic circumstances, and three factors tapping individual factors. The family-related factors were family structure (assessed as 'intact' if the cohort member lived continuously with both original parents until age 10 or 'otherwise'), parental social class at birth, socio-economic disadvantage at age 5, and mother's educational qualifications at age 5. Parental social class was measured with the Registrar General's measure of social class which defines social class according to job status and the associated education, prestige or lifestyle, and is assessed by the current or last held job. In the BCS70 it was coded on a 6-point scale ranging from professional (I) to unskilled (V). In cases in which there was no father the mother's social class was used. For ease of interpretation the coding was reversed so that a high score (ranging from 1 to 6) indicated a high social position. On average social class was 3.572 (SD = 1.215). Socio-economic disadvantage at age 5 was assessed using a summative index giving an overall score of material disadvantage that ranged from 0 to 3 on the basis of presence or absence of three variables. These were: overcrowding ($\geqslant 1$ person per room), no housing tenure, and shared use or no access to a bathroom, indoor lavatory and hot water (Schoon et al., 2002). The average socio-economic disadvantage score was 0.612 (SD = 0.802). Finally, mother's education was assessed when the cohort member was aged 5 and was coded (1), the mother had some qualifications, or (-1), the mother had no qualifications. The individual factors were birthweight, academic attainment and emotional and behavioural problems at age 5. Birthweight was normal if it was above 2,500 gr. Birthweight (for those cohort members with valid data) was normal for 3573 (94.8%) cohort children. At age 5 academic attainment was measured with the Human Figure Drawing test, developed by Goodenough (1926) and Harris (1963), which is a modified version of the Draw-a-Man test and has been evaluated as a measure of intelligence. Emotional and behavioural problems in childhood were assessed with 27 items of the Rutter 'A' Health and Behaviour Checklist (Rutter et al., 1970) described in

Study I of Chapter 2. The average general ability (z-score ranging from -5 to 3) was 0.10 (SD = 1.063), and the average Rutter 'A' score (ranging from 0 to 33) was 8.824 (SD = 4.988).

Results

Figures 4.2 and 4.3 show the results of the multiple linear regression analyses (separately by gender) carried out to explore the independent role of father involvement in children's educational attainment, even after controlling for mother involvement and other confounding factors. As can be seen in the figures, although father involvement was an insignificant predictor of later educational attainment in men, it was positively related to educational attainment in women. For both genders, internal locus of control and mother involvement at age 10 were positively related to educational attainment by age 26. Self-esteem was insignificantly associated with educational attainment. In both genders social class, general ability, and mother's educational attainment were positively (and socio-economic disadvantage was negatively) related to educational attainment. Uniquely in women, emotional and behavioural problems at age 5 were negatively related to educational attainment. The amount of variance in educational attainment accounted for by the variables in the models was 30% in both men and women. Although father involvement was not linked to educational attainment via its impact on child's self-esteem or locus of control, it was found that locus of control mediated the relationship between self-esteem and educational attainment in both genders, and that mother involvement mediated the relationship between father involvement and educational attainment in men. In other words, self-esteem affected educational attainment via its effect in increasing locus of control, and father involvement affected sons' educational attainment via its effect in mother involvement. An explanation why mother's interest mediated the relationship between father's interest and sons' educational attainment might be that child-oriented men select child-oriented women to be the mothers of their children or that fathers who are 'involved' with their sons encourage mothers to be even more involved.

This study suffered from some important limitations. First, of course, only those cohort members with complete data on age 10 – mother's interest in child's education, father's interest in child's education, self-esteem and locus of control – and on age 26 – educational attainment – were included in the study. Second, parental interest in the child's education was just a 1-item question completed by the child's teacher. Related to this it is questionable if the measure is sensitive enough given that over half the mothers and fathers were given the highest interest rating by the teacher. Third, as Feinstein and Symons (1999) noted, parental interest is likely to be

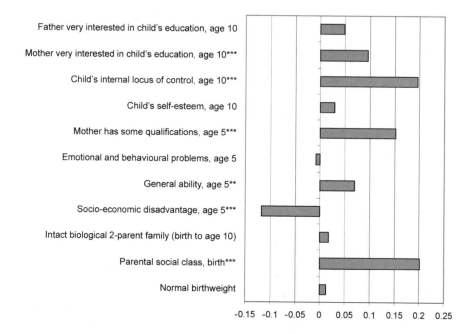

Figure 4.2   Standardised regression coefficients (βs) predicting men's educational attainment at age 26 from father and mother involvement at age 10 in BCS70 ($N = 1326$)
Notes: **$p < 0.01$; ***$p < 0.001$

endogenous (parents show high levels of interest in children who do exceptionally well in school) which makes any discussion on implications even more difficult.

SUMMARY AND CONCLUSIONS

This chapter describes two longitudinal studies (Studies I and IV) and two cross-sectional studies (Studies II and III) which explored the role of father involvement, controlling for mother involvement, in children's academic outcomes. The children's outcomes were educational attainment in adult life (Studies I and IV), academic motivation (Study II), and career maturity (Study III) in adolescence. Not only were the outcomes different (although related), but father involvement was also assessed at different ages and with different measures. In particular, father involvement was measured in the cross-sectional studies with four child-reported items asking children

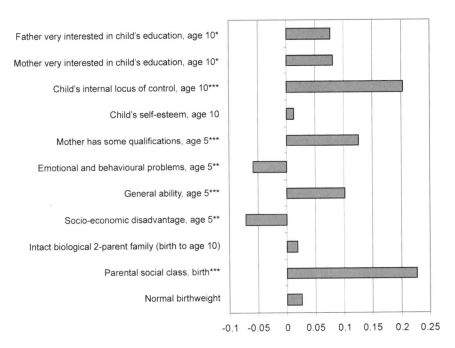

Figure 4.3 Standardised regression coefficients (βs) predicting women's educational attainment at age 26 from father and mother involvement at age 10 in BCS70 ($N = 1578$)
Notes: *$p < 0.05$; **$p < 0.01$; ***$p < 0.001$

whether their father figures spend time with them, talk through their worries with them, take an interest in their school work, and help with their plans for the future. In contrast, in Study I (which used data from sweeps of the NCDS) father involvement was assessed by the child's parent (usually the mother) and teacher with four items completed when the child was aged 7 (in 1965): 'father takes outings with the child', 'father manages the child', 'father reads to the child' and 'father is interested in the child's education'. In Study IV (which used data from sweeps of the 1970 British Cohort Study (BCS70) which traced all children born between 5 and 11 April 1970 in Britain) father involvement was measured with only one of these items ('father is interested in the child's education') when the child was age 10.

The results from the multivariate analyses carried out showed that high socio-economic status predicted educational attainment only in the longitudinal studies (Studies I and IV), whereas non-intact family structure was associated with low educational attainment in the 1958 birth cohort (Study I) and with negative attitudes to school in Study II. Although Study III found that father involvement was not related to children's career maturity, Study II showed that father involvement was associated with both sons' and daughters' academic motivation, although given the cross-sectional nature of the dataset used for that study, the direction of causality could not be determined. Perhaps more interestingly, both longitudinal studies described in this chapter (Studies I and IV) showed that even after controlling for early mother involvement, early father involvement was associated with later educational attainment in daughters. Only the study using the NCDS dataset (Study I) showed that father involvement was also related to educational attainment in sons (although in the BCS70 study, father involvement did affect sons' educational attainment indirectly, via its effect in raising mother involvement). What needs to be remembered, however, is that at age 7 father involvement in the NCDS was measured with four items, whereas in BCS70 (Study IV) only the item assessing the father's interest in the child's education was asked. Feinstein and Symons (1999), also using the NCDS dataset, showed that father's and mother's interest in the child's education was one of the major influences on attainment. In explaining the significant effect of parental interest on attainment, Feinstein and Symons suggested that parental interest in the child's education reflects both the 'public' and the 'private' time of parents: *public time* refers to the establishment of a home structure for learning, and *private time* refers to active involvement with the education of children, correcting homework for example (p. 303). It seems that the other three indicators of paternal involvement at age 7 ('father reads to child', 'takes outings with the child', and 'father takes an equal to mother's role in managing the child') also reflect both these factors.

CHAPTER 5

FATHER INVOLVEMENT AND CHILDREN'S AGGRESSIVE BEHAVIOUR

INTRODUCTION

Although the body of literature on familial and in particular parenting correlates of children's externalising behaviour problems is large, relatively less is known about the independent role of fathering and mothering. Some recent studies have shown that father's harsh parenting is associated with externalising child behaviour, even after controlling for mother's harsh parenting. This chapter describes three studies (two longitudinal and one cross-sectional) carried out to explore links between father involvement and adolescent children's externalising behaviour. The first explored the role of father involvement in children in trouble with the police, the second the role of father involvement in children's bullying behaviour, and the third the role of father involvement in recovery from externalising behaviour problems.

PREDICTORS OF CHILDREN'S EXTERNALISING BEHAVIOUR PROBLEMS

Not much is known about the independent role of fathering and mothering in children's externalising behaviour problems, although the body of literature on familial correlates (Loeber & Hay, 1998; Perry, Perry & Boldizar, 1990) and in particular parenting correlates (Steinberg, Mounts, Lamborn & Dornbusch, 1991) is large. Externalising behaviour problems, known as oppositional defiant disorder in DSM-IV (American Psychiatric Association, 1994), are defined as a recurrent pattern of negativistic, defiant, hostile behaviour including tempers, non-compliance, and spiteful, angry and resentful behaviour.[1] For example, poor childrearing, and in particular

---

[1] By contrast, the central feature of *internalising* disorders is disordered mood or emotion. Like externalising disorders, depressive and anxiety disorders (which constitute the internalising

poor supervision, harsh discipline, parental disharmony, rejection of the child and low involvement (Scott, 1998), are consistently shown to be related to externalising behaviour problems (Farrington, 1994). In fact, Taylor, McGue and Iacono (2000), in line with Loeber and Stouthamer-Loeber (1987), showed that family's 'contextual' factors such as socio-economic status were not strong predictors of juvenile delinquency (an expression of severe externalising behaviour problems), arguing that individual differences in delinquency are associated with environmental factors shared by children in a family, such as parenting style, but not between parents and their children, such as socio-economic status. In his review of the causes of aggressive behaviour in childhood and adolescence, Scott (1998) also concluded that twin and adoption studies suggest that there is 'a large shared (family) environmental effect, a moderate non-shared (unique) environmental effect, and a modest genetic effect' (p. 203).

Earlier, Eaves et al. (1997) similarly showed that although there is evidence of a substantial genetic component among children with externalising behaviour problems there is also considerable evidence that such children are more likely to develop a conduct or antisocial disorder where there are associated family adversities, conflicted family relationships, punitive childrearing practices and maternal depression. Cohen, Brook, Cohen, Velez and Garcia (1991), in a longitudinal study from early childhood through late adolescence, showed that the key influences on the expression of externalising disorders were the presence of the following factors eight years earlier: neighbourhood crime, residential instability, parental socio-pathy, parental mental illness, remarriage, maternal inattention, and power-assertive discipline. Reading difficulties have also been consistently associated with externalising behaviour problems (Patterson, DeBaryshe & Ramsey, 1989) but whether reading retardation leads to a behavioural disorder or whether behaviour problems pre-exist reading difficulties is not clear. Others have focused more on identifying protective factors or on delineating trajectories of change for externalising problems. Various researchers, for instance, have shown that high self-esteem, good coping skills, school achievement, involvement in extra-curriculum activities and positive relationship with parents, peers and adults have all been shown to be protective against externalising behavioural problems (Loesel & Bliesener, 1994; Merikangas & Angst, 1994; Sweeting & West, 1995). More recently, Galambos, Barker and Almeida (2003) showed that parents' firm behavioural control rather than support was associated with limiting children's anti-social behaviour.

[1](continued) disorders) encompass a variety of diagnoses. DSM-III-R (American Psychiatric Association, 1987), for instance, includes more than 10 anxiety disorders and 3 categories of morbid depression. Both the Rutter 'A' and Goodman's Strengths and Difficulties Questionnaires (described earlier in the book) assess internalising as well as externalising behaviour problems in children.

Below I will describe three studies that Ann Buchanan and I carried out to explore the role of father involvement in recovery from externalising behaviour problems (Study III), and two manifestations of externalising behavioural problems: delinquency (Study I) and bullying (Study II). With regards to delinquency, Farrington (1995), using longitudinal data from the Cambridge Study of Delinquent Development, showed that young people who become involved in crime at the earliest ages – before they are 14 – tend to become the most persistent offenders, with longer criminal careers. This is particularly important given that the life-time likelihood of acquiring at least one criminal conviction is greater than commonly realised (more than 40% males and 10% females are likely to be found guilty or cautioned for an indictable offence at some point during their lives), and that young offenders are versatile in committing other types of antisocial behaviour, such as heavy drinking, drug-taking, dangerous driving and promiscuous sex, which makes delinquency only one element in a much larger syndrome of antisocial behaviour. The 'peak' ages at which young people are most likely to be found guilty or cautioned are between the ages of 15 and 19. Criminal involvement typically starts before the age of 15, but declines markedly once young people reach their 20s. Powerful correlates of juvenile delinquency are difficult temperament (Lyons-Ruth, 1996), low intelligence and poor academic performance (Hinshaw, 1992). On the other hand, impulsiveness, hyperactivity, restlessness and attention problems (which compose elements of the cluster of externalising behaviour problems) are associated with both low attainment in school and inability to foresee the consequences of offending (Farrington, 1996). Parental psychiatric problems, marital discord (Laucht et al., 2000) and non-intact family structure (Kemppainen, Jokelainen, Isohanni, Jaervelin & Raesaenen, 2002; Simons, Lin, Gordon, Conger & Lorenz, 1999) are also among the major familial risk factors of juvenile offending. Criminality in the family is another risk factor (Farrington, Barnes & Lambert, 1996), especially for boys (Fergusson & Horwood, 1999). Low socio-economic status (assessed by low family income and poor housing, rather than low prestige of the parents' occupations) of the parental family (Farrington, 1995) is also associated with juvenile delinquency although not consistently (Loeber & Stouthamer-Loeber, 1987; Taylor et al., 2000). Finally, having delinquent peers is associated with delinquency although it is not clear if membership of a delinquent peer group leads to offending or whether delinquents simply gravitate towards each other's company, or both (Farrington, 1996).

Bullying, on the other hand, is a special form of aggression. It is generally conceived as repeated unprovoked aggressive behaviour in which the perpetrator or perpetrators are more powerful than the person or persons being attacked. The prevalence of bullying at schools varies according to country, geographical locations, the age of the children sampled, the method of data collection and how bullying was conducted. Bullying can take several forms. It can be physical, verbal or indirect (Björkqvist, Österman & Kaukiainen, 1992), relational (Crick et al., 1999) or generic (which denotes non-specific descriptions of victimisation, which include any of the other forms of victimisation). Bullying behaviour at school is predictive of delinquency later in life (Baldry & Farrington, 2000; Khatri, Kupersmidt & Patterson, 2000; Rigby & Cox, 1996), and is frequent. In England alone 10% of secondary school pupils reported being bullied 'sometimes' or 'more frequently' and 6% admitted taking part in bullying others (Whitney & Smith, 1993). Bullying is not uncommon among primary school children, too. Also in the UK, Wolke, Woods, Bloomfield and Karstadt (2000) showed that among primary school children 4.3% were direct bullies, 39.8% were victims, and 10.2% both bullied and were victimised frequently (bully/victims). The rates for relational bullying were 1.1% bullies, 37.9% victims and 5.9% bully/victims. Regarding gender differences, boys are more numerous in the bully category and are bullied by other boys (rarely by girls), but girls experience bullying from both genders (Smith, 2000). Bullying is also strongly associated with both emotional and behavioural problems (Khatri et al., 2000). In their study, Wolke et al. (2000) showed that all primary school age children involved in direct bullying had significantly increased total behaviour problems, hyperactivity, conduct problems, and peer problem scores, and lower prosocial behaviour scores (as assessed with the Strengths and Difficulties Questionnaire) compared to those not involved in bullying. Findings were similar (but less pronounced) for relational bullying involvement and behaviour problems for bully/victims and victims.

THE ROLE OF THE FATHER IN CHILDREN'S EXTERNALISING BEHAVIOUR PROBLEMS

Those studies that have looked at the role of fathers in children's conduct problems or delinquent behaviour showed that conflict with fathers (Liu, 2004) and fathers' negativity and fathers' harsh or neglectful parenting (Biller & Lopez Kimpton, 1997; DeKlyen et al., 1998) are significantly associated with externalising child behaviour. More recently Chang, Schwartz, Dodge and McBride-Chang (2003) showed that fathers' harsh parenting had a stronger effect than mothers' harsh parenting in the children's aggression. In addition, fathers' harsh parenting affected sons more than daughters, whereas there was no gender differential effect with mothers' harsh parenting. Australian studies have shown that paternal physical parenting style increased adolescent sons' (but decreased adolescent daughters') self-reported delinquency scores (Heaven et al.,

2004), and that paternal bonding was an important correlate of delinquency, even after controlling for maternal bonding (Mak, 1994). In a similar vein, Aldous and Mulligan (2002) showed that in two-parent families fathers' active care of difficult-to-raise preschoolers was related to fewer problems in children later, independently of mother's care. Along the same lines, Harris et al. (1998) showed that even after controlling for mother involvement and a change in mother's closeness, both low father involvement and decreasing closeness between fathers and adolescents in intact families predicted delinquency in adult life, and Simons et al. (1999) showed that the association between divorce and children's externalising problems was in fact explained (at least in boys) by the compromised quality of mother's parenting and of father's involvement in parenting. Kosterman, Haggerty, Spoth and Redmond (2004) showed that socialisation experiences with fathers was directly related to the antisocial behaviour of daughters (with more prosocial socialisation protecting against antisocial behaviour), but not sons, in early adolescence. Sons were influenced indirectly by their fathers; paternal bonding promoted prosocial beliefs which, in turn, inhibited sons' antisocial behaviour.

With regards to bullying, in particular, although several links between parenting or family characteristics and bullying behaviour have been identified (Baldry & Farrington, 2000), as with other child outcomes, the independent effects of fathering are rarely distinguished from those of mothering. From what has been found, however, it seems that father absence (Berdondini & Smith, 1996) and father's own bullying behaviour at school (Farrington, 1993) are significant risk factors. Farrington (1993), who assessed bullying and antisocial behaviour, in a sample of 411 London males from the age of 8, and in their resident children aged 3–15 when the men were aged 32, showed strong evidence of continuity in bullying, with 30% of men who had been identified as bullies at age 14 reporting that their children were bullies, compared with 17% of men who had not been bullies. There is also evidence that antisocial personality disorder and alcohol or drug abuse in fathers are associated with problems of conduct and aggression in children and adolescents (Fals-Stewart, Kelley, Fincham, Golden & Logsdon, 2004; Goetting, 1994; Phares, 1996). Smith and Farrington (2004) more recently showed that having an antisocial father was associated with early conduct problems, with later antisocial behaviour, and with assortative mating with a convicted partner. Jaffee et al. (2003), in their sample of 5-year-old twin pairs and their parents, relatedly showed that although not living with one's biological father was associated with more conduct problems when the father engaged in low levels of antisocial behaviour, living with one's father was associated with more conduct problems when the father engaged in high levels of antisocial behaviour.

STUDY I: THE ROLE OF FATHER INVOLVEMENT IN EARLY CHILDHOOD IN ADOLESCENT DELINQUENCY

Using longitudinal data from the National Child Development Study, this study investigated the independent role of father involvement at age 7 in delinquency at age 16, controlling for the effect on mother involvement and known risk factors (Flouri & Buchanan, 2002). In addition, it examined whether father involvement is a more important predictor of juvenile delinquency when mother involvement is low rather than high, and whether growing up in a non-intact family affects the association between parental involvement and juvenile delinquency.

Measures

Trouble with the police at age 16 (assessed with a 1-item dichotomous variable) was used as a proxy for juvenile offending. Because adolescents often engage in delinquent behaviours of which their parents are unaware, probably the most accurate assessment of delinquency is obtained when the parental and teachers' reports are combined (Hart, Lahey, Loeber & Hanson, 1994; Piacentini, Cohen & Cohen, 1992). Therefore, in this study a cohort member had been in trouble with the police by age 16 if the parent (the mother in 90.8% of the cases) or the teacher had reported him or her to be. In all 16.4% of boys and 5.1% of girls were reported to have been in trouble with the police. The prevalence rate for males compares with the 20.7% of males who had been convicted of one or more offences by the age of 16 in the Cambridge Study in Delinquency Development carried out at roughly the same time as the NCDS, which again compares well with official national statistics for males born in the same year as the Cambridge Study and the National Child Development Study cohort members (Home Office Statistical Bulletin, 1987, 1989). The slightly lower prevalence rate in our study may be due to the fact that teacher and parent reports, rather than official crime records, were used and therefore they are likely to underestimate the actual prevalence rate. In all, 6768 cases had complete data on both trouble with the police at age 16 and father and mother involvement at age 7. This was our initial sample.

The variables that were controlled for were familial and individual risk factors. Of the individual risk factors, cognitive ability, emotional and behavioural problems, and academic motivation (all measured as in Study III of Chapter 3) were controlled for. Of the family-related risk factors, age 7 mental health problems in the parental home, domestic tension (both assessed as in Study III of Chapter 3), and family structure (assessed as intact if the child's mother and father at age 7 were his or her natural parents vs all other situations) were controlled for. In all, 97% of the cohort members lived in intact families. In addition, age 7 parental alcoholism and age 7 parental criminality (both assessed by the Health Visitor's report whether 'alcoholism is one of the difficulties in this family', and whether the 'family has required the services of the Probation Officer', respectively) were adjusted for. Of the 6768 cohort members, 5924 had valid data on parental alcoholism and 6124 had valid data on parental criminality. Parental alcoholism and parental criminality were a problem for 48 and 85 cohort members, respectively. Markers of socio-economic disadvantage were low parental socio-economic status ('manual' vs 'non-manual') at child's birth, age 7 large sibship size (number of children under age 21 in the household), and high residential mobility (number of family moves since the child's birth until age 7).

Results

Because boys were more than three times as likely as girls to be involved with the police at age 16 (chi-square = 219.440, df:1, $p < 0.001$) logistic regression was carried out separately for each gender. For both boys and girls academic motivation was negatively (and family size was positively) related to teacher- or parent-reported trouble with the police at age 16. For boys only, however, trouble with the police was also significantly related to low IQ, low father involvement in childhood and parental criminality. Uniquely for girls, non-intact family structure at age 7 was significantly associated with later trouble with the police. The study found no evidence that father involvement is a more important predictor of juvenile delinquency when mother involvement is low rather than high, or that growing up in a non-intact family affects the association between parental involvement and juvenile delinquency.

STUDY II: FATHER INVOLVEMENT AND ADOLESCENT BULLYING BEHAVIOUR

This study (Flouri & Buchanan, 2003c) explored the independent effect of father involvement in adolescent bullying behaviour after controlling for mother involvement, the child's age and gender, parental socio-economic status and family structure. The data for this study came from a confidential questionnaire researching the views and experiences of 1147 adolescents aged between 14 and 18 in the UK. In all, 493 (43%) boys and 652 (56.8%) girls took part in the study (2 adolescents did not state their gender). Three thousand anonymous questionnaires were distributed into schools and youth clubs where entire classes or groups undertook to complete them usually within the school day or youth club setting. Most of the sample lived in England, were aged between 14 and 15 years (84.9%) and were White (83.8%). Of the 1147 adolescents, 43.8% were aged 14, 40.4% were aged 15, 6.4% were aged 16, 5.3% were aged 17, and 3.2% were aged 18 years. Seven hundred and ninety-five adolescents (69.3%) reported that they live with both their parents. Of the remaining 352 adolescents, 263 (22.9%) reported that they live with their mother and 38 (3.3%) with their father. Of the 1147 adolescents who took part in the study, 229 (20%) reported that they had received free school meals at some point during their schooling, which (as also discussed in Study VI of Chapter 3) compares well with the 19.8% of pupils known to be eligible for free meals in nursery and primary schools and the 17.5% of pupils known to be eligible for free meals in secondary schools in England (Statistics of Education, 1998). However, only 78 (6.8%) reported that no one in their family worked, which (as also discussed in Study VI of Chapter 3) is significantly lower than the average proportion of workless households in Britain (19%) (Office for National Statistics, 1998).

Measures

Bullying behaviour was assessed with a 4-item 5-point scale. Participants had to report whether they had done any of the following in the last fortnight: 'bullied someone', 'spread rumours about someone', 'deliberately hurt someone', and 'deliberately left someone out'. Cronbach's alpha was 0.70. Of the 1147 adolescents who took part in the study 868 (75.7%) reported that they had not taken part in any form of bullying in the previous fortnight. Only 31 adolescents (2.7%) reported that they had been engaged in all four forms of bullying included in the questionnaire during the previous fortnight. Father involvement and mother involvement were assessed as in Study VI of Chapter 3. Cronbach's alphas for the father involvement and the mother involvement scales were 0.83 and 0.80, respectively. Socio-economic status, family structure, age and gender were also measured as in Study VI of Chapter 3.

Results

The multiple linear regression analysis carried out to predict bullying behaviour in the sample showed that, as expected, boys tended to engage in bullying behaviour more than girls. None of the other socio-demographic variables of age, family structure, and family socio-economic status was significant in predicting bullying behaviour. Both mother involvement and father involvement were, however, negatively associated with bullying behaviour (in fact, the father and the mother involvement effects were quite similar (beta = −0.11, and beta = −0.14, respectively)), although the amount of variance explained in the regression model was modest at 7%. Although the study found no evidence to support the notion that the child's gender or family structure changes the salience of fathers for children's bullying behaviour, it showed that father involvement was more important when mother involvement was low rather than high.

STUDY III: FATHER'S INTEREST IN THE CHILD'S EDUCATION IN ADOLESCENCE AND CHILD'S RECOVERY FROM EXTERNALISING BEHAVIOUR PROBLEMS

This study (Buchanan & Flouri, 2001), using longitudinal data from the childhood sweeps of the National Child Development Study, explored the role of father involvement at age 16 (the teacher-reported father's interest in child's education at age 16) and other 'protective' factors (good reading skills at age 11, good relationships with parents at age 16, and good school attendance at age 16) in recovery from externalising behaviour problems after age 7, after controlling for known risk factors.

Measures

'Recovery' from externalising behaviour problems after age 7 was assessed (using the Rutter 'A' Health and Behaviour Checklist) as follows: children who were designated in the 'externalising' subgroup at 7 were deemed to have 'recovered' if they were not in the top 20% of children with emotional and behavioural problems at age 11 *and* 16. Thus, in light of the evidence that children with externalising disorders may develop depression in adult life (e.g. Eaves et al., 1997), we considered both externalising and internalising scores when assessing recovery. As explained in Study IV of Chapter 3, a factor analysis carried out on the items of the shortened (23 items) Rutter 'A' to examine its dimensionality in this sample confirmed that the 'internalising' behaviour problems subgroup was based on the total score for positive responses to having headaches, stomach aches, sleep problems, worries, and being solitary, miserable and fearful. The 'externalising' behaviour problems subgroup was based on the total score for positive responses to being fidgety, destroying things, fighting, not being liked and being irritable, disobedient and unsettled. Children in the top 20% of the total emotional and behavioural problems score from the shortened Rutter 'A' were designated as showing some disorder. Children with an 'internalising' score exceeding their 'externalising' score were designated as having an 'internalising' problem, while those with a 'externalising' score exceeding their 'internalising' score were designated as having an 'externalising' problem. Children who had equal internalising and externalising scores, the comorbid group, were omitted from the analysis due to the group's small sample size at each age. As in Study IV of Chapter 3 this study used information obtained initially from 6441 individuals for whom there were complete psychological data at ages 7, 11, 16 and 33 years. Eight hundred and sixty children who were mentally disabled or who had chronic illness or disability were not included in this analysis. Of these 6441 cohort members, 3748 had never exhibited emotional or behavioural problems whereas 662 had at least once showed disruptive behaviour in their childhood. Therefore, the sample in our study was these 4410 individuals. The factors controlled for were gender, socio-economic status of parents at birth (manual vs non-manual) and domestic tensions at age 7 (all assessed as in Study I of Chapter 2). Family structure was 'birth' (vs 'otherwise') if cohort members lived with their birth parents until age 16 and had no experience of severe disadvantage or care (assessed as in Study IV of Chapter 3). Parental mental health was 'ill' if the Health Visitor reported evidence of mental health difficulties in the family at age 7, or if either parent had a psychiatric chronic condition at age 11, or if either parent had a diagnosis of psychiatric illness at age 16. The variables that constituted the 'risk factors' grouping were family residential mobility (three or more family moves since child's birth until child was aged 7), clumsiness (child is clumsy, according to the teacher at age 7, or the medical doctor at age 11 or 16), social services involvement (the family has been in contact with the Children's Department at age 7 or 11, or with the Social Services at age 16), and involvement with the police (the family has been in contact with the Probation Officer at age 7 or 11, or in prison at age 11, or the child has been in trouble with the police/has been to criminal court/has been in contact with the police or probation at age 16). The variables that constituted the 'protective factors' grouping were father's interest in the child's education at age 16 (teacher's report), good school attendance at age 16 (child's school attendance was 90% or more), good reading skills at age 11 (top one-third of score on reading test), and self-reported good relationships with parents at age 16 (cohort member indicates either 'very true' or 'usually true' that he or she gets on with mother or father). The protective and risk factors groupings were linear summaries of these individual factors.

Results

Of the 7 year olds with emotional and behavioural problems (top 20% scores of the Rutter 'A' Checklist), 43% went on to have emotional and behavioural problems when they were aged 11, and 43% went on to have emotional and behavioural problems when they were aged 16. Similarly, of the 11 year olds with emotional and behavioural problems, 50% continued to have emotional and behavioural problems at age 16.

With regards to externalising behaviour problems in particular, 662 children (of the 4410 children of the study) had at least once (at ages 7, 11 or 16) exhibited externalising behaviour problems. One hundred and seventy-seven children had externalising behaviour problems at age 7 only, 158 at age 11 only, 156 at age 16 only, 39 at ages 7 and 11, 39 at ages 7 and 16, 45 at ages 11 and 16, and 48 at all ages (ages 7, 11 and 16).

The logistic regression analysis carried out to explore predictors of recovery from externalising behaviour problems showed that although individually the protective factors were associated with recovery at the bivariate level, as a group they were not significantly related to recovery at the multivariate model. At the multivariate level only the grouping of risk factors for psychological maladjustment was negatively associated with recovery.

SUMMARY AND CONCLUSIONS

This chapter described one cross-sectional (Study II) and two longitudinal studies (both using data from the National Child Development Study) carried out to explore links between father involvement and children's externalising behaviour problems. Father involvement in Study I was measured with four items asked when the cohort children were aged 7 ('father reads to the child', 'father takes outings with the child', 'father takes an equal to mother's role in managing the child', and 'father is interested in the child's education'), whereas father involvement in Study II was assessed with four items asking (the child) if the father spends time with the child, talks through the child's worries with the child, takes an interest in the child's school work, and helps with the child's plans for the future.

The studies described in this chapter showed that father's involvement was negatively related to risk for trouble with the police in adolescence in boys (Study I), and to adolescent bullying behaviour in both boys and girls (Study II), even after controlling for mother involvement. Furthermore, father involvement was more important in decreasing bullying behaviour when mother involvement was low rather than high. Growing up in a non-intact family did not affect the association between father involvement and adolescent delinquency or that between father involvement and bullying. Although mother involvement was negatively related to bullying behaviour in Study II it was not related to trouble with the police in Study I. Non-intact family structure was not related to bullying behaviour or to recovery from externalising behaviour problems, although it was related to risk for trouble with the police in adolescence in girls. This is in line with Amato and Keith's (1991) finding that a stepfather may offset the loss of a biological father for boys but not for girls, as girls may view a stepfather as taking the mother away, with adolescent girls likely to find the presence of a stepfather especially stressful due to an interrupted closeness with the mother or exposure to sexual tension with the stepfather (see Foley et al., 2004, for a discussion). It also echoes Kemppainen et al.'s (2002) earlier finding that the absence of the father during childhood was the strongest risk factor in predicting female criminality in a 1966 birth cohort in Finland.

Contrary to our hypothesis, father's interest in the child's education (assessed by the child's teacher at age 16) was not related to recovery from externalising behavioural problems (Study III). This finding, however, is in line with other research (Galambos et al., 2003; Herman, Dornbusch, Herron & Herting, 1997b) showing that in limiting externalising behaviour problems parents' firm behavioural control rather than support (which probably taps some of the aspects of 'high involvement' as operationalised in Study III) is most effective. Parental support has been shown to be related to positive children's outcomes in other domains, such as academic achievement and psychosocial well-being and competence (see Galambos et al., 2003, for a discussion). As shown in Chapter 3, father involvement was related to children's self-reported life satisfaction, happiness and absence of psychological distress, all three of which indeed tap broad aspects of psychosocial well-being.

Caution should be exercised before generalising from these findings, however. In Study I both father involvement at age 7 and trouble with the police by age 16 were teacher- and parent-reported. As parent and teacher reports were used rather than official crime records, the actual prevalence rate may well have been underestimated. Furthermore, no information was provided as to how frequent and how serious the trouble with the police was or how early it started. In Study II, on the other hand, both the nature of bullying and father involvement were assessed by the children themselves and so self-presentation bias cannot be discounted. Furthermore, the amount of variance in bullying accounted for was very modest, and father's own aggression was not controlled for. In addition, the study was, of course, cross-sectional. This means that it is possible that since children who bully are 'generally oppositional, defiant, and aggressive towards adults (including teachers and parents)' (Olweus, 1993, p. 59) they may elicit low levels of father involvement. Or, conversely, they may bully because they lack father involvement. Finally, as with all findings from the studies described so far in the book, these findings do not pertain to a 'high risk' group for externalising behaviour problems, children with absent fathers or father figures. As Smith and Farrington (2004) noted, absent fathers are likely to be younger at the time of their children's birth, and are more likely than older fathers to share a range of risk factors and antisocial behaviours. Absent, antisocial fathers may transmit genetic risk to their children, as well as exacerbating the financial difficulties and stress characterising lone-parent families. Therefore, it is not clear if these findings are consistent with the 'protective' role of father involvement investigated here and not simply with a genetic explanation of continuity of antisocial behaviour.

However, Studies I and II differed in the operationalisation of both father involvement and adolescent outcomes, in the study design, as well as in the cohorts examined. (In the first study, trouble with the police in adolescence was assessed in 1974, whereas in the second, adolescent bullying behaviour was assessed in 2000.) Then, rather than shedding doubts on the generalisability of the findings, that actually provides further evidence for the link between father involvement and adolescents' externalising behaviours. The studies described in this chapter showed that perhaps father involvement may have been an under-researched correlate of these behaviours. Future studies should try to explore the pathways of influence, and identify in which contexts father involvement has the most impact.

CHAPTER 6

FATHER INVOLVEMENT AND CHILDREN'S QUALITY OF RELATIONSHIPS

INTRODUCTION

Although studies have shown that parenting affects a child's ability to relate to others, no study has so far directly explored the independent contributions of father involvement and mother involvement in children's quality of relationships with important others later in life: i.e. their parents in adolescence and their partners in adult life. This chapter presents a study using longitudinal data from sweeps of the National Child Development Study to explore if father involvement at age 7 is related to closeness to father at age 16 and closeness to mother at age 16 independently of mother involvement at age 7 and confounding factors, and if closeness to father at age 16 is related to quality of relations with partner at age 33 independently of feelings of closeness to mother at age 16 and confounding factors.

PREDICTORS OF QUALITY OF PERSONAL RELATIONSHIPS

Personal relationships are an important research focus in psychology. Close personal relationships, such as those between intimate partners and between parents and their children, provide the social context in which individual lives develop (Van der Broucke et al., 1995) and as such are of interest to child psychologists. Given the well-established link between interparental conflict and children's maladjustment (Davies & Cummings, 1994; Grych & Fincham, 1990), as well as that between dissatisfaction with partner and depression (Gagnon, Hersen, Kabacoff & Van Hasselt, 1999), research on quality of close relationships is also of interest to clinical and developmental psychologists. Furthermore, among those married, quality of the relationship between spouses predicts marital demographic outcomes. Various researchers have used the constructs of rewards, barriers and alternatives to study marital cohesion (Previti & Amato, 2003). Rewards (such as satisfaction with the spouse as a companion or with the sexual relationship) involve the positive outcomes associated with being in a relationship, barriers (such as having worries about financial independence, being religious or having children) encompass psychological forces that restrain people from leaving relationships, and alternatives reflect the attractiveness of potential partners other than one's spouse (as well as the attractiveness of having no partner at all). Many researchers showed that people's perceptions of rewards, barriers and alternatives determine whether a marriage ends in divorce (Previti & Amato, 2003; White & Booth, 1991).

Several individual, structural and family-related factors have been shown in previous research to affect both marital outcomes and quality of the parent–child relationship in adolescence. For instance, there is evidence (Baer, 1999) that closeness to parents in adolescence is greater in intact families as compared to single-parent families (see also Chapter 2) and that family structure is also related to children's partnerships in later life. For instance, in the USA, Teachman (2004) showed that, with the exception of parental death, any time spent in an alternative family increased the likelihood that a woman cohabits before marriage, and Wolfinger (2003) showed that parental divorce raised the likelihood of teenage marriage, but those who had experienced parental divorce were disproportionately likely to avoid marriage if they remained single past the age of 20. Similarly, Teachman (2003) showed that US women who experienced more transitions in childhood living arrangements, and who lived with other than married, biological parents, formed premarital cohabiting unions faster than other women. Furthermore, rates of first marriage were higher among women who lived with a step-parent, and were lower among women who lived with a parent and that parent's cohabiting partner. With regards to the association between parental background and quality of relationships with one's spouse, rather than marital outcomes *per se*, Webster, Orbuch and House (1995) had shown earlier that although single-parent childhood family structures did not appear to affect children's adult marital quality and perceived stability, among adults in relatively unhappy marriages, both adult children of divorce and adults who never lived with their father reported significantly higher chances of divorce than those from two-parent families.

Furthermore, among those in relatively unhappy marriages, children of divorce more often reported patterns of interaction that are likely to strain a marital relationship. These findings are in line with more recent research showing that adults with divorced parents, compared with adults with continuously married parents, report more marital problems and are more likely to see their own marriages end in divorce (Amato, 1999). Research that has explored the role of parental background, not in marital outcomes or in quality of the relationship between intimate partners as such but in antecedents of both, has also pointed in useful directions. For instance, King (2002) showed that although parental divorce was negatively associated with trust in offspring which was, in turn, related to quality of personal relationships, these effects largely disappeared once the quality of the past parent–adolescent relationship was taken into account. The one exception, interestingly, was trust in fathers, where children of divorced remained at higher risk of mistrust.

Similarly, there is evidence that, apart from the structure of the parental family, the context in which relationships between family members develop predicts children's later relationship outcomes with both parents and partners. For instance, there is evidence that good sibling relationships (Bussell et al., 1999) are positively related to good parent–child relationships. More recently, Sabatelli and Bartle-Haring (2003) showed that both husbands' and wives' perceptions of their family-of-origin experiences (i.e. father–mother, father–child and mother–child relationships characterised by respect, empathy, a tolerance for individuality, and confirmation or acceptance) emerged as significant factors influencing their marital adjustment. On the other hand, mental health difficulties in either the children (Hurd, Wooding & Noller, 1999) or the parents (Cummings & Davies, 1999) are negatively related to the quality of the parent–child relationship. Parental ill mental health, in particular, strongly predicts offspring ill mental health (Hammen, Rudolph, Weisz, Rao & Burge, 1999), which, given the strong link between depression and dissatisfaction with one's intimate partner, is particularly significant.

A lot more research has been carried out to explore links between quality of the interparental relationship and the children's later relationships outcomes. For instance, there is consistent evidence showing that conflictual relationships and parental resolution styles of conflict are related both to offspring conflictual relations and resolution styles (Dadds, Atkinson, Turner, Blums & Lendich, 1999; Du Rocher Schudlich, Shamir & Cummings, 2004) and to poor quality of the parent–child relationship (Turner & Barrett, 1998).

Finally, with regards to barriers that, as discussed earlier, have been found to predict the quality of the relationship between intimate partners or spouses, having children (Graham, Fischer, Fitzpatrick & Bina, 2000) and being religious (Mahoney et al., 1999) have been strongly linked to marital satisfaction, as have high social class and high educational attainment (Albrecht, 1979), both of which are also related to the quality of the parent–child relationship (Wentzel, 1994).

PARENTING AND LATER PERSONAL RELATIONSHIPS

Parenting experiences predict the later quality of the relationship with one's parent. In particular there is evidence that earlier parental involvement predicts later closeness to parent. Closeness to mother, for instance, has been related to earlier maternal care (Hill, Mackie, Banner, Kondryn & Blair, 1999) and, similarly, closeness to father to earlier father involvement (Almeida & Galambos, 1991; Herman & McHale, 1993). Parenting also affects children's ability to relate to people other than their parents (Watson & Gross, 2000) and, in fact, predicts offspring's current marital quality (Belt & Abidin, 1996). Zimmermann (2004), for instance, recently showed that adolescents' secure attachments with their parents were related to their friendship quality. Conger, Cui, Bryant and Elder (2000) showed that nurturant-involved parenting in the family of origin predicted warm, supportive, and low hostility relations in children's early adult romantic relationships. These competent behaviours were positively associated with relationship quality for the early adult couple and also mediated the connection between parenting and relationship quality.

There are several reasons why one should expect the quality of one's relationship with one's parents to be related to the quality of one's relationship with one's partner later in life. Firstly, attachment theory emphasises the role of parent–child relationships in developing children's internal working models of relationships, with recent research suggesting that securely attached adolescents are able to develop successful and satisfying relationships in adulthood (Roisman, Madsen, Hennighausen, Sroufe & Collins, 2001). Secondly, according to social learning theory, parents transmit ideas about opposite-sex relationships to their children via modelling. Children observe how their parents relate to them and use this experiential knowledge as part of a foundation for developing intimacy in their own relationships (Gray & Steinberg, 1999b).

THE ROLE OF FATHERS

So far no study has directly explored the independent contributions of father involvement and mother involvement in children's quality of relationships with their parents in adolescence and with their partners in adult life. Studies that have explored links between dimensions of fathering and relationship outcomes have pointed in useful directions. For example, studies exploring links between the parental family system, father's parenting and relationship outcomes in children have shown that interparental conflict is associated with fathers' hostility towards children which, in turn, leads to problematic relationships with peers (Du Rocher

Schudlich et al., 2004; Stocker & Youngblade, 1999). Carson and Parke (1996) showed that fathers who typically responded to their preschoolers' negative affect displays with negative affect of their own had children who shared less, were more aggressive, and avoided others, and MacKinnon-Lewis, Castellino, Brody and Fincham (2001) showed that fathers' earlier negative behaviour predicted negative attributions in their adolescent children. Working with the attachment perspective, Ducharme, Doyle and Markiewicz (2002) showed that adolescents who were securely attached to their mother described less affectively negative interactions with parents, whereas adolescents who were securely attached to their father reported less conflict in their interactions with peers. Earlier, Franz, McClelland and Weineberger (1991) established a connection between experiencing close, loving father involvement at age 5 and positive adult outcomes, such as long-term marriages, successful parenthood and close friendships. Focusing more on the self-reported quality of interpersonal relationships rather than demographic outcomes such as union formation behaviour, Burns and Dunlop (1998) showed that maternal and paternal care in adolescence were positively related to adult children's attitudes to relationships and intimacy with peers, their satisfaction with their current close relationships, and the amount of conflict within these relationships. Relatedly, Hill, Kondryn, Mackie, McNally and Eden (2003) showed that, even after controlling for relationships with mothers, lack of paternal encouragement was associated with poor close relationships in young adults.

Recent studies have also started to explore gender differences in the link between fathering and children's quality of personal relationships later in life. For example, Möller and Stattin (2001) showed that, in Sweden, boys who shared an affectionate and trustful relationship with their fathers in adolescence felt satisfaction with their romantic partners in midlife, but the same was not true for girls. Along the same lines, Risch, Jodl and Eccles (2004) more recently showed that both African American and European American boys who felt close to their biological custodial fathers, biological non-custodial fathers and stepfathers felt less likely to divorce in the future than boys who did not feel close to their fathers, but the same was not true for girls. An explanation might be that adolescent girls generally feel more positive about marriage and the role of wife and mother as a result of their socialisation, and so fathers are less likely to influence girls' attitudes (Risch et al., 2004). Chang et al. (2003) showed that mothers' harsh parenting style affected the children's emotion regulation more strongly than fathers' style, whereas fathers' harsh parenting had a stronger effect on the children's aggression. In addition, fathers' harsh parenting affected sons more than daughters, whereas there was no gender differential effect with mothers' harsh parenting.

This chapter describes a study I carried out with Ann Buchanan in 2002 (Flouri & Buchanan, 2002b) using the NCDS dataset (see Study I of Chapter 2) to explore the independent effects of father involvement and mother involvement in good relationships with parents in adolescence, and those of closeness to mother and closeness to father in good relationships with partners in later life. In particular, the study explored whether father involvement at age 7 is related to closeness to father and closeness to mother at age 16 independently of mother involvement at age 7 and confounding factors, and if closeness to father at age 16 is related to quality of relations with partner at age 33 independently of feelings of closeness to mother at age 16 and confounding factors. In addition, the study attempted to shed some light as to how the proposed link between father involvement and offspring's quality of personal relations later in life might work. Because low father involvement and distant father–child relationships have been linked with the child's psychological maladjustment (see Chapter 3) and, in turn, are associated with poor quality of personal relations, the study investigated whether the child's psychological maladjustment at age 16 mediates the relationship between father involvement at age 7 and closeness to father at age 16, and, equally, if the child's psychological distress at age 33 mediates the relationship between closeness to father at age 16 and satisfaction with one's partner at age 33. Finally, the study checked for moderator effects. Firstly, the study explored the association between father involvement and offspring outcomes, and also explored whether the association between closeness to father and offspring marital quality is stronger for sons or for daughters. Secondly, the study examined whether father involvement is more important to offspring outcomes when mother involvement is low rather than high, and, related to this, if the relationship between closeness to fathers and satisfaction with one's partner is stronger when closeness to mothers is low rather than high.

STUDY I: THE ROLE OF FATHER INVOLVEMENT IN CLOSENESS TO PARENTS IN ADOLESCENCE, AND THE ROLE OF CLOSENESS TO FATHER IN CLOSENESS TO PARTNER IN ADULT LIFE

Measures

Closeness to father and closeness to mother at age 16 were measured with two 1-item self-reports. Cohort members had to indicate on a 5-point scale (ranging from 1 to 5) the extent to which 'they get on well' with their father, and the extent to which 'they get on well' with their mother. Quality of relationships with siblings at age 16 was also assessed with a 1-item 5-point scale (ranging from 1 to 5) asking cohort members how often they 'quarrel with a brother or sister'. Marital quality at age 33 was measured with a self-reported questionnaire based on a modified version of the Locke–Wallace Marital Adjustment Test (Locke & Wallace, 1959), a well-validated measure of marital satisfaction (Freeston & Plechaty, 1997), ranging from 0 to 55. Cohort members were asked to indicate the degree to which they agreed/disagreed with their partners on each of the following 11 situations: 'handling family finances', 'how to spend spare time', 'showing affection for each other', 'liking the same friends', 'having sex together', 'behaving generally in the right and decent way towards other people', 'sharing household tasks', 'outlook on life', 'relationships with parents or parents-in-law', 'deciding if or when to have children', and 'how children should be brought up'. Responses ranged from 'never talking about it' (0) to 'nearly always agreeing with partner' (5). In all, 6350 cases had complete data on both the Locke–Wallace scale at age 33 and closeness to mother and father at age 16. This was the initial sample. Mean scores were 4.06 (SD = 0.94) for closeness to father at age 16, 4.24 (SD = 0.81) for closeness to mother at age 16, 2.44 (SD = 1.20) for frequency of quarrelling with sibling at age 16, and 42.39 (SD = 7.70) for marital adjustment at age 33. Cronbach's alpha of the Locke–Wallace scale was 0.83.

Parental socio-economic status at birth, father and mother involvement at age 7, domestic tension, and parental ill mental heath, age 16 emotional and behavioural problems, age 16 academic motivation, age 20 educational attainment, and age 33 psychological distress were assessed as in Study III of Chapter 3. The parental family structure was 'intact' if the cohort member had continuously lived with both natural parents until age 16 and was 'non-intact' in all other situations. We also controlled for age 33 socio-economic status ('non-manual' vs 'manual'), parent status (has children or not), and religion (belongs to religion or not). Of the 6350 cohort members, 3351 (52.8%) reported that they belong to a religion and 4496 (79.5%) had children. Although 5188 (86.7%) were born to families of non-manual socio-economic status, 4205 (70%) were in non-manual occupations at age 33 (but rather than showing evidence of downward mobility, perhaps this difference is related to the different ways of coding socio-economic status in 1958, when the cohort members were born, and in 1991, when the cohort members were aged 33). The majority of cohort members grew up in continuously intact families (N = 3927 or 90.7%) and in homes not characterised by domestic tension (N = 4750 or 95.8%) or mental health problems (N = 5104 or 97.5%).

Results

Figures 6.1, 6.2 and 6.3 show the results of the multiple linear regression analyses carried out to predict closeness to mother and father in

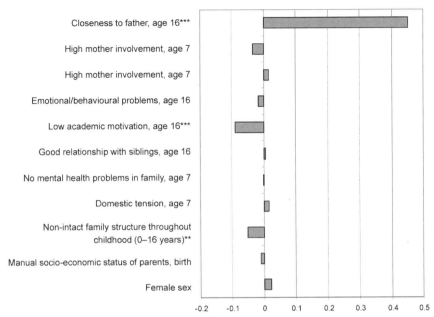

Figure 6.1 Standardised regression coefficients (β) predicting self-reported closeness to mother at age 16 from father involvement at age 7, closeness to father at age 16 and known confounding factors ($N = 2037$)
Notes: **$p < 0.01$; ***$p < 0.001$

adolescence and marital quality in adult life. As can be seen in Figure 6.1, compared to their counterparts, adolescents from intact families, those with better relationships with their fathers and those with higher academic motivation were more likely to report better relationships with their mothers at age 16. The amount of variance in feelings of closeness to mother explained by the variables in the model was 24%. Figure 6.2 shows the results of the regression analysis carried out to predict closeness to father at age 16. As can be seen, academic motivation and quality of relationships with mother were also positively related to quality of relationships with father. Unlike the mother–child relations model, however, family structure was unrelated to quality of the father–child relationship, emotional and behavioural problems were negatively related to quality of relations with father, and, compared to girls, boys were more likely to report better relations with their fathers. The amount of variance in feelings of closeness to father explained by the variables in the model was 26%. Figure 6.3 shows the regression analysis results for marital adjustment at age 33. It was found that, compared with their counterparts, women, people with higher educational qualifications, and those with lower current psychological distress were more likely to report better relationships with their partners. Good relationships with mothers, fathers and siblings in adolescence were

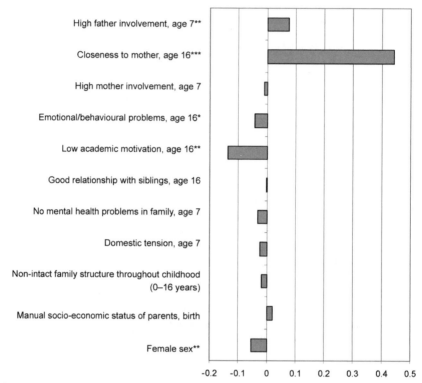

Figure 6.2 Standardised regression coefficients (β) predicting self-reported closeness to father at age 16 from father involvement at age 7 and known confounding factors (N = 2037)
Notes: *p < 0.05; **p < 0.01; ***p < .001

all positively related to good relationships with partners in adult life. The amount of variance in marital adjustment at age 33 explained by the variables in the model was low, at 8%.

Regarding the mediation hypotheses, there was no evidence that a child's emotional and behavioural problems mediated the relationship between father involvement in childhood and the child's feelings of closeness to father in adolescence, or that psychological distress mediated the relationship between closeness to father in adolescence and marital satisfaction in adult life. The association between father involvement at age 7 and relations with mother at age 16 was not stronger for sons than for daughters. However, closeness to father was more strongly related to closeness to mother for sons than for daughters. The impact of father involvement did not vary with the degree of mother involvement in predicting quality of the father–child relationship in adolescence. Whereas the association between mother involvement at age 7 and relations with

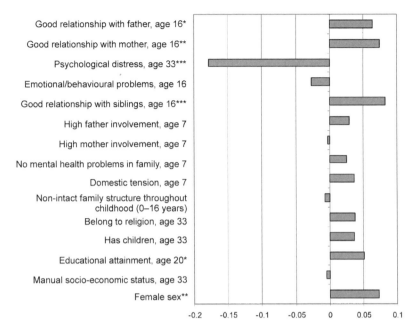

Figure 6.3   Standardised regression coefficients (β) predicting self-reported marital adjustment at age 33 from father involvement at age 7, closeness to father at age 16 and known confounding factors (N = 1843)
Notes: *p < 0.05; **p < 0.01; ***p < 0.001

father at age 16 was not stronger for daughters than for sons, the association between father involvement at age 7 and relations with father at age 16 suggests that closeness to father at age 16 was more strongly related to the level of father involvement at age 7 for daughters than for sons. Regarding marital quality, the relationship between marital adjustment at age 33 and father involvement at age 7 did not depend on the level of mother involvement at age 7, and the relationship between father involvement in childhood and marital adjustment in adult life was not stronger for sons than for daughters. Similarly, the interaction terms calculated between mother–child relations and father–child relations in adolescence and between father–child relations in adolescence and gender were insignificant, suggesting that the relationship between marital adjustment at age 33 and father–child relations at age 16 did not depend on the quality of mother–child relations or on the child's gender.

SUMMARY AND CONCLUSIONS

This study showed that closeness to mothers and closeness to fathers in adolescence were explained by different factors. Whereas good child–mother relations in adolescence were associated with good father–child relations, intact family structures and high academic motivation, closeness to fathers was unrelated to family structure but was instead explained by fathers' involvement in childhood and closeness to mothers, and was greater for boys, adolescents with fewer emotional and behavioural problems, and the academically motivated. The study found no evidence suggesting that the impact of father involvement varies with the degree of mother involvement. However, it was found that in adolescence the quality of relations with the father was more strongly related to the quality of relations with the mother for sons than for daughters, and that quality of relations with the father was more strongly related to the level of father involvement in childhood for daughters than for sons.

These findings are in line with other research showing that quality of relationships with mother is related to quality of relationships with father (Dunn, Davies, O'Connor & Sturgess, 2000), and that boys feel closer to their fathers than girls (although in this study boys and girls reported similar levels of closeness to their mothers). Interestingly, in both boys and girls, academic motivation was positively related to closeness to both mothers and fathers. As, however, both academic motivation and closeness to parents were measured at the same time, it is not clear if feeling close to parents leads adolescents to have positive attitudes to school, or if being academically motivated makes adolescents feel close to their parents. The other interesting finding was that whereas levels of closeness to mother were not related to levels of mother involvement earlier in life, fathers had to be involved early in their children's lives for their children to feel close to them in adolescence. The finding of the linkage between father involvement and closeness to father is consistent with Almeida, Wethington and McDonald's (2001) earlier study showing that when fathers spend more time in childcare activities they are more likely to engage in supportive interactions with their children (although they are also more likely to have conflictual interactions with their children). This study showed that feelings of closeness to fathers appear to be 'earned', especially for girls. Although in both boys and girls father involvement at age 7 was related to feelings of closeness at age 16, the association between father involvement and later closeness to father was stronger in girls than it was in boys. However, the finding that mother involvement was not related to closeness to mother later in life is in contrast with Hill et al. (1999) who showed that adult children's current closeness to mother was related to maternal care in childhood. An explanation might be that in Hill et al.'s (1999) study both closeness to mother and maternal care were assessed concurrently, which suggests that as maternal care was recalled (rather than prospectively assessed, as in this study) it is possible that current circumstances (e.g. current feelings of closeness to mother) colour past experiences (perceived maternal care in childhood). This study found no evidence to suggest that closeness to father compensates for distant mother–adolescent relations (and vice versa). However, it showed that the linkage between closeness to mother and closeness to father was stronger for sons than it was for daughters. These findings suggest that closeness to father and closeness to mother are interrelated but distinct.

The study also showed that marital adjustment at age 33 was related to good relationships with siblings, mother and father in adolescence. These findings lend further support to other evidence linking good relationships in the parental home with good relationships with spouses later in life (Sabatelli & Bartle-Haring, 2003). Also supporting previous findings (see Hetherington, 2003, for a review) marital adjustment was rated as better by women and those with higher educational qualifications, and was negatively related to psychological distress. The negative association between psychological distress and marital adjustment is in accord with the findings of Kiecolt-Glaser and Newton (2001) and, more recently, Hetherington (2003). Hetherington (2003), for instance, found that the frequency of doctors' or hospital visits was three times higher for unhappily married or recently divorced women than for happily married women. Marital problems affected men, too, although in different ways. Although health problems were higher in recently divorced men than in married men, many of the problems they exhibited seemed to be related to lifestyle issues, such as irregular daily routines of sleeping and eating, unhealthy diets, alcohol and drug abuse, and risk-taking activities.

The study found no evidence to show that a child's emotional and behavioural problems mediated the relationship between father involvement in childhood and the child's feelings of closeness to father in adolescence, or that psychological distress mediated the relationship between closeness to father in adolescence and marital satisfaction in adult life. In other words, early father involvement was not linked to feelings of closeness to father in adolescence by decreasing the child's emotional and behavioural problems, and closeness to father in adolescence was not related to marital adjustment in adult life by decreasing psychological distress. It seems, therefore, that in this study fathers affected later relationship outcomes in their children, not by promoting their children's mental health, at least directly.

This study suffered from some important limitations, however. First, selection factors (such as attitudes towards marriage, number and type of previous unions, a premarital birth) were not controlled for. Second, the study did not explore whether the age 33 partnership whose perceived quality was assessed was marriage or cohabitation. This is important given that research has shown that people choose riskier partners when cohabiting than when marrying. For example, completing high school, stable employment and high earnings are less important prerequisites for cohabitation than for marriage (Clarkberg, 1999), and they are all related to the quality of the intimate relationship (Fox, Benson, DeMaris & Van Wyk, 2002). Third, no information was collected on social networks which would be significant given the links between marital outcomes and the structural patterns of spouses' social and support networks, such as density, or network overlap (Bradbury, Fincham & Beach, 2000). Fourth, assessment of the overall family 'climate' in the parental home was tapped simply by the Health Visitor's 1-item assessment of evidence of domestic tension when cohort members were aged 7 or by the cohort members' assessment of the quality of their relationships with their parents and siblings when the members were aged 16. This is important in light of the evidence showing that, consistent with a general social learning model of relationship violence, all forms of family-of-origin violence are predictive of all forms of relationship abuse (Kwong, Bartholomew, Henderson & Trinke, 2003), which, although it is not tantamount to relationship quality, is nonetheless related to it. In addition, this study did not assess the quality of parenting. Swinford, DeMaris, Cernkovich and Giordano (2000) found that harsh physical punishment in childhood was both directly and indirectly (via leading to adolescent and young adult problem behaviour) related to greater perpetration of intimate partner violence towards women in adult life. Although 'involved' fathers and 'involved' mothers are not likely to use coercive or physical punishment, the quality of the parental involvement at age 7 in the NCDS cohort was not assessed. Again, it is likely that parents who were 'highly involved' in the NCDS (i.e. frequently took outings with their children, frequently read to their children, and were very interested in their children's education) were also warm, affectionate or authoritative, and were therefore likely to have well-adjusted children (Maccoby, 2000). However, as this information was not available on the NCDS this explanation could not be tested in this dataset. Fifth, other concurrent predictors of quality of intimate relationships, such as economic distress, were not controlled for. The study did control for current socio-economic status but it did not include subjective feelings of economic distress or hardship, which are related to quality of the intimate relationship. Fox et al. (2002), for instance, demonstrated the importance of the two partners' feelings of financial well-being in elevating or reducing the risk of intimate partner violence towards women. Sixth, the findings from this study are only applicable to children who grew up with a father figure, a mother figure and at least one sibling in adolescence, and who at the age of 33 were partnered, too. Although these were not perhaps unusual family circumstances in those born in 1958 in Britain, it is likely that this picture represents a smaller percentage of the population today in Britain and indeed elsewhere, too. Finally, the amount of variance in closeness to mother at age 16, closeness to father at age 16, and marital adjustment at age 33 explained in our models was modest (at 24% and 26%, respectively) or low (only 8% of the variance in marital adjustment was explained by the variables shown in Figure 6.3). But given all the factors in an individual's life that might contribute to the outcomes of personal relationships later in life, it is not surprising that parental involvement and closeness to parents early in life played a modest role. Despite its limitations, this study showed that parental involvement in early childhood could predict children's feelings of closeness to parents in adolescence, and that perceived good relationships with parents in adolescence could predict the quality of a relationship with intimate partners 17 years later.

CHAPTER 7

FATHER INVOLVEMENT AND CHILDREN'S SOCIO-ECONOMIC OUTCOMES

INTRODUCTION

Although research has explored links between father's absence and children's socio-economic outcomes (see Chapter 1), a lot less is known about the role of father involvement in children's socio-economic outcomes. However, the link between father involvement and children's later attainments is a plausible one given the associations between father involvement and academic achievement (see Chapter 4) and between father involvement and psychological adjustment (see Chapters 3 and 5), which are related to socio-economic outcomes and attainments. This chapter describes four studies carried out to explore associations between father involvement and socio-economic outcomes in children. Studies I, II and III explore long-term socio-economic outcomes (age 33) associated with early father involvement (age 7) using longitudinal data from the National Child Development Study. The age 33 outcomes were labour force participation (Study I), socio-economic disadvantage, operationalised as experience of homelessness, living in subsidised housing, and receiving state benefits (Study II), and materialism/postmaterialism (Study III). Following on Study III and using cross-sectional data, Study IV explored the link between father involvement and children's materialism in adolescence.

PREDICTORS OF SOCIO-ECONOMIC OUTCOMES (SOCIO-ECONOMIC STATUS AND SOCIO-ECONOMIC DISADVANTAGE)

I: Socio-economic status

Although the original status-attainment model (Blau & Duncan, 1967) stressed the significance of parental socio-economic status for offspring socio-economic status, more recent models introduced human agency into the process of status attainment, such as educational and occupational aspirations, as a mediator between background factors and educational and socio-economic outcomes. Still, the (usually longitudinal) research establishing links between parents' socio-economic status and children's socio-economic status is continuously expanding. One of the most persistent research priorities in the sociological literature on poverty, for instance, is explaining intergenerational poverty. Corcoran (1995) discussed how early arguments over the 'culture of poverty' assumed considerable intergenerational transmission of poverty, but differed over whether this was due to cultural inadequacies of the poor or to structural barriers and discrimination faced by the poor. He described four new theoretical perspectives developed to explain intergenerational poverty in the United States: the resources model, the correlated disadvantages model, the welfare culture model, and Wilson's 'underclass' model. The resources model emphasises how the lack of material resources of poor parents affects children's socio-economic outcomes: poor families have little money, time or energy to devote to developing their children's human capital (e.g. schooling), have little time for supervising children, are less plugged into job-finding networks and, as they can afford housing only in disadvantaged neighbourhoods, live in areas that provide lower-quality schools, fewer role models, less social control, and fewer job networks. The correlated disadvantages thesis is that it is not parental poverty *per se* but other disadvantages, associated with parental poverty, that keep children in poverty too. For instance, poor parents are less effective in developing their children's human capital as they themselves have less schooling than non-poor parents. Poor families are also more likely to be lone-parent families, the children of which have higher rates of high-school dropout, teen pregnancy and joblessness (due to the distress of losing a parent, and to reduced parental involvement and supervision (see Chapter 1)). The 'welfare culture' model suggests that children in families and communities that rely on welfare inherit self-defeating work attitudes and poor work ethics from the community, as the stigma associated with being in welfare disappears. Wilson's (1987) underclass model, finally, also stresses the role of the community and particularly social isolation in children's socio-economic outcomes. It applies, however, primarily to ethnic minority poor (as the White poor in the USA are very unlikely to reside in very poor neighbourhoods). Wilson's main thesis is that exposure to neighbourhood poverty reinforces the damaging consequences of individual disadvantage. The model suggests that when the proportion of middle-class Black residents drops in inner-city areas important socialising institutions such as churches and community organisations (which were supported by middle-class residents and exposed poor residents to mainstream alternatives) weaken. As a consequence, the remaining poor residents have reduced connections to job-finding networks for mainstream jobs, and few examples of mainstream success, which limits their expectations about what is possible for them (see Corcoran, 1995, for a full discussion).

At the same time it has been argued that parental socio-economic status predicts child's socio-economic status because parents' socio-economic status is an indicator of the social context in which the child develops, but also reflects hereditary influences which are related to both academic functioning and health (Plomin & Bergeman, 1991), which are, in turn, related to socio-economic outcomes. It is, however, increasingly accepted that genetic factors are only part of the large cluster of influences on socio-economic outcomes. In any case, the influence of parental social class on academic achievement is generally found to be of moderate size (Schoon et al., 2002), suggesting that intervening experiences and influences are of importance.

II: Socio-economic disadvantage

Socio-economic status is not the only socio-economic outcome that has been studied in relation to early experiences and circumstances. Substantial research has been carried out on early precursors of socio-economic disadvantage. Socio-economic disadvantage is associated with a variety of cofactors, such as poor living conditions, overcrowding, or lack of resources (Schoon et al., 2002), which measures of socio-economic status, such as prestige of current or last occupation and housing tenure (or car ownership), provide only limited insight into. Recent studies have started to include alongside the conventional measures of socio-economic status proximal indicators of socio-economic disadvantage such as receipt of social security benefits (e.g. income support, supplementary or unemployment benefits) (Power, Matthews & Manor, 1998), years on benefits and money worries (Graham & Blackburn, 1998), and measures of deprivation, such as overcrowding (Wardle, Robb & Johnson, 2002) and lack of basic household amenities (Schoon et al., 2002). Material circumstances are often measured as equivalent net family income (adjusted for family size and composition with weightings from supplementary-benefit scales), and financial difficulties (if not subjectively assessed) are often measured by frequency of mortgage or rent arrears (Power et al., 1998).

The idea is that, although related to an individual's relative position in society (i.e. socio-economic status), socio-economic disadvantage also encompasses poverty and the dynamic aspects of social exclusion. Social exclusion, in particular, embraces a view of poverty concerned with multiple aspects of deprivation, with the role of neighbourhood, and with process and dynamics over time. The terms 'poverty', 'deprivation' and 'social exclusion' are sometimes used interchangeably as synonyms for each other. However, poverty is generally interpreted as income related, deprivation is related to quality of life, and social exclusion refers to the process whereby individuals become deprived, although sometimes it implies an inability to fully participate in social and economic activities that influence decision-making (Pringle & Walsh, 1999). Poverty has been assessed empirically (see Bradshaw & Finch, 2003) by measuring income (income poverty), by establishing a relative lack of certain items or activities which are perceived as necessary (deprivation), or by asking people whether they feel poor or deprived (subjective poverty). For example, the conventional measure of relative poverty in the European Union is a net household income less than 60% of the median (Atkinson, Cantillon, Marlier & Nolan, 2002). In Britain, Bradshaw and Finch (2003) showed that although there was little overlap in the group of people defined as poor by these three dimensions, the more dimensions on which people were poor, the more they were unlike the non-poor and the poor on only one dimension in their characteristics and their social exclusion (operationalised as exclusion from the labour market, exclusion from services, and exclusion from social relations). In particular, those who were poor on all three dimensions (the cumulatively poor) were more likely than the other poor groups (necessities poor, subjective poor, low-income poor and no poor) to be women, lone parents, large families, and to have no workers in the household. The cumulatively poor were also more likely than the other poor groups to be labour market excluded, lacking two or more services, unable to participate in three or more activities, and be confined (by fear of going out).

A lot of empirical research from social scientists has been carried out to explore predictors of adult socio-economic disadvantage, and their findings have supported several of the arguments described above by Corcoran (1995). For example, as with social class, socio-economic disadvantage is usually intergenerational, and, even when it is not, it can be predicted from early factors. Horrell, Humphries and Voth (2001), who used evidence from Britain during industrialisation to explore the effects of early deprivation on children's human capital acquisition, showed not only that the poverty of one generation could prejudice the life chances of the next independently of individual merit, but also that a common misfortune, such as the loss of a father, precipitated a slide into destitution. According to Horrell et al. (2001) the reason why the loss of a father affected children's human capital formation is that, as the mother had to go out to work, the reduction of domestic production damaged the child's accumulation human capital (time substitution effect), and that the woman could not earn enough to fully compensate for the loss of income earned by the father (income substitution effect), which meant that often children had to join the labour force. This usually ensured survival, but also retarded human capital acquisition (as the extra income was insufficient to offset the energy expended at work, the acceptance of a dead-end job or the termination of schooling) (Horrell et al., 2001, p. 342).

Studies with more recent samples also demonstrate the importance of schooling for children's socio-economic outcomes. Poor educational attainment remains one of the strongest predictors of both unemployment and socio-economic disadvantage (Brook & Newcomb, 1995; Rönkä & Pulkkinen, 1995) and is a strong protective factor against an experience of homelessness in high-risk groups (Bassuk et al., 1997). Other factors that have been linked to either disadvantage or escape from disadvantage for those at risk of being disadvantaged (protective factors) include variables that are mainly linked to educational attainment (Duncan & Brooks-Gunn, 1997; Macmillan and Hagan, 2004) or to ill mental health and deviant behaviours (Chen & Kaplan, 2003) both of which affect socio-economic outcomes. For instance, growing up in an intact family has a positive effect on children's academic achievement and cognitive ability (Mulkey, Crain & Harrington, 1992), and being married predicts escape from poverty for the children of the poor (Caputo, 1997). With regards to unemployment, for instance, Kokko, Pulkkinen and Puustinen (2000) recently showed that early externalising problems directly predicted long-term unemployment in adulthood, whereas internalising problems predicted long-term unemployment indirectly (via poor educational attainment). Drinking problems are also related to low work involvement (Brook & Newcomb, 1995), an unstable career line (Rönkä & Pulkkinen, 1995) and unemployment (Sanford et al., 1994), whereas low IQ scores, family conflict, lack of attachment to school (Caspi et al., 1998), adolescent delinquency (Bellair & Roscigno, 2000), absence of adolescent work experience (Mortimer & Johnson, 1998) and childhood peer relationships problems (Woodward & Fergusson, 2000) have been found to increase the risk of unemployment. These variables have also been recognised as precipitating factors associated with homelessness (Bassuk et al., 1997) and socio-economic disadvantage (Duncan & Brooks-Gunn, 1997). Experience of childhood physical and sexual abuse (Herman et al., 1997a) and experience of intimate violence (Browne & Bassuk, 1997) have been especially linked with homelessness in women. Social scientists have also extensively studied the impact of the structural parameters of the family group, especially size of the sibship group, on educational and other status outcomes (Steelman, Powell, Werum & Carter, 2002). The resource dilution model (see also Chapter 2), for instance, suggests that siblings dilute the parents' tangible and intangible resources, which results in an inverse relationship between sibship size and offspring academic achievement and cognitive ability (Downey, 1995). Or, the inverse relationhip between sibship size and children's intelligence or attainments is because people with lower IQ tend to have both larger families and children with lower IQ (see Steelman et al., 2002, for a review). It is being increasingly accepted, however, that individual risk factors for socio-economic disadvantage do not exert their effect in isolation, but it is usually the number of factors and their combined effect that determine outcomes (Ackerman, Schoff, Levinson, Youngstrom & Izard, 1999). Although the relation between any single risk factor and subsequent outcomes tends to be weak, multiple-risk models are generally good predictors of subsequent outcomes (Evans, 2004).

CHILDHOOD ENVIRONMENT AND SOCIO-ECONOMIC OUTCOMES: SOCIAL CAUSATION OR SOCIAL SELECTION?

In terms of theory it is, of course, important to establish whether socio-economic disadvantage is a cause or a consequence of the individual-level attributes with which it is correlated (Caspi et al., 1998). The contribution of childhood environment to socio-economic disadvantage in adult life is often discussed from one of two perspectives: social selection and social causation. Social selection refers to the process whereby certain persons selectively enter certain life contexts, and social causation refers to the process whereby certain life contexts shape subsequent behaviour and development.

Causation and selection hypotheses have been tested in a systematic way in studies which, looking at the social epidemiology of health inequality, explore links between socio-economic disadvantage and ill health (see Schoon et al., 2003, for a review). A frequently cited study by McDonough, Duncan, Williams and House (1997) found that income level was a strong predictor of adult mortality in the United States, especially for persons under the age of 65 years. Persistent low income was particularly consequential for mortality, whereas income instability was important among middle-income individuals. More recently, Korpi (2001) showed that ill health increased the risk of both becoming and remaining unemployed, although there was also unequivocal evidence of worsening of health status due to unemployment. Similarly, van de Mheen, Stronks, Schrijvers and Mackenbach (1999) had found that although neither upward nor downward mobility was affected by health problems, health problems were significantly associated with a later higher risk of mobility out of employment and a later lower risk of mobility into employment. Mulatu and Schooler (2002) showed that socio-economic status (rather than socio-economic disadvantage) positively affects physical health and health positively affects socio-economic status, but the causal path from socio-economic status to health was stronger than the reverse. A substantial part of the effect of socio-economic status on health was due to differences in psychological distress, and less to differences in health-related lifestyles and behaviours, whereas in terms of the effects of health on socio-economic status, differences in weight and sleeping behaviour were more important than psychological distress. Looking particularly at the association between socio-economic status and mental health, Ritsher, Warner, Johnson and Dohrenwend (2001) found evidence for an effect of parental socio-economic status on offspring depression (social causation) but not for an effect of either parental or offspring depression on offspring socio-economic status (social selection). Power, Manor and Matthews (1999), who used data from the 1958 British birth cohort, investigated both timing and duration effects of socio-economic status on self-rated health at age 33 and explored whether health risks are modified by changing socio-economic status. They showed that timing was not a major factor. Instead, socio-economic status from birth to age 33 had a cumulative effect on poor health. In addition, the odds of poor health increased by 15% in men and 18% in women with a 1-unit decrease in social position (i.e. the lifetime socio-economic status score). Power et al. (1999) therefore empirically tested all three general hypotheses on how exposure to social risk can be linked to later health-related outcomes (see Hallqvist, Lynch, Bartley, Lang & Blane, 2004, for a description). The first hypothesis suggests that there are stages or critical periods in the individual's development in which an increased sensitivity to the influence of external agents may have crucial effects on later health. Research pursuing this hypothesis usually investigates the influence of the 'timing' of risk. The second hypothesis suggests that exposures or insults gradually accumulate to increase the risk of chronic disease and mortality, and that cumulative differential lifetime exposure is the main explanation to observed socio-economic differences in risk of disease. The third hypothesis considers how individuals change between different categories of the social structure once or several times during the life course. Hallqvist et al. (2004) drew attention to the danger of confounding between accumulation and possibly more complex combinations of critical periods of exposure and social mobility.

Duration and timing effects have also been explored in studies looking at early factors associated with later socio-economic (rather than health) outcomes. There is increasing awareness that persistent adversity over time might have effects on children's behaviour beyond the effects of intermittent or concurrent adversity (Ackerman, Brown & Izard, 2004). McLoyd (1998) had shown how persistent poverty had more detrimental effects on school achievement (which, as explained above, predicts socio-economic outcomes) than transitory poverty (although children experiencing both types of poverty generally did less well than never-poor children). In particular, McLoyd (1998) found that higher rates of perinatal complications, reduced access to resources that buffer the negative effects of perinatal complications, increased exposure to lead and less home-based cognitive stimulation partly accounted for diminished cognitive functioning in poor children. These factors, along with lower teacher expectations and poorer academic-readiness skills, also appeared to contribute to lower levels of school achievement among poor children. Research has also looked at the role of the timing of risk in later socio-economic outcomes. Using data collected from both the 1958 birth cohort and the 1970 birth cohort in Britain, Schoon et al. (2002) showed that the influence of concurrent risk on academic achievement and subsequent social class attainment was greatest during early childhood for both cohorts.

FATHER'S AND MOTHER'S PARENTING AND CHILDREN'S SOCIO-ECONOMIC OUTCOMES

There are several reasons to expect parenting to be related to children's socio-economic outcomes. First, poor parenting behaviours increase the odds that a child will engage in antisocial behaviour or substance use and will perform poorly in school or drop out (see Chapters 4 and 5), which are related to low attainments in adult life. Second, children who have a close relationship with their parents are likely to have better access to family resources, which in turn contribute to the acquisition of academic skills (Coleman, 1988) and access to job-finding networks. Third, parenting is related both to parental socio-economic status and parents' experience of adversities (see Chapter 2), and so the link between parenting and children's socio-economic circumstances might be simply because parents' socio-economic circumstances are related to both. Indeed, the relatively few empirical studies that explored mothers' and fathers' parenting in relation to children's socio-economic outcomes in various countries have shown promising results. In the United States, for instance, Amato (1994) found that closeness to fathers and mothers during childhood was positively related to adult daughters' and sons' educational and occupational mobility. More recently, Wiesner, Vondracek, Capaldi and Porfeli (2003) showed that, even after controlling for family structure, parents' socio-economic status, parental expectations, and children's conduct and mental health problems, academic achievement, delinquency, and relations with deviant peers, low parental involvement predicted long-term relative to short-term unemployment in young men, and poor parental discipline predicted long-term unemployment relative to college education. In Britain, Bond and Saunders (1999) using data from the National Child

Development Study explored the role of parental aspirations and parents' interest in the child's education in sons' occupational attainment in adult life. They showed that although parents' aspirations for their child's education did not directly influence the child's achieved occupational grade, they influenced the child's aspirations which then affected the child's academic motivation and subsequent qualifications. Furthermore, parents' aspirations for their child at age 7 influenced parents' interest and involvement in their child's education at both age 11 and age 16. In turn, parents' interest in the child's education affected the child's ability test scores, which were related to later educational and subsequent occupational attainment. More recently, Kokko and Pulkkinen (2000) in Finland showed that their measure of child-centred parenting (a composite index of good relationships between the parents, positive memories of the father, maternal support and supervision and absence of physical punishment) was negatively related to later long-term unemployment.

Some research has also been carried out on the role of parenting as a moderator of the relationship between background factors and offspring socio-economic outcomes. Theoretically this research approach is construed within the general framework of investigating resilience (i.e. better than expected outcomes) or prevention (i.e. avoidance of adverse outcomes) in individuals exposed to risk (Luthar, Cicchetti & Becker, 2000). For example, Hagan, Macmillan and Wheaton (1996) showed that the negative effects of family migration were significantly more pronounced in families with uninvolved fathers and unsupportive mothers. In those families the diminished social capital provided by parents did not compensate for the community social capital lost as a result of a family's move. Schoon, Parsons and Sacker (2004), who compared adult attainments of socially advantaged and socially disadvantaged adolescents, showed that although social disadvantage was a significant risk factor for educational failure, poor consequent adjustment in work and poor health-related outcomes, parents' educational aspirations for their children were significantly associated with educational resilience among socially disadvantaged individuals.

Using longitudinal data from the NCDS (see Study I of Chapter 2), Studies I and II sought to show if father involvement in childhood is negatively associated with unemployment (Study I) and socio-economic disadvantage, operationalised as homelessness, living in subsidised housing, and receiving state benefits (Study II). Unemployment is a factor likely to be important in the process of accumulating disadvantage (as it is related to both poverty and social exclusion). Entering unemployment is a drastic example of downward social mobility, and one that is likely to have a substantial impact on subsequent mobility chances. Time spent unemployed and frequency of unemployment spells are better indicators than simply labour force participation outcome ('employed' vs 'unemployed'). On the other hand, state benefits receipt and subsidised housing tap income poverty, whereas homelessness is an extreme form of disadvantage as lack of accommodation is combined with deprivation, income poverty and social exclusion (Kennedy & Fitzpatrick, 2001). In particular, Studies I and II explored whether father involvement at age 7 is related to these adult outcomes (measured at age 33) after controlling for mother involvement at age 7 and known confounding variables. The confounding factors controlled for reflected both individual and familial influences that previous research has identified as predictors of these outcomes. Both studies also checked for moderator effects, and in particular whether the association between early father involvement and socio-economic outcomes in adult life was stronger for sons or daughters, when mother involvement was low or high, and in intact or non-intact families. Finally, because socio-economic disadvantage is intergenerational, it was also explored whether father involvement moderates the effect of families' socio-economic status in children's later socio-economic outcomes.

STUDY I: THE ROLE OF FATHER INVOLVEMENT AT AGE 7 IN LABOUR FORCE PARTICIPATION OUTCOME (EMPLOYED VS UNEMPLOYED) AT AGE 33

At age 33, 11 369 NCDS cohort members were traced. All 11 369 cohort members had valid data on current economic activity. Of those, 4% were unemployed and 79% were part- or full-time employed or self-employed. Another 17% who were not in the labour force (but were in full-time education, disabled or stayed at home to care for others) were excluded from the analysis. In all, 5023 cohort members had valid data on mother involvement at age 7, father involvement at age 7 and labour force participation at age 33. Of the 5023 cohort members, 4795 (95.5%) were employed and 228 (4.5%) were unemployed. This was the initial sample for this study.

Measures

Parental socio-economic status at birth, age 7 father involvement, mother's involvement, domestic tension, parental ill mental health, and child's emotional and behavioural problems, as well as age 11 cognitive ability, age 16 academic motivation, age 20 educational attainment and age 33 psychological distress and partner status were measured as in Study III of Chapter 3. Family structure at age 7 was also controlled for and it was 'intact' (if the child's mother and father figures were the natural parents) or 'non-intact' (in all other situations). In all, 97.2% of the participants were in intact families and 2.8% were in non-intact families at age 7. Other factors controlled for were the teacher's report at age 16 on whether the cohort child had been in trouble with the police or not, the cohort member's report at age 16 on whether he or she had any work experience, and self-reported frequency of drinking (which was measured on a 5-point scale anchored with 'most days' (1) and 'never' (5)) at age 23. Of the cohort members with valid data in these variables, 5.2% had been in trouble with the police and 39.8% had a part-time job at age 16. The average frequency of drinking at age 23 was 2.23 (SD = 1.04).

Results

The logistic regression analysis carried out to predict age 33 labour force participation outcome (unemployed vs part- or full-time employed or self-employed) showed that father involvement at age 7 was not a statistically significant predictor of labour force participation at age 33. However, mother involvement was positively related to labour force participation in men. Educational attainment and presence of partner were positively (and current psychological distress was negatively) related to labour force participation in adult life (for full details, see Flouri & Buchanan, 2002e). The association between early father involvement and labour force participation outcome in adult life was not stronger for sons than for daughters, or in intact than in non-intact families. The impact of father involvement did not vary with the degree of mother involvement and father involvement did not moderate the relationship between parental family's socio-economic status and labour force participation outcome.

Discussion

This study showed that father involvement at age 7 could not predict labour force participation outcome (employed vs unemployed) at age 33. Apart from the usual limitations associated with using the NCDS to explore father involvement in later children's outcomes (for a discussion see Chapter 3), there are particular limitations pertaining to this piece of research. In particular, the operationalisation of labour force participation outcome in this study was somewhat not sensitive enough. Labour force participation outcome was current employment status rather than the total amount of unemployment over a given period or the number of bouts of unemployment within a certain period. Despite this, it is noteworthy that men with 'involved' mothers at age 7 were more likely than men with less involved mothers at age 7 to be employed 26 years later.

STUDY II: THE ROLE OF FATHER INVOLVEMENT AT AGE 7 IN AGE 33 SOCIO-ECONOMIC DISADVANTAGE (RECEIVING STATE BENEFITS, LIVING IN SUBSIDISED HOUSING, AND HAVING EXPERIENCED HOMELESSNESS SINCE AGE 23)

Socio-economic disadvantage at age 33 was measured as homelessness, living on subsidised housing, and receiving state benefits. Homelessness was assessed by a self-report dichotomous item at age 33 which asked cohort members whether they had been homeless in the past 10 years. Self-reported state benefits receipt was assessed as follows: cohort members or their partners received at least one of the following three benefits: supplementary benefit/income support, unemployment benefit and income support, and family credit. Finally, people lived in subsidised housing if they lived in sheltered housing, homeless hostel or prison/remand centre, or if their home was rented from the local authority or a housing association. In all, of the 11 369 cohort members traced at age 33, 11 362 had valid responses on homelessness. Of those, 3.8% said that they had been homeless in the past 10 years. Of the 11 253 cohort members with valid responses on state benefits receipt, 10% said that they received some form of state support. Finally, of the 11 369 participants with valid responses on subsidised housing, 14.2% said that they lived in subsidised housing. In all, 5880 cohort members had valid data on mother involvement at age 7, father involvement at age 7 and the three socio-economic disadvantage indicators at age 33 described above. This was our initial sample for this study (for full details see Flouri & Buchanan, 2004a).

Measures

Parental socio-economic status at birth, age 7 family structure, father involvement, mother involvement, domestic tension, parental ill mental health, and child's emotional and behavioural problems, as well as age 11 cognitive ability, age 16 academic motivation, age 20 educational attainment and age 33 psychological distress and partner status were measured as in Study I described above. Other factors controlled for were age 7 sibship size (number of children under age 21 in the family) and age 7 residential mobility (number of family moves since the child's birth), as well as age 16 (parent- or teacher-reported) trouble with the police, and age 33 parent status (has children or not). Of the 5880 cohort members with valid data, 460 (9.3%) were reported to have been in trouble with the police at age 16, and 3990 (67.8%) had children at age 33. The average number of family moves (ranging from 0 to 22) since the cohort member's birth until age 7 was 1.11 (SD = 1.41). The average number of children under age 21 (including those living away) in the parental household when the cohort member was aged 7 (ranging from 1 to 14) was 3.04 (SD = 1.57).

Results

The three indicators of socio-economic disadvantage explored were interrelated. In particular, those who had experienced homelessness tended to both receive state benefits (chi-square = 57.158, df: 1, $p < 0.001$), and live in subsidised housing (chi-square = 65.641, df: 1, $p < 0.001$), and those who received state benefits tended to live in subsidised housing (chi-square = 782.964, df: 1, $p < 0.001$). Both father involvement and mother involvement at age 7 were negatively related to socio-economic disadvantage at age 33. In particular, children whose father and mother were involved with them at age 7 were less likely to report at age 33 that they have experienced homelessness ($t = 3.19$, df: 5868, $p < 0.001$, and $t = 2.63$, df: 231.76, $p < 0.01$, respectively), that they receive state benefits ($t = 9.11$, df: 5878, $p < 0.001$, and $t = 9.97$, df: 5878, $p < 0.001$, respectively), and that they live in subsidised housing ($t = 12.32$, df: 5878, $p < 0.001$, and $t = 14.60$, df: 936.20, $p < 0.001$, respectively).

To explore the role of father involvement at age 7 independently of mother's involvement and confounding factors in age 33 homelessness, living in subsidised housing and receiving state benefits, six logistic regressions were carried out in total (one regression model separately by gender for each indicator of socio-economic disadvantage). The analyses were carried out separately by gender as women were more likely than men to both live in subsidised housing and receive state benefits (chi-square = 13.10, df: 1, $p < 0.001$, and chi-square = 39.20, df: 1, $p < 0.001$, respectively) although they were as likely as men to have experienced homelessness (chi-square = 1.28, df: 1, $p > 0.05$).

It was found that for both genders an experience of homelessness was related to absence of partner, but in men it was also related to current psychological distress and sibship size in childhood. State benefits receipt was related in both genders to absence of partner and low educational attainment, but in women it was also associated with presence of children, and in men with current psychological distress, low academic motivation in adolescence and large sibship size in childhood. Finally, for both men and women, living in subsidised housing at age 33 was predicted from low educational qualifications and current psychological distress, but it was also predicted from absence of partner in women and from large sibship size and non-intact family structure in men.

The only significant father involvement interaction effects were as follows. First, father involvement and mother involvement were more strongly interrelated in families whose daughters were not living in subsidised houses at age 33 than in those whose daughters were living in subsidised houses. Second, in families of manual socio-economic status, son's experience of homelessness was strongly related to low levels of father involvement in childhood. Whereas early father involvement in non-manual families was similar between men who had experienced homelessness and men who had never experienced homelessness (mean = 2.108, SD = 1.104, and mean = 2.253, SD = 1.176, respectively), early father involvement in manual families was significantly lower in men who had an adult experience of homelessness than in men who had never been homeless (mean = 1.533, SD = 0.990, and mean = 1.718, SD = 1.094, respectively).

Discussion

This study showed that although early father involvement could not directly predict any of the three children's adult outcomes (experience of homelessness, state benefits receipt, and living in subsidised housing) at the multivariate level, it had a protective role against an experience of homelessness in men from lower socio-economic groups.

Even though these findings could be misused for 'victim blaming', 'unpacking' parenting can be very fruitful in future adult outcomes research. To suggest that parenting and individual factors early in life can have some statistical power in predicting socio-economic disadvantage later in life is not to argue that being poor – or worse, being on the streets – is the result of moral laxity or personal and family defects.

PREDICTORS OF MATERIALISM

Materialism is usually conceptualised as a value and is, therefore, an enduring belief that has a 'transcendental quality' guiding actions and attitudes across times and situations. Materialism, usually defined as 'the importance a consumer attaches to worldly possessions' (Belk, 1985, p. 265), is one of the 'survival' as opposed to 'self-expression' values that psychological research usually investigates within the parental socialisation paradigm (Kasser, Ryan, Zax & Sameroff, 1995). According to Inglehart and Baker (2000), self-expression values tap a syndrome of trust, tolerance, subjective well-being, political activism and self-expression that emerges in post-industrial societies with high levels of security. Self-expression-oriented individuals (and societies) value environmental protection, the women's movement, tolerance of outgroups, and rising demand participation and decision-making in economic and political life. In contrast, survival values are shaped by economic scarcity and insecurity which, in politics, are conducive to xenophobia, a need for strong decisive leaders and deference to authority. Societies and individuals that emphasise survival values show relatively low levels of subjective well-being, report relatively poor health, are relatively intolerant to outgroups, are low on support for gender equality, are relatively low on environmental activism, and are relatively favourable to authoritarian government (Inglehart, 2000).

Psychological research has started, since the 1990s, to develop an interest in materialism mainly because of the substantial evidence linking materialism and psychological maladjustment (see Kasser, 2002, for a review). For instance, cross-sectional studies have linked materialism with neuroticism (Mick, 1996), desire for conformity (Schroeder & Dugal, 1995), susceptibility to peer influence (Flouri, 1999), psychological distress (Kasser & Ryan, 1993), low self-esteem (Richins & Dawson, 1992), and dissatisfaction with life and life domains (see Burroughs & Rindfleisch, 2002, for a review). Longitudinal studies have also found supporting evidence. Cohen and Cohen (1996), for instance, showed that adolescents who endorsed materialistic values (defined by the extent to which adolescents admired 'having expensive possessions', 'wearing expensive clothes' and 'being pretty or handsome') were more likely than those who did not to subsequently exhibit externalising behaviour symptoms such as attention deficit disorder and conduct disorder symptoms. At the same time, however, materialism has been associated with achievement motivation and goal-directedness (Netemeyer, Burton & Lichtenstein, 1995), which, as aspects of agency, are related to successful life outcomes (Bandura, 2001).

With regards to the measurement of materialism, Inglehart (1990) identified postmaterialist societies in which individuals emphasise such values as belonging and self-expression instead of material possessions, and classified respondents as possessing 'materialist' or 'postmaterialist' values by the social goals they valued. In the shortened version of his index, materialist and postmaterialist values were measured by asking respondents to rank order four political goals; these goals were 'maintaining order in the nation', 'fighting rising prices', 'protecting freedom of speech' and 'giving people more say in important government decisions'. People whose first and second choices were the first two values were considered materialists; those whose first and second choices were the last two values were postmaterialists; and those whose first and second choices were a materialist and a postmaterialist value constituted the 'mixed' group. Others define materialism as 'the importance an individual attaches to worldly possessions' (Belk, 1985, p. 265), and operationalise it as either a trait (Belk, 1985) or a value (Richins & Dawson, 1992) opposing positive mental heath states. Richins (1987), for instance, assessed materialism by measuring acquisition centrality, acquisition as the pursuit of happiness, and possession-defined success. Although, however, the definition and measurement of materialism offered by Richins (1987) and Inglehart (1990) differ from each other, they both share a basic understanding of materialism as the importance a consumer attaches to worldly possessions, and as the emphasis on individualistic as opposed to societal concerns.

With regards to the aetiology of materialism, Inglehart (1990) proposed two hypotheses to explain support for materialism/postmaterialism: his scarcity hypothesis argued that people value things in short supply, and his socialisation hypothesis argued that individuals' values (retained throughout adult life) reflect the economic conditions at the time they reached adulthood. He also argued that contemporary factors may influence the adoption of postmaterialist values. Education, for instance, new middle-class membership and low integration (i.e. low religiosity, not married and no children) have strong effects on the adoption of postmaterialist values whereas frequent religious services attendance and support for traditional gender roles are related to materialist values (Inglehart, 1990). Experience of childhood poverty and feelings of economic insecurity are related to adoption of materialist values in adult life (Sangster & Reynolds, 1996). Family disruption as a process and a factor associated with feelings of insecurity in children has also been explored in relation to materialism, but empirical studies have shown mixed results. While some studies have shown that family disruption is associated with offspring materialist values (Rindfleisch, Burroughs & Denton, 1997), others have found no association (Flouri, 1999).

Father's and mother's parenting and children's materialism

Psychological research, on the other hand, tends to demonstrate the importance of parental socialisation and parenting in materialism (Flouri, 1999). The usual research approach echoes basic organismic theories which suggest that environments that do not support growth and self-expression are associated with valuing financial success relatively more than prosocial values (Kasser & Ryan, 1993). Recent research, however, has shown that closeness to fathers is positively related with materialism (Marks, 1997) whereas closeness to mothers is negatively related with materialism (Flouri, 1999). An explanation might be that the issues relating to materialism are more likely to be discussed by men than by women. Therefore, those close to their mothers would be imbued with the sense that materialist concerns are of less importance. In contrast, those close to their fathers would be more exposed to economic and security issues and thus regard them as important (Marks, 1997). Supporting evidence for this might also be found in studies showing that the greater the father's influence in the family, the greater the children's level of group-based social anti-egalitarianism (Sidanius & Pena, 2003).

In terms of theory there are several reasons why father involvement (rather than closeness to father) would be negatively related to child materialism. First, father involvement is likely to reflect the father's warm and authoritative parenting which promotes the development of autonomy and self-direction (Barber, 1996), both of which are inversely related to materialism. Second, fathers who are involved in childcare are likely to hold gender equity attitudes (see Chapter 2) and self-expression values in general which are likely to be positively related to children's self-expression values, in accordance with the identification theory of the transmission of values, which suggests that because values are schemata (i.e. learned cognitive structures) about what is important or desirable in life, they are learned through a process of identification with important others (Guastello & Peissig, 1998). Third, low father involvement is likely to be associated with family poverty or parental low socio-economic status (see Chapter 2) and so the link between the father's low involvement and the child's survival values, such as materialism, might be because socio-economic disadvantage or low socio-economic status is associated with both.

Following this line of research, Studies III and IV explored links between materialism and father's parenting, controlling for mother's parenting and confounding factors. In particular, Study III, using longitudinal data from sweeps of the National Child Development Study, explored links between materialism at age 33, father involvement at age 7 and closeness to father at age 16, and Study IV, using data from the Families in the Millennium Study, explored links between materialism and father involvement in adolescence. In addition, because it has been shown that, when parental involvement is low, young people turn to their peers for support (Churchill & Moschis, 1979), Study IV explored whether perceived social support from friends was more strongly related to materialism when father involvement was low rather than high. The role of perceived social support from friends was not explored in Study III as this information was not available in the NCDS.

STUDY III: FATHER INVOLVEMENT AT AGE 7, CLOSENESS TO FATHER AT AGE 16, AND MATERIALISM AT AGE 33

This study used longitudinal data from the NCDS to explore the role of the father early in life in the child's materialism in adulthood (for full details see Flouri, 2003). In the NCDS, materialist and postmaterialist values were assessed with Inglehart's (1990) 4-item measure at age 33. Of the 11 363 cohort members about whom there was information at age 33, 11 227 respondents had complete data on materialism/postmaterialism. Of those, 17.9% were materialists, 18% postmaterialists and 64.1% belonged in the mixed category. The mixed group was omitted from the analysis. Therefore, the samples for this study were the 2009 materialists and the 2021 postmaterialists.

Measures

Father involvement at age 7 and closeness to father at age 16 were measured as in Study I of Chapter 6. The factors controlled for were mother involvement at age 7 and closeness to mother at age 16 (also measured as in Study I of Chapter 6), as well as the confounding variables (falling under the broad domains of 'familial and economic insecurity', 'education', 'contemporary influences' and 'mental health') that the parental sociali- sation paradigm has identified as important. Economic insecurity was tapped with the following seven measures: parental socio-economic status when the child was born, mother's education, father's education, number of family moves since the child's birth until age 7, and evidence of domestic tension and financial difficulties in the family. Evidence of financial difficulties in the family was assessed using a composite measure (of the Health Visitor's report at age 7 and receipt of free school meals at ages 11 and 16) as follows: If the Health Visitor did not report the family to be in financial difficulties when the cohort member was aged 7, or if no one in the family received free school meals when the cohort member was aged 11 or 16, then there was no evidence of financial difficulties in the family as the cohort member was growing up. If the Health Visitor reported the family to be in financial difficulties when the cohort member was aged 7, or if anyone in the family received free school meals when the cohort member was aged 11 or 16, then there was evidence of financial difficulties in the family as the cohort member was growing up. Of the study participants with valid data on financial difficulties in all childhood sweeps, 534 (22.6%) had experienced financial difficulties in childhood (7–16 years). Non-intact parental family structure in childhood, as proxy for both familial and economic insecurity, was also controlled for. In particular, family structure was 'intact' if the cohort child lived continuously with both natural parents until age 16, or 'non-intact' in all other situations.

Educational attainment was operationalised as in Study III of Chapter 3. The contemporaneous factors controlled for were current (age 33) socio- economic status (i.e. 'manual' vs 'non-manual'), having a partner or not, having children or not, and belonging to a religion or not. Finally, mental health was operationalised as externalising and internalising behaviour problems. In this study they were measured at age 7, as in Elliott and Richards (1991) who extracted two main 7-item factors from the Rutter 'A' Health and Behaviour Checklist. The two factors were 'disruptive behaviour' (which corresponds to externalising behaviour problems) and 'unhappy and worried' (which corresponds to internalising behaviour problems). The Rutter 'A' items used were those 14 items that were asked in all three childhood sweeps (ages 7, 11 and 16) in the NCDS. The externalising behaviour problems items were, for example: the child is disobedient at home, fights with other children, is irritable and quick to fly off the handle, destroys own or others' belongings, is squirmy or fidgety, and has difficulty settling to anything. The internalising behaviour problems items were, for example: the child worries about many things, is upset by new situations, is bullied by other children, is miserable or tearful, and prefers to do things alone. The average externalising behaviour problems score (ranging from 0 to 12) was 2.88 (SD = 2.16), and the average internalising behaviour problems score (ranging from 0 to 10) was 2.69 (SD = 1.85).

Results

Figures 7.1 and 7.2 show the logistic regression analyses results (carried out separately by gender) predicting age 33 materialism/postmaterialism in the NCDS.

As can be seen, financial difficulties in childhood were predictive of men's postmaterialism later in life, educational attainment predicted both men's and women's postmaterialist values, whereas religiosity (in men) and presence of partner (in women) were negatively related to postmaterialism. Poor relations with father in adolescence were predictive of postmaterialist values at age 33 in women, a finding which replicated similar results by Marks (1997).

Discussion

This study showed that even after controlling for family's socio-economic background, parental family structure, financial difficulties in childhood, current socio-economic status, educational attainment, religion, and other confounding variables, poor father–daughter relations in adolescence were predictive of postmaterialism 16 years later. A major limitation of the study, however, was that materialism/postmaterialism was measured using rankings and therefore the 'ipsative' problem could not be avoided. Related to this, materialism was assessed with a 4-item battery and therefore measurement error cannot be discounted. In that respect,

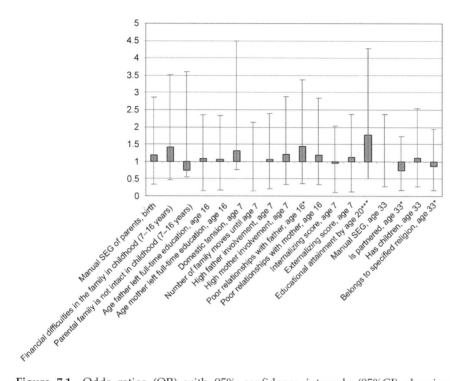

Figure 7.1 Odds ratios (OR) with 95% confidence intervals (95%CI) showing predictors of materialism/postmaterialism at age 33 in NCDS women (*N* = 380) *Notes*: *$p < 0.05$; ***$p < 0.001$

Inglehart's 12-item index, or a scaled measure of materialism, would have been more appropriate, but such measures were not available in the NCDS. Another limitation is that parent's own values were not controlled for again as this information was not available in the NCDS. Finally, other important environmental influences on materialism, such as peers, were left unexamined. Study IV addressed most of these issues.

STUDY IV: FATHER INVOLVEMENT AND CHILDREN'S MATERIALISM IN ADOLESCENCE

This study used different measures to explore links between father involvement and children's materialism in the children's sample of the FMS (see Study II of Chapter 2). Father involvement was measured as in Study II of Chapter 2. Materialism was measured using Richins' (1987) scale, a 5-item 5-point scale, anchored with 'strongly disagree' and 'strongly agree'. Items included: 'I would like to be rich enough to buy

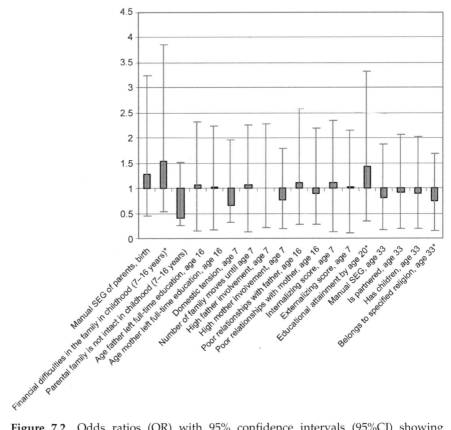

Figure 7.2 Odds ratios (OR) with 95% confidence intervals (95%CI) showing predictors of materialism/postmaterialism at age 33 in NCDS men ($N = 408$)
*Notes: *$p < 0.05$

anything I want' and 'It's really true that money can buy happiness'. The scale (ranging from 5 to 25) had a mean score of 13.91 (SD = 4.69) and Cronbach's alpha 0.72. The variables controlled for (all assessed as in Study II of Chapter 2) were: socio-economic status (assessed by receipt of free school meals), child's gender, child's age, family structure ('intact' or 'otherwise'), child's emotional and behavioural problems (assessed with the Strengths and Difficulties Questionnaire), child's self-esteem (assessed with seven items from Rosenberg's (1965) Self-Esteem Scale), mother involvement and interparental conflict. This study also controlled for goal-directedness and peer influence. Goal-directedness was measured with the Modified Goal-Directedness Scale (Schmitt-Rodermund & Vondracek, 1999), a 3-item 5-point scale including such items as 'I have clear goals for the future (even if it takes time to reach them)'. The scale (ranging from 3 to 15) had a Cronbach's alpha of 0.76, and a mean score of 11.55

(SD = 2.76). Peer influence was measured with the Modified Perceived Social Support from Friends scale (Procidano & Heller, 1983), a 4-item 3-point scale ranging from 4 to 12. Sample items were: 'My friends enjoy hearing about what I think', and 'I have a deep, sharing relationship with a number of friends'. Cronbach's alpha was 0.64, and the scale's mean score was 9.62 (SD = 1.80).

Results

As can be seen in Figure 7.3, mother involvement was negatively related to materialism, but father involvement was unrelated to materialism. Interparental conflict, goal-directedness, age, and emotional and behavioural problems were positively related to materialism. Compared to girls, boys scored higher on materialism. The amount of variance in materialism explained by the factors shown in Figure 7.3 was 11%. As expected, peer support was more strongly related to materialism when father involvement was low rather than high (for full details see Flouri, in press).

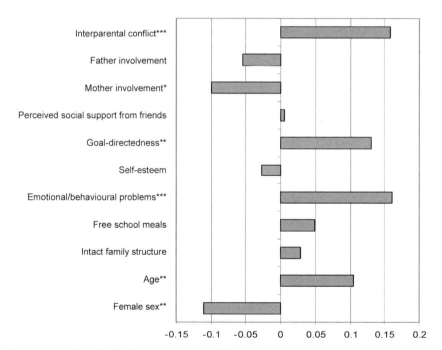

Figure 7.3 Standardised regression coefficients (β) predicting children's materialism (N = 747)
Notes: *p < 0.05; **p < 0.01; ***p < 0.001

SUMMARY AND CONCLUSIONS

This chapter described four studies, three longitudinal (all using data from sweeps of the NCDS) and one cross-sectional (Study IV), carried out to explore links between paternal parenting (assessed as father involvement in all studies, and as both father involvement and closeness to father in Study III) and children's socio-economic outcomes. Father involvement was measured differently in Studies I, II and III, and IV. Father involvement in Studies I, II and III was assessed with four items asked when the cohort children were aged 7 ('father reads to the child', 'father takes outings with the child', 'father takes an equal to mother's role in managing the child', and 'father is interested in the child's education'), whereas father involvement in Study IV was measured with the child-reported Modified Inventory of Father Involvement (Hawkins et al., 2002), which assesses the child's perception of the father's competence in the parenting role. The socio-economic outcomes predicted were somewhat disparate too. First, the outcomes were placed in different life stages. All three longitudinal studies explored age 33 outcomes, whereas the cross-sectional study explored outcomes in adolescence. Second, the outcomes involved different life domains. Study I looked at labour force participation, Study II at homelessness and income poverty and Studies III and IV at values. This is significant; even though unemployment, homelessness and income poverty are interrelated, they are not inter-changeable. Even Studies III and IV, which looked at the same value (materialism), measured it quite differently. In Study III materialism was a political and value orientation mapped across Inglehart's (2000) survival vs self-expression dimension, which taps a syndrome of trust, tolerance, political activism and self-expression that emerges in post-industrial societies with high levels of security. In Study IV materialism was operationalised and measured as the importance one attaches to material possessions, which again, although related, is not tantamount to materialism as a political and value orientation. Inglehart's materialism is perhaps conceptually less close to consumer materialism than it is to support for the 'Protestant' work ethic, achievement motivation, mastery over problems, and general 'toughness'.

Despite these issues, which make comparisons between studies difficult, all four studies showed some support for the usefulness of exploring the contextual dimensions of the family environment in relation to children's socio-economic outcomes. For instance, Study I showed that even after controlling for factors associated with adult unemployment, mother involvement at age 7 was negatively associated with unemployment in sons at age 33. Study II found that, again in sons but not in daughters of manual workers, father involvement at age 7 was negatively associated with an experience of homelessness by age 33. Study IV showed that mother involvement was negatively related to materialism in adolescence, and that peer influence was more strongly related to materialism when father involvement was low rather than high. This chapter, however, did not present unequivocally positive parenting (and in particular fathering) 'effects': Study III showed that, in women, poor relations with father in adolescence predicted postmaterialist values in adult life.

Before trying to explain this last finding it might be worth trying to discuss the 'positive effects' first. The finding that mother (but not father) involvement in childhood was negatively related to men's unemployment echoes the finding of Study IV of Chapter 4 that, in men, mother (but not father) involvement was positively related to educational attainment in adult life even after controlling for the family's socio-economic character-istics and individual factors in childhood. Mother involvement was also negatively related to adolescent materialism, which echoes earlier findings that closeness to mother was negatively related to materialism in both adolescents (Flouri, 1999) and adults (Marks, 1997). On the other hand, the finding that father involvement was negatively associated with working-class men's experience of homelessness in adult life represents an imperfect example of 'intergenerational mobility' (according to sociologists) or 'resilience' (according to psychologists): father involvement was related to avoidance of homelessness in 'high-risk' individuals, namely working-class men (Quigley, Raphael & Smolensky, 2001). The second and final 'positive' father involvement effect was also a moderator effect: father involvement 'protected' against materialism when peer influence, a risk factor for materialism, was high rather than low (Study IV). It is interesting that in these three studies all statistically significant father involvement findings were interaction effects.

These positive parenting – and, in particular, fathering – 'effects' aside, Study III showed that a distant relation with the father in adolescence was positively related to the daughter's postmaterialism in adult life. Marks (1997) also showed that closeness to father in adolescence was positively related to materialism in adult life (in both men and women, however). Marks' explanation was that since issues related to materialism are more likely to be discussed by men than by women, those daughters who were close to their father would be more exposed to economic and security issues and thus view them as important. But why was closeness to father related to materialism only in daughters in this study? An explanation might be that girls who reported feeling close to their father in 1974 may have not been socialised according to typical masculine and feminine stereotypes (which one assumes were more powerful then than they are today), and so grew up to hold 'masculine' (e.g. materialist) values. In contrast, because boys were socialised to value financial success as a part of their masculine identity, a close father–adolescent relationship may not have been necessary to promote materialism in sons.

These studies suffered from several limitations, however. First, the measurement of most adult outcomes in the longitudinal studies was perhaps simplistic. Labour force participation at age 33 was simply the cohort member's self-report on whether he or she 'is currently employed' or 'is currently unemployed'. The total amount of unemployment over a given period or the number of bouts of unemployment within a certain period would have been more informative indices. Similarly, homelessness at age 33 was measured as 'experience of homelessness in the last 10 years' instead of perhaps the total amount of homelessness in the last 10 years or the number of bouts of homelessness in that period, which, of course, leaves unanswered important questions such as: How long must one be without housing to consider oneself homeless? Is it enough to be without housing for just one night, or is a longer period necessary? What about squatters or people living in substandard housing, or the 'precariously housed' who may not be literally homeless but are just one misfortune away from losing the house (Rossi, 1989)? Poverty at age 33, on the other hand, was measured as living in subsidised housing and as receiving state benefits, which probably measure income poverty, but not subjective poverty or deprivation. Bradshaw and Finch (2003), however, showed that there was little overlap of these poverty dimensions (income poverty, subjective poverty and deprivation) which suggests that it is not clear who exactly were the poor cohort members of the study. Bradshaw and Finch (2003) offered several explanations why there was little overlap in the poverty dimensions found in their study. First, because there are cases in transition; for example, there are households who have lost a worker and are now income poor but not (yet) lacking necessities (deprived). Second, because there is 'false consciousness'; for example, there are people who do not feel poor (subjectively poor) despite being both income poor and lacking in socially perceived necessities (deprived). Third, because housing costs were not controlled for; for example, at a 'before housing costs' equivalent income level, households with high housing costs are more likely to feel deprived than households with low housing costs. Fourth, because perceptions of poverty vary according to how resources are distributed in the household. Borrowing Bradshaw and Finch's (2003) example, a female non-bread-winner cohort member may feel poor because her partner does not share his income with her.

Materialism in Study III, on the other hand, was not measured simplistically although it was also measured imperfectly. Materialism/postmaterialism was measured using rankings and therefore the 'ipsative' problem could not be avoided. Furthermore, it was measured with Inglehart's 4-item rather than 12-item battery, and therefore measurement error cannot be discounted.

Another limitation of the studies presented here was that several confounding variables were not controlled for. Studies I and II in particular did not adjust for the effect of childhood socio-economic disadvantage, which is important given the links between experience of childhood adversities and poor adult attainments (Corcoran, 1995). Related to this, parents' educational and occupational aspirations, which mediate the relationship between background factors and educational and socio-economic outcomes, were not controlled for. Bond and Saunders (1999), who also used data from the NCDS, showed that although parents' aspirations for their sons' education did not directly influence their sons' achieved occupational grade, they influenced their sons' aspirations which then affected their academic motivation and subsequent qualifications. It would have been particularly interesting to see if the father's aspirations could be associated with positive socio-economic outcomes in 'high-risk' groups, and to explore pathways of influence of the father's aspirations in both sons' and daughters' attainments. In addition, the role of peers was not addressed in any of the longitudinal studies. Peer relationships problems have been linked to later unemployment (Woodward & Fergusson, 2000) usually through poor educational attainment and higher rates of criminal conviction (Healey, Knapp & Farrington, 2004), and to homelessness, especially in high-risk groups (Kingree, Stephens, Braithwaite & Griffin, 1999). Finally, ethnicity, which is related to both socio-economic disadvantage (Blackwell, 2003) and values (Silver & Dowley, 2000), was not controlled for. With regards to both materialism studies, on the other hand, neither Study III nor Study IV controlled for parents' values, which are directly related to children's values in accordance with the identification theory of the transmission of values, or for other environmental factors that may contribute to the development of values, such as schools and the media (Kasser, 2002).

Despite these limitations, all three longitudinal studies showed strong evidence for the link between educational attainment and socio-economic outcomes, and between psychological distress and socio-economic outcomes. In particular, even after controlling for several confounding variables, educational attainment at age 20 was negatively related to unemployment, state benefits receipt, living in subsidised housing, and materialism at age 33 in both men and women. Psychological distress was positively related to unemployment and living in subsidised housing in both genders and to state benefits receipt and homelessness in men. As, however, both socio-economic outcomes and psychological distress were measured concurrently, it is not clear if psychological distress was the cause or the effect of these adversities. In line with previous research, religion and the presence of a partner were negatively related to materialism/ postmaterialism. The presence of a partner was also negatively related to all four adult adversities (unemployment, homelessness, state benefits receipt, and living in subsidised housing) explored in this chapter, which echoes previous findings about the small but consistent effects of being partnered in positive outcomes. Being partnered or married usually generates well-being because a partner can act as a buffer in difficult times, and through the emotional and economic support she or he provides (Diener et al., 1999). Generally speaking, parental family structure was not related to children's values or to most of the children's adversities in adult life. In fact, the association between non-intact family structure in childhood and living in subsidised housing at age 33 in men was the only statistically significant family structure effect in all four studies presented in this chapter. It was only in men again that sibship size was positively associated with homelessness, receiving state benefits and living in subsidised housing. These findings are in line with Kuo and Hauser (1997) who also showed that sibship size was more important for the educational attainment of men than it was for that of women.

The findings presented in this chapter, that certain individual factors were associated with entry to or escape from adversity, should not, however, distract one (a) from the fact that perceptions of the poor – by those not in poor circumstances – still tend to reflect attitudes and stereotypes that attribute poverty to personal failings rather than socio-economic structures and systems and to ignore strengths and competencies in these groups (Quadagno, 1994), or (b) from the fact that social policy and anti-poverty programmes continue to reflect some of these stereotypes (Bullock, 1995).

CHAPTER 8

NON-RESIDENT FATHERS' PARENTING: DETERMINANTS AND CHILDREN'S PSYCHOLOGICAL OUTCOMES

INTRODUCTION

As discussed in Chapter 1, in father-absent families the fathering dimensions that are usually explored in relation to child outcomes are non-resident fathers' economic support for their children, frequency (but also sometimes regularity and/or quality) of contact, and involvement. Diminished levels of non-resident fathers' contact or involvement, for example, have been implied as driving at least part of the association between fathers' absence and children's adverse outcomes. Generally speaking, it seems that although payment of child support has been associated with positive children's educational outcomes across studies, the effects of non-resident fathers' contact and involvement require careful specification. Research exploring factors associated with non-resident fathers' parenting has identified several structural as well as individual determinants, with recent studies starting to explore not only what predicts non-resident fathers' continuing involvement and contact with their children, but what determines fathers' transition to non-residence in the first place. This chapter presents a cross-sectional study which, using data from 520 teenagers with non-resident fathers from the Families in the Millennium Study, explores both determinants of non-resident fathers' involvement and contact with their children, and children's psychological outcomes associated with involvement and contact.

THE 'OUTCOMES'

Although there is strong evidence for the positive role of non-resident fathers' payment of child support for children's outcomes (Graham & Beller, 2002; Hetherington & Stanley-Hagan, 1997), as these economic contributions improve children's standards of living, health, educational attainment and general well-being (Seltzer, 1994), the evidence for the effects of non-resident fathers' contact is either weak (Seltzer, 1994) or mixed (Amato & Gilbreth, 1999). In one study, boys and younger children, but not girls or older children, were better adjusted with frequent and regular contact with their fathers (Stewart, Copeland, Chester, Malley & Barenbaum, 1997). There is also evidence that levels of interparental conflict significantly moderate the 'effects' of contact in children. Although in the context of low conflict, frequent visits between fathers and children tend to be associated with better child adjustment, where interparental conflict is intense, more frequent visits are linked to poorer adjustment, presumably because of the opportunities for more direct exposure of the children to parental aggression and pressures (Hetherington & Kelly, 2002). Other studies also show that careful specification is required before generalising from their findings. For instance, Simons, Whitbeck, Beaman and Conger (1994) showed that non-resident fathers' involvement was negatively related to adolescents' externalising but not internalising behaviour problems, and more recently Stewart (2003) showed that only certain measures of authoritative parenting of non-resident fathers' involvement were associated with child outcomes, and that not all types of father–child contact (such as participating in leisure activities) influenced children's well-being. An explanation might be that because of time constraints, most non-resident fathers have primarily recreational relationships with their children and so they do not engage in authoritative parenting such as helping with homework or talking over personal problems, which is consistently related to positive child outcomes (Gray & Steinberg, 1999a). Another reason might be that a close, 'parent-like' contact with the non-resident father is associated with better relations with both parents which is related to better children's outcomes (Clarke-Stewart & Hayward, 1996). Amato and Gilbreth (1999) showed in their meta-analysis that, across studies, payment of child support was associated with children's academic success, and fewer externalising problems, and that contact was significantly but modestly associated with academic success and lack of internalising problems. They also concluded that how often non-resident fathers saw their children was less important than what they did when they were with their children. It should be pointed out, however, that the effect size of the associations between non-resident fathers' *contact* and children's academic success and emotional/behavioural problems increased significantly in studies published between 1989 and 1998, as compared with the results of studies published between 1970 and 1988 (Dunn, 2004), perhaps suggesting that recent cohorts of non-resident fathers are more committed to the parental role (Amato & Gilbreth, 1999).

Indirect support for the importance of the quality of the father's parenting irrespective of family structure can be found in studies showing that even prior to family dissolution, children from families that subsequently dissolved performed less well than peers whose parents remained married. Sun and Li (2001), for instance, showed that American families at the predisruption stage were characterised by a shortage of financial, cultural, human and social capital, even after demographics were controlled. In addition, some parental investment measures yielded a smaller educational return for students whose families subsequently dissolved than for those whose parents remained married. Sun and Li (2001) suggested that the negative postdisruption effects on children's academic achievement can be either largely or completely predicted by academic performance and investment differences at the predisruption stage. Providing further support for the significance of explaining the relationship between father absence and child outcomes, Ram and Hou (2003), using data from cycles of the National Longitudinal Surveys of Children in Canada, showed that the scarcity of material resources mediated the relationship between family structure and cognitive outcomes, whereas the diminution of familial resources – especially those related to parenting style (ineffective parenting) and psychological well-being of parents (depression) – mediated the relationship between family structure and emotional and behavioural outcomes.

Recent studies generally define with greater precision both the populations and the child behavioural domains in which the role of the non-resident father is likely to be influential. For example, in the United States, Peters and Mullis (1997) found positive effects of child support income on cognitive test scores in adolescence, but not on later outcome measures such as educational attainment, earnings, and labour market experience, and Argys, Peters, Brooks-Gunn and Smith (1998) showed that the positive child support effects in children's cognitive outcomes were stronger for Blacks in their divorced/separated families sample and for Whites in their non-marital-birth sample. Manning and Lamb (2003) found that it was closeness to non-resident father that was positively associated with both academic and behavioural outcomes in adolescents. In particular, even after controlling for family structure, socio-demographic characteristics, family stability and parenting, closeness to father was positively associated with grade point average and college expectations, and was negatively associated with suspension/expulsion, delinquency and school problems (operationalised as the degree, since the start of the school year, the adolescent has had problems getting along with teachers, paying attention in school, getting homework done, and getting along with other students). In the United Kingdom, Dunn et al. (2004) showed that child–non-resident father contact and relationships were related to young children's adjustment and that these associations were stronger for children from single-parent families than for those with stepfathers, and for those whose mothers had been first pregnant as teenagers. Earlier, in the United States, Perloff and Buckner (1996) showed that contact with fathers had a modest beneficial effect on behaviour in children on welfare, although negative traits of fathers (e.g. substance abuse, physical violence) were associated with increased child behaviour problems.

As discussed in Chapter 1, diminished levels of non-resident fathers' contact or involvement have been implied as driving at least part of the association between fathers' absence and children's adverse outcomes. As with recent studies on non-resident fathers' involvement, recent studies on father absence also specify with precision both the father and child populations and the child adjustment domains that father absence is purported to influence. Following up community samples of girls in the United States and New Zealand, Ellis et al. (2003), for example, showed stronger and more consistent evidence of effects of father absence on daughters' early sexual activity and teenage pregnancy than on mental health or academic achievement. This elevated risk was either not explained (in the US study) or only partly explained (in the New Zealand study) by familial, ecological and personal disadvantages associated with father absence. In the United States, Dunifon and Kowaleski-Jones (2002) found single motherhood to be associated with reduced well-being and low academic achievement among European American children, but not African American children, and Delaire and Kalil (2002) showed that American adolescents living with their single mothers and at least one grandparent in multigenerational households had developmental outcomes that were at least as good and often better than the outcomes of teenagers in married families. More recently, Harper and McLanahan (2004) showed that although a sizeable portion of the risk of youth incarceration among American adolescent males that appeared to be due to father absence could actually be attributed to other factors, such as teen motherhood, low parent education, racial inequalities and poverty, adolescents in father-absent households still faced elevated incarceration risks. However, the adolescents who faced the highest incarceration risks were those in step-parent families, including father–stepmother families. Earlier, Thomas, Farrell and Barnes (1996) showed that for White (but not for Black) adolescent males, non-resident father involvement buffered the negative effects of single-mother families on delinquency, heavy drinking and illicit drug use. Furthermore, although the highest rates of problem behaviour were found among White male adolescents in single-mother families without the support of a non-resident father, for Black male adolescents there were actually fewer problem behaviours when non-resident fathers were not involved. Similarly, King, Harris and Heard (2004) showed evidence for racial and ethnic diversity in non-resident father involvement by demonstrating that the greatest loss of social capital by living apart from their fathers was experienced by White youth with less-educated fathers. King et al. (2004) showed that of all ethnic groups of non-resident fathers in the United States, White fathers fall at the two extremes, with the lowest levels of father involvement reported for White fathers with a high school education or less and the highest levels of involvement reported for White fathers with high levels of education. In contrast, Hispanic, Black and Asian non-resident fathers exhibit fewer significant differences by education, with levels of involvement falling between the two extremes exhibited by White fathers. King et al. (2004) concluded that White youth with less educated fathers may be at greatest risk of sustained loss of social capital, as their non-resident fathers are less involved than minority fathers and highly educated White fathers. Although their levels of contact are not significantly lower than those of minority youth, they stand out as having the lowest levels of talking with their fathers, and they report being less close to them. King et al. (2004) suggested that such educational differences are less pronounced for minorities, and especially Blacks, because Black women have been historically involved in the labour force and so Black men have been less likely to be the sole breadwinners, with implications for family and gender roles and for power relations. Black marriages are more egalitarian than White marriages, with Black husbands more likely than White husbands to share housework and childcare. Greater equality between spouses in Black families has led to greater participation by Black fathers in childrearing that obscures educational differences. Indirect support for these theses was also provided recently by Plotnick, Garfinkel, McLanahan and Ku (2004) who investigated the hypothesis that stricter child support enforcement may reduce teenage childbearing by raising the costs of fatherhood.[1] Plotnick et al. (2004) using data from the US National Longitudinal Survey of Youth showed that during the early 1980s, teens living in states with higher rates of paternity establishment were less likely to have children, and that this relationship was stronger for non-Hispanic Whites than for non-Hispanic Blacks.

In addition, non-structural factors, such as cultural values, may influence the types of activities in which minority non-resident fathers engage with their children. For example, the stronger role of religion in the lives of Black and Hispanic Americans may encourage minority fathers to attend religious services or to become involved in church-related activities with

[1]Other researchers in the United States have also claimed that failing to establish child support obligations for non-resident fathers simply because their incomes are initially low does not appear justified. Phillips and Garfinkel (1993) showed that incomes of non-marital fathers, which typically are low in the beginning, increase dramatically over the years after paternity establishment often to a level comparable with the incomes of divorced fathers. Compliance with child support orders is generally problematic, with US national data indicating that only 39% of the custodial mothers received all the child support owed to them in 1995 (Scoon-Rogers, 1999).

their children more so than other groups. In any case in the United States Blacks are more likely to visit their absent children than are non-Blacks (King, 1994), and family values and kinship ties – which predict continued involvement with non-resident children (Cooksey & Craig, 1998) – are more important in Blacks (King et al., 2004). Recent studies also suggest that more attention should be paid to characteristics other than race or ethnic group membership of non-resident fathers when determining their role in child development. There is evidence, for instance, that fathers of children born to teenage mothers show problem behaviours, which may negatively influence their ability to engage in successful parenting (Ekéus & Christensson, 2003), which in turn is related to positive child outcomes. Providing further supporting evidence for this, Jaffee et al. (2003) in the United Kingdom showed that the less time fathers lived with their children, the more conduct problems their children had, but only if the fathers engaged in low levels of antisocial behaviour. In contrast, when fathers engaged in high levels of antisocial behaviour, the more time they lived with their children the more conduct problems their children had. The role of the non-resident father's conduct problems in children's outcomes has actually been variously stressed in studies examining the contrary way that policy and practice have tended to operate in many countries concerning violence against women on one hand and against children on the other. Eriksson and Hester (2001) discussed how, although the arrangements made for children's contact with parents after parents have separated or divorced are important with regard to the ongoing safety of women and children who have left violent men, fatherhood in the context of separation and divorce has tended to be construed as inherently non-violent, with consequences for women, child safety and children's welfare. Furthermore, mothers are dissatisfied with high levels of father contact when the father is or has been violent, which is especially significant given that mother's dissatisfaction with high levels of contact is negatively related to children's well-being. King and Heard (1999), for instance, showed that American children who had a father living elsewhere were least well off in families in which mothers were dissatisfied with high levels of father contact.

THE 'DETERMINANTS'

Establishing exactly how much contact between the non-resident father and the child is taking place is difficult as the answer depends on which study is relied on, what is being measured, and who is asked (Hunt & Roberts, 2004). Custodial mothers report less contact than non-resident fathers, and formerly married fathers have more contact than ex-cohabitants and those who have never lived together (Maclean & Eekelaar, 1997). Blackwell and

Dawe (2003) in Britain, using data from the National Statistics Omnibus Survey, demonstrated that the perceptions of resident parents and non-resident parents about face-to-face contact differ from one another. For instance, although 14% of non-resident parents reported that they never see their children, 28% of resident parents said that the non-resident parent never sees the child. Of non-resident parents, 77% said they saw their children either every day, or at least once a week, or at least once a month. Responses from resident parents indicated that only 60% saw their children either every day, or at least once a week, or at least once a month. There is a similar discrepancy in the reported levels of indirect contact (telephone calls, letters, emails and texts). Whereas 12% of non-resident parents reported that they never had indirect contact with their children, the resident parent responses reported that 29% of non-resident parents never had indirect contact with their children. What is consistently shown, however, is that compared with non-resident fathers, non-resident mothers are more likely to visit frequently, assume more parenting functions, and less often cease contact with their children (see Kelly & Emery, 2003, for a discussion), and that as time goes by, after separation or divorce, children typically have less and less contact with the non-custodial parent. Within a couple of years after divorce, for instance, 30% to 40% of American children no longer see their non-resident parent, and about 20% to 30% see their parent as often as once a week (see Clarke-Stewart & Hayward, 1996, for a discussion). British figures are not dissimilar. Bradshaw and Millar (1991) showed that 40% of fathers have no contact after two years. Note, however, that more recent studies suggest that children and their non-resident fathers may now be seeing each other more frequently (Amato & Gilbreth, 1999). Hetherington and Kelly (2002) report that between 18% and 25% of American children have no contact with their fathers two to three years after divorce.

Research that explored factors associated with the non-resident fathers' continued involvement with their children has identified several structural as well as individual predictors of continued non-resident fathers' involvement with their children. Most empirical research on 'visitation' or 'contact' links payment of child support with payment of visits, and American data show the likelihood of any visits to be 15% higher and the frequency 20% higher if a father pays any child support (see Graham & Beller, 2002, for a review). Fathers' positive perception of the paternal role (Ihinger-Tallman, Pasley & Buehler, 1993), close proximity (Blackwell & Dawe, 2003) and education (Hetherington & Stanley-Hagan, 1997), and levels of involvement before separation (Whiteside & Becker, 2000), generally predict father involvement, although it seems that even more important is the quality of the father's relationship with the child's mother (Amato & Rezac, 1994; Cutrona, Hessling, Bacon & Russell, 1998) as a good relationship with the custodial mother is usually related to greater access to information about and therefore a greater understanding of the child, which, in turn, may increase his altruism towards the child (Carlson & McLanahan, 2001). Quality of the parents' romantic relationship was also one of the most powerful predictors of father involvement in young disadvantaged fathers (Gavin et al., 2002) and in unmarried fathers (Johnson, 2001). In particular, Johnson (2001) showed that his sample of unmarried American fathers were more likely to be non-resident if they were not romantically involved with the child's mother, and Gavin et al. (2002) showed that although the father's employment status, the maternal grandmother's education, and the father's relationship with the baby's maternal grandmother were associated with paternal involvement, involvement in their African American fathers was predicted most strongly by the quality of the parents' romantic relationship. Rangarajan and Gleason (1998) also showed that among fathers of children born to teenage mothers (the group among non-custodial fathers having perhaps the most difficult time in providing economic support to their children) the fathers' employment status and education led to more economic support but not to large increases in the amount of time fathers spend with their children, suggesting that factors such as commitment to the child and the relationship with the child's mother may be influential. More recent American research looking at factors determining involvement with children born to adolescent mothers has also emphasised the importance of exploring the role of the maternal grandmothers who occupy a central position in the lives of adolescent mothers and their children, serve as gatekeepers, either supporting or inhibiting the non-resident fathers' involvement (Krishnakumar & Black, 2003), and buffer the negative effects of strain in the adolescent mothers' relationships with their children's non-resident biological fathers[2] (Gee & Rhodes, 2003).

Time since parents separated has, as explained above, also been found to predict levels of contact. In Britain, Blackwell and Dawe (2003) using responses from resident parents showed that only about a third (32%) of those children whose parents separated three years ago or more saw their non-resident parent at least once a week compared with over 50% of children whose parents separated less than three years ago (70% of children whose parents separated less than a year ago, 64% of children whose parents separated one year to less than two years ago, and 56% of children

[2]The majority of African American adolescent mothers continue to reside with their child in the home of the maternal grandmother, who often assumes traditionally parental roles such as financial provision and assistance with caregiving. Welfare reform adopted in the late 1990s is likely to increase this trend, given the requirement that adolescent mothers live with a parent, legal guardian, or other adult relative if they wish to receive financial benefits (Gavin et al., 2002).

whose parents separated two years to less than three years ago[3]). Certain child characteristics have also sometimes been shown to affect non-resident father involvement. For example, non-resident fathers are more likely to be involved with their sons than with their daughters (Ihinger-Tallman et al., 1993) – although they are more likely to talk with daughters than they are with sons (Cooksey & Craig, 1998) – and when children are older (Hetherington & Stanley-Hagan, 1997). There is also some evidence that children's emotional and behavioural problems may diminish non-resident father involvement (Simons et al., 1994), and that sons feel closer than daughters to their non-resident fathers (King et al., 2004). Note, however, that as much of this research is cross-sectional it is difficult to establish if fathers find it easier to get involved with well-adjusted children, or if children are well-adjusted because their fathers are involved (see also Chapters 2 and 3 for a discussion).

In the United Kingdom, Maclean and Eekelaar (1997) showed that non-resident fathers decrease their involvement when either they or their former spouse remarry as a remarriage makes it more difficult for the non-resident father to balance old and new relationships. However, other research which differentiated between type of men's new partnerships showed that it was men who are most linked to the traditional family life (i.e. those who are currently married) that are most likely to maintain ties with their previous offspring. However, Seltzer's (1991) finding that remarried fathers are more economically stable, coupled with the evidence linking payment of child support and involvement (Graham & Beller, 2002), might mean that this is because remarried fathers are simply more able to pay child support. Further exploring whether the life-course decisions that fathers make 'crowd out' their involvement with their non-resident children, Cooksey and Craig (1998) showed that it is when fathers reside with only biological children that they are less likely to see their children from former relationships. In other words, additional stepchildren do not produce the same crowding-out effect. Manning and Smock (2000) also provided evidence supporting the claim that fathers 'swap' families when they form new ones but only when the trade-off is between new biological children living inside fathers' households and existing biological children living outside fathers' households. Recent studies have also

[3]Note that while this pattern of results did not change when the non-resident parents' responses were used, the proportion of children reported to have direct contact with their non-resident parent was much larger for each of the separation period groups. For instance, when non-resident parents' responses were used, just over a half (53%) of children whose parents had been separated for at least three years had direct contact with their non-resident parent at least once a week compared with around four-fifths of children whose parents had separated more recently (79% of children whose parents separated less than a year ago, 84% of children whose parents separated one to less than two years ago, and 79% of children whose parents separated two to less than three years ago).

stressed the lack of clarity concerning postdivorce enactment of the father role (Leite & McKenry, 2002) as an important factor of non-resident fathers' low levels of involvement with their children. Other father characteristics that have been explored as predictors of contact include ethnicity and socio-economic status (with the prevailing argument actually being that racial/ethnic differences in non-resident fathers' involvement reflect socio-economic differences) and it seems that there is evidence to support that both factors have some influence. Better-educated parents are more likely to conform to social expectations of close ties between parents and children despite separation, whereas more well-off non-resident parents are better able to incur the costs associated with visitation and participation in activities. In contrast, poverty and unemployment may demoralise fathers who cannot provide financially for their children, leading fathers to withdraw from participating in their children's lives, and mothers to feel less compelled to foster or even allow the father's involvement (see King et al., 2004, for a discussion). In the United Kingdom, Blackwell and Dawe (2003) showed that children whose resident parent was White were more likely than those whose resident parent was non-White to have weekly direct contact with their non-resident parent (44% compared with 32%), whereas children whose resident parent was in a lower occupations socio-economic group were more likely than children whose resident parent was in a higher or intermediate occupations group to never have contact with their non-resident parent (30% compared with 16% and 12% respectively). In the United States, King et al. (2004), who investigated ethnicity and socio-economic status as determinants of non-resident fathers' involvement in White, Black, Hispanic and Asian adolescents, similarly found that White adolescents have significantly higher levels of both overnight visits and inperson, phone or letter contact with their non-resident fathers compared to Black and Hispanic adolescents, although when contact was measured as 'any contact at all' Black–White differences disappeared, and Hispanic adolescents consistently stood out as being most likely not to have any contact (77%, compared with 87% of Whites, 86% of Blacks, and 92% of Asians). King et al. (2004) also interestingly showed that particular ethnic groups are significantly higher or lower on a particular activity with their non-resident fathers. White adolescents stood out on their comparatively high incidence of playing sports with their fathers (24% vs 17% of Blacks and 15% of Hispanics), Black adolescents stood out on their high rate of attending religious services with their fathers (17% vs 11% of Whites), and Hispanic adolescents stood out with the highest percentage who have worked on a school project (16% vs 10% of Whites). King et al. (2004) showed that after controlling for father's education, mother's education, household income, family structure, marital birth, father's country of birth, and adolescent's age and gender in their study, White adolescents had the highest levels of overnight visits and levels of face-to-face, phone or letter contact, although differences were reduced. The higher incidence of playing sports among Whites was still evident in comparison to Hispanics, but was no longer significantly different from Blacks. At the multivariate level Blacks also exhibited a higher frequency of working on school projects with their fathers compared to Whites, and Hispanics were significantly more likely to talk about dating and about problems compared to Whites. Significantly, the addition of these controls (father's education, mother's education, household income, family structure, marital birth, father's country of birth, and adolescent's age and gender) increased differences in ratings of closeness to fathers, with Black adolescents reporting that they were closer to their non-resident father than White adolescents. With regards to the role of the non-resident father's education, King et al. (2004) showed that the father's level of education differentiated levels of involvement more so for Whites than for minority fathers (see also the discussion in the preceding section on the 'outcomes'). Whereas among highly educated fathers ethnic group differences were relatively minor, among less-educated fathers White fathers were the least involved with their children. What many studies have not taken into account, however, when predicting changes in father involvement following divorce or parental separation are levels of involvement before separation (Kelly & Emery, 2003), as many non-resident fathers were minimally involved even when they were co-resident (but see Whiteside & Becker, 2000).

Recent studies have started to explore not what predicts non-resident fathers' continuing involvement with their children, but what determines fathers' transition to non-residence in the first place. This is important given that many fathers are initially 'resident'. In the United States alone the majority (83%) of fathers reside with their biological children when those children are born (Bumpass & Lu, 2000). Gupta, Smock and Manning (2004) explored factors associated with US fathers' transition to non-residence in a sample of more than 1000 men who became fathers during the period from 1968 to 1997 and were resident with their biological children when those children were born. They found that the probability of non-residence decreased significantly as both fathers' and mothers' incomes increased, suggesting that women's incomes may have stabilising rather than disruptive effects on family life, as was previously suggested. Earlier, Johnson (2001) had shown that his sample of unmarried American fathers were more likely to be non-resident if they were not romantically involved with the child's mother. The sex composition of children has also been explored as a factor influencing divorce or fathers' transition to non-residence. As shown in Chapter 2, there is evidence from studies both in the United States (Morgan et al., 1988) and elsewhere (Bose & South, 2003) that families with a daughter have a higher divorce risk than families with a son. Morgan and colleagues, using retrospective US data from 1980, showed that having sons reduced the risk of divorce by about 9%. The explanation is that, in general, sons are simply more valued over daughters. Arnold (1997), who provided a detailed study of 44 countries with demographic and health surveys in the period from 1986 to 1995, found son preference in a range of different countries – demonstrating that such preferences do not emerge from a single set of historical and cultural experiences – and daughter preference only in the Caribbean region. Although more recent studies in industrialised countries (Diekmann & Schmidheiny, 2004) did not support the general hypothesis that sons contribute more to marital stability than daughters (as in industrialised countries people tend to have more egalitarian attitudes in general), there is some evidence that the sex composition of children does continue to be important. Andersson and Woldemicael (2001) found that Swedish parents of two children were less likely to divorce if they had one child of each sex – the preferred sex composition of children in Sweden.

Jaffee et al. (2001) explored how early childhood experiences could predict father's non-residence among the 'high-risk' group of young fathers. Using longitudinal data from the Dunedin Multidisciplinary Health and Development Study – a study of a New Zealand cohort of children born between 1 April 1972 and 31 March 1973 – they explored whether disadvantaged family background predicted both early (ages 14–26 years) and absent fatherhood. They found that being born to a teenage mother, the number of years spent living with a single parent, a history of conduct problems, initiation of sexual activity before age 16, and leaving school before age 16 all increased the likelihood of becoming a father at an early age. In addition, among those cohort members who had become fathers between the ages of 14 and 26, the amount of time a father spent living with his first-born child decreased significantly if the quality of his relationship with his own parents had been poor, if he initiated sexual activity before age 16, and if he had a history of conduct problems. Even after controlling for the father's age at the child's birth, poor parent–child relationship quality and a history of conduct problems remained significant predictors of the amount of time a young father lived with his first-born child. Jaffee et al. (2001) also found that, after controlling for marital status, young fathers who lived only some or none of the time with their child had lower socio-economic status, were unemployed for longer, were more residentially mobile, and had more children than fathers who lived full-time with their child. In addition, compared to young fathers who lived full-time with their child, young fathers who lived only some or none of the time with their child had higher scores on negative emotionality, reported more symptoms of anxiety, marijuana dependency and alcohol dependency, spent more months disabled by a mental health or drug problem, engaged in more types of criminal offences, had more criminal convictions, and reported more partner and child abuse.

Finally, in the United States McLanahan and Carlson (2002) moved from investigating individual- and family-level predictors of father's non-residence to reviewing the existing evidence on how public policies have affected childbearing and non-resident father involvement. They showed that efforts to encourage greater father involvement, by focusing almost exclusively on increasing absent fathers' child support payments, reaps only minimal benefits for poor children because absent fathers often have few resources and little incentive to make support payments. Similarly, efforts to increase the emotional involvement of unmarried fathers with their children have produced disappointing results, but there is some evidence that such programmes can make a difference when targeting fathers at the time of a child's birth (see also Chapter 2). In contrast, efforts focusing on preventing unwanted pregnancy among teen girls especially have met with some success (see also Plotnick et al., 2004), with those programmes seeking to alter adolescents' life opportunities in addition to providing education or family planning services holding the most promise.

In 2001 Ann Buchanan and I used data from 520 British teenagers with non-resident fathers who had taken part in our Families in the Millennium Study (see Study I in Chapter 3) to explore both the determinants of non-resident fathers' involvement and contact with their children, and children's psychological outcomes associated with involvement and contact (Flouri, under review – b).

STUDY I: NON-RESIDENT FATHERS' PARENTING: DETERMINANTS AND CHILDREN'S PSYCHOLOGICAL OUTCOMES

The original pool for this study was the 2218 sample of 11 to 18-year-old children who took part in the Families in the Millennium Study (for more information see Study I of Chapter 3). Of the 1091 parents who took part in the study, the number of non-resident fathers was 22 and therefore only the children's responses were used. For 2184 children there was information regarding the structure of their family. Of those, 520 reported that their father was not living with them. This was the study's sample size. In all, data from 277 (53.7%) boys and 239 (46.3%) girls were available. The mean age of the children was 13.36 (SD = 1.60) years. There was an even distribution of responses across the three schools, with 31% of the children coming from the inner-city school, 29.9% from the suburban school and

39.1% from the rural school. In all, 28.1% of the children reported that they were on free school meals. The majority were White British (68.3%), followed by Caribbean (4.6%), White and Black Caribbean (3.8%) and any other White (3.8%). The non-resident father figure was the biological father for the majority of the cases (83.2%), although for 13.4% of the cases it was the stepfather, and for 2.2% 'other'. For 98.1% of the cases the mother figure was the child's biological mother. For the highest proportion of children (31.3%) the parents were separated for 10 years or more. Only for 7.2% of the children had the parents never lived together, and 8.8% of the children reported that their parents were recently separated (a year or less ago). The majority (50.6%) saw their father at least once a week, although 7.8% of the children reported that they never see their father.

Because it was deemed insensitive to ask children whether their non-resident father paid child support, we did not include this question in the children's questionnaire. However, we asked the children to report on their non-resident father's involvement and frequency of contact. Father involvement and mother involvement were measured with the Hawkins et al. (2002) Modified Inventory of Father Involvement (IFI) (see Study I of Chapter 3). In this study the mean child-reported father involvement (ranging from 26 to 130) was 96.42 (SD = 27.21), and the mean child-reported mother involvement (ranging from 31 to 130) was 111.81 (SD = 16.72). Frequency of contact was assessed with one item asking children to state how often they see their non-resident father. Responses were: 'At least once a week' (1), 'At least once a month' (2), 'At least every 3 months' (3), 'At least every 6 months' (4), 'At least once a year' (5), 'Once every 2 years or less' (6), and 'Never' (7). The mean frequency of contact was 2.55 (SD = 2.05). Child-reported time since parental separation was 'A year or less' (1), '2–5 years' (2), '6–9 years' (3), '10 years or more' (4), and 'Never lived together' (5). The mean time since parents' separation was 3.03 (SD = 1.10). Children also stated whether their mother and father lived with another partner. In all, 53.2% of the children reported that their mother did not live with another partner, and 42.8% said that their father did not live with another partner. The child's characteristics that were included in this study were (see Study II of Chapter 2 and Study I of Chapter 3) child-reported gender, age and emotional and behavioural problems (assessed with the self-report version of the Strengths and Difficulties Questionnaire (SDQ)). As explained in Chapter 2, the established SDQ cut-off scores classify roughly 20% of children in community samples as borderline/abnormal. In this sample, 21.7% of the children were assessed to be in the borderline/abnormal range for emotional symptoms, 39.8% were in the borderline/abnormal range for conduct problems, 32.3% were in the borderline/abnormal range for hyperactivity, 27.1% were in the borderline/abnormal range for peer problems, 39.1% were in the borderline/abnormal range for prosocial behaviour, and 39.5% were in the borderline/abnormal range for total difficulties, suggesting that the children in this sample were at an elevated risk for emotional and behavioural problems. The socio-economic status of parents was assessed with receipt of free school meals. Children assessed interparental conflict by completing nine items from Grych et al.'s (1992) Children's Perception of Interparental Conflict Scale. In this sample, the mean interparental conflict (ranging from 9 to 27) was 14.15 (SD = 4.55). Cronbach's alpha was 0.85.

Results

As expected, frequency of visitation was related to father involvement ($r = 0.37$, $p < 0.001$) which, in turn, was related to mother involvement ($r = 0.43$, $p < 0.001$). Child-reported interparental conflict was negatively related to child-reported non-resident father's involvement ($r = -0.15$, $p < 0.05$), but was insignificantly related to child-reported non-resident father's low frequency of contact ($r = 0.01$, $p > 0.05$). At the bivariate level the only statistically significant correlates (apart from interparental conflict, father's contact, and mother's involvement) of non-resident father's involvement were child's prosocial behaviour ($r = 0.16$, $p < 0.01$), time since parents separated ($r = -0.14$, $p < 0.05$), and child's age ($r = -0.13$, $p < 0.05$). The only statistically significant correlates (apart from father involvement) of non-resident father's low frequency of visitation were child's emotional symptoms ($r = 0.10$, $p < 0.05$), child's hyperactivity ($r = 0.10$), and time since parents separated ($r = 0.30$, $p < 0.001$). Therefore although neither father involvement nor father contact was related to total difficulties, they were both related to specific SDQ subscales.

The results from the multiple linear regression analyses carried out to explore what predicts both non-resident fathers' frequency of contact and involvement with the child are shown in Figures 8.1 and 8.2. As can be seen, time elapsed since parental separation was the only factor that was (negatively) related to frequency of visitation. With regards to factors associated with a non-resident father's involvement, father involvement with the child was positively related to mother involvement and was negatively related to interparental conflict. Both regression models were significant ($F(8, 218) = 2.846$, $p < 0.01$, and $F(8, 183) = 6.613$, $p < 0.001$, respectively) but the amount of variance in father involvement and father contact explained by the variables in the models was quite modest (6% and 19%, respectively). Subsequent regression analyses (not shown here) were carried out to explore predictors of the nine IFI subscales, namely discipline, school encouragement, mother support, providing, talking together, praise, developing talents, reading support, and attentiveness.

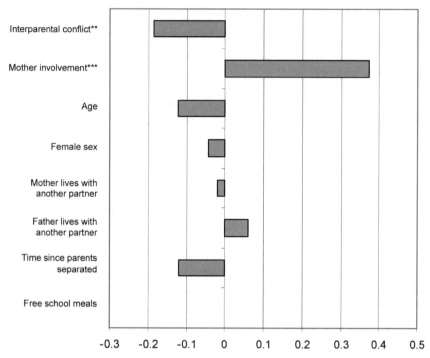

Figure 8.1 Standardised regression coefficients (β) predicting non-resident (biological or social) father's involvement ($N = 192$) (children's reports)
Notes: **$p < 0.01$; ***$p < 0.001$

Results showed that mother involvement predicted all nine aspects of father involvement. Interparental conflict was negatively associated with all but discipline. Age was inversely related to discipline, time and talking together, praise, reading and homework support, and attentiveness. Fathers who were not re-partnered were rated higher in reading and homework support (see Flouri, under review – b).

The next part of the study explored the role of non-resident father's involvement and non-resident father's contact in children's psychological outcomes as assessed with the Strengths and Difficulties Questionnaire (SDQ). Figure 8.3 shows the results of the multiple linear regression on the 25-item SDQ. As can be seen, the only factors significantly associated with children's emotional and behavioural well-being were mother involvement and low interparental conflict. The amount of the variance in emotional and behavioural problems was 19% and the regression model was statistically significant ($F(10, 139) = 4.466$, $p < 0.001$).

Next, the relationship between non-resident father's involvement and frequency of visitation and children's emotional and behavioural problems

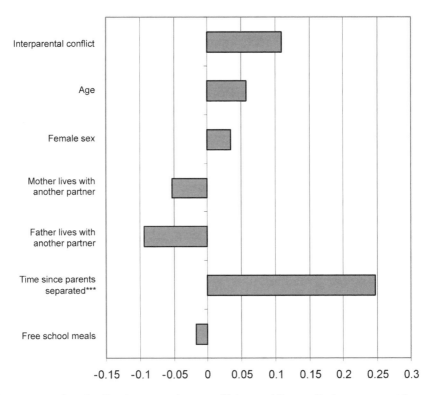

Figure 8.2 Standardised regression coefficients (β) predicting non-resident (biological or social) father's low frequency of visitation ($N = 278$) (children's reports)
Note: ***$p < 0.001$

in the borderline/abnormal range was explored. Figures 8.4 to 8.9 show the risk associated with each of the SDQ subscales.

SUMMARY AND CONCLUSIONS

This study used data from 520 British adolescents (whose biological or social father was not living with them) in order to explore factors associated with non-resident father contact and non-resident father involvement, and children's psychological outcomes associated with non-resident father contact and involvement. The study showed that, at both the bivariate and the multivariate level, neither non-resident father involvement nor non-resident father's frequency of visitation was related to the child's global emotional and behavioural well-being. Instead, what predicted the child's emotional and behavioural problems, adjusting for controls, was mother

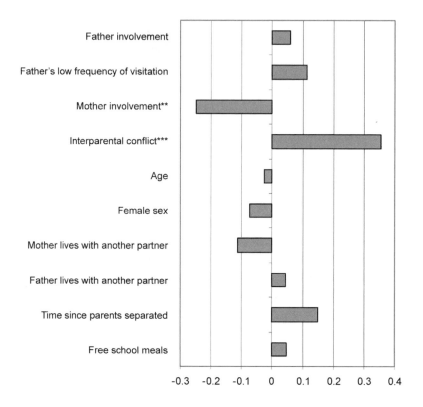

Figure 8.3 Standardised regression coefficients (β) predicting children's emotional and behavioural problems from non-resident (biological or social) father's involvement and contact ($N = 150$) (children's reports)
Notes: **$p < 0.01$; ***$p < 0.001$

involvement and interparental conflict. Looking at links between non-resident fathering and children's emotional and behavioural problems in the clinical range, father's frequency of contact was negatively related to conduct disorder, and father involvement was negatively related to severe peer problems.

Special caution should be exercised in generalising from these findings. To start with, as this study is cross-sectional it is not possible to establish causality. It may be, for example, that children fare better because their mothers are involved, or that mothers find it easier to get involved with well-adjusted children. With regards to the children's reports of their non-resident fathers, on the other hand, it is possible that children with non-

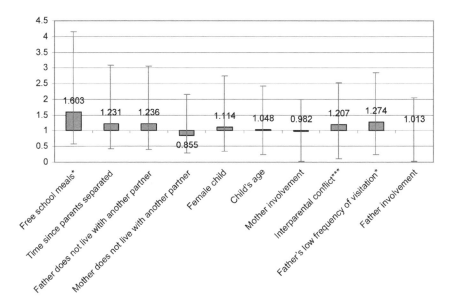

Figure 8.4 Odds ratios (OR) with 95% confidence intervals (95% CI) predicting children's severe total difficulties from non-resident (biological or social) father's involvement and contact (children's reports)
Notes: $^*p < 0.05$; $^{***}p < 0.001$

resident fathers may feel disadvantaged when they compare themselves with children from intact families and so they might choose to present their relationship with their non-resident father as better or worse than reality. Perhaps more importantly, this study did not ask whether these children received any child support from their non-resident fathers as children may not have known or may have considered such a question insensitive. However, it is quite likely that the positive effects of frequency of visitation for children's severe externalising behaviour problems observed in this study may be at least partly due to the payment of child support, as greater contact with fathers tends to be associated with more child support being paid. Child support, in turn, helps to move families out of income poverty which predicts children's externalising behaviour problems (see Chapter 4). In addition, the study did not look at the number and the type of changes that had occurred in both the father's and the mother's families. This is important, as many changes (e.g. remarriages, the introduction of step- and halfsiblings, changes in economic resources, geographical moves) occur in most separated families (Ahrons & Tanner, 2003). The study asked children only to report whether their resident mother and non-resident father lived with another partner or not, and so no information was available on these other factors affecting involvement, such as non-resident father's

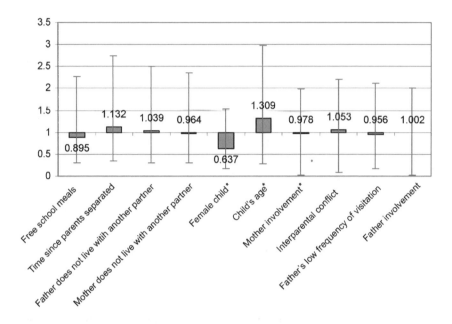

Figure 8.5   Odds ratios (OR) with 95% confidence intervals (95% CI) predicting children's severe prosocial behaviour problems from non-resident (biological or social) father's involvement and contact (children's reports)
Notes: $*p < 0.05$; $**p < 0.01$

geographical distance from the child and presence of new co-resident children. In addition, the children of the study were not asked to report on the regularity and duration of contact with their father, or if the father was absent for reasons other than the presumably romantic separation from the mother (work-related reasons, for example). Given that the reported father figure varied widely in this sample (recall that the non-resident father was the biological father for 83.2% of the children), it is reasonable to expect that the reasons for the father's non-residence (which determine father involvement) also varied widely. How father's non-residence was defined by the children might also have varied. Lin, Schaeffer, Seltzer and Tuschen (2004) showed that when children whose parents had divorced spend most nights with their mother, mothers are more likely than fathers to state that the children 'live with' their mother, suggesting that family researchers can no longer rely on simple questions to capture complex living arrangements. This study asked children to state who they lived with 'most of the time', but it did not differentiate between children with essentially 'two homes' and children who hardly ever see their father. Finally, the study explored predictors of non-resident father's frequency of face-to-face contact. Therefore, in this study, no contact meant no face-to-face contact rather

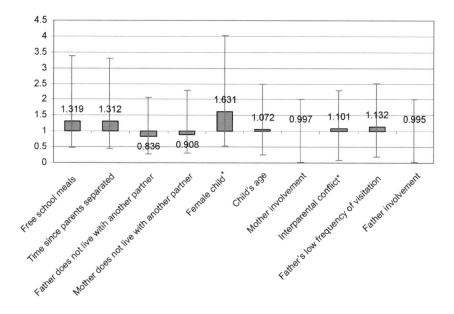

Figure 8.6 Odds ratios (OR) with 95% confidence intervals (95% CI) predicting children's severe emotional symptoms from non-resident (biological or social) father's involvement and contact (children's reports)
Note: *$p < 0.05$

than no communication of any kind (e.g. talking on the phone, e-mailing and letters). However, contact can vary along several dimensions apart from the nature of communication (face-to-face, or communication by telephone/e-mail/letter) such as frequency, regularity and continuity (Bradshaw, Stimson, Skinner & Williams, 1999). In this study duration and regularity of contact were similarly not assessed. Clearly, it is important to have all these limitations in mind when trying to generalise from the findings of this study.

In addition, this study did not test whether the relationship between non-resident father's involvement and children's psychological outcomes was stronger for boys or girls or when mother involvement was low or high (Amato, 1994). Finally, it did not explore if non-resident father's involvement was more strongly related to children's emotional and behavioural well-being when interparental conflict was low rather than high, which is significant given the evidence that, in high conflict, father

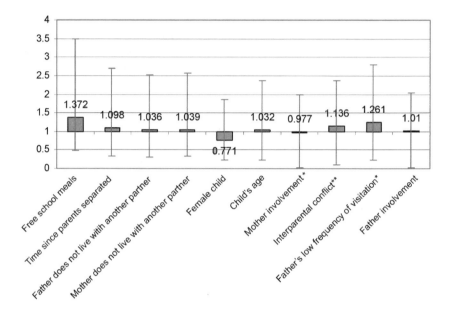

Figure 8.7 Odds ratios (OR) with 95% confidence intervals (95% CI) predicting children's conduct disorder from non-resident (biological or social) father's involvement and contact (children's reports)
Notes: *$p < 0.05$; **$p < 0.01$

involvement may not be beneficial for children (Buchanan, Hunt, Bretherton & Bream, 2001).

It is also important to consider several factors, not necessarily limitations, that set the context in which this study's findings should be seen. First, the age of the children should be considered, especially in light of the evidence that the effect of divorce is more harmful among younger children than among adolescents, whereas the converse is true in the case of remarriage (Hines, 1997). It seems that most children of disrupted families manifest emotional and behavioural problems during early childhood, which lessen with age, especially when they come into greater contact with the outside world in school and peer groups. This study also explored reports of adolescents of a wide range of ages (ages 11–18). Second, the study did not look at non-resident fathers' reports of children's emotional and behavioural problems and their perceived levels of involvement and contact. In this study, as mentioned above, it was not possible to use fathers' reports as only 22 non-resident fathers returned questionnaires. It would have been at the very least interesting to explore

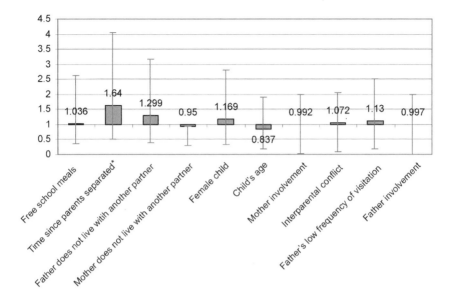

Figure 8.8   Odds ratios (OR) with 95% confidence intervals (95% CI) predicting children's hyperactivity disorder from non-resident (biological or social) father's involvement and contact (children's reports)
Note: *$p < 0.05$

these too, as non-resident fathers' reports of their parenting and their children's emotional and behavioural problems are generally different from mothers' and children's reports of non-resident fathers' parenting (Blackwell & Dawe, 2003) and children's emotional and behavioural problems (Luoma et al., 2004). Studies, however, generally suggest that requiring the non-resident father's participation in research screens out the more antisocial and socio-economically disadvantaged families (Pfiffner, McBurnett & Rathouz, 2001), which would, of course, make the sample of this study very selective. Third, it would also have been useful to explore the role of familial resources in this group of children in more detail in light of the evidence that it is their decline in father-absent families that explains children's worse emotional and behavioural outcomes. Ram and Hou (2003) showed that economic factors contributed a small part to the explanation of differences between children in intact and disrupted (step-parent or lone-parent) families in terms of their emotional and behavioural problems. Even in the case of cognitive outcomes, their contribution was not impressive. However, familial resources (in particular, parental depression, ineffective parenting and family dysfunction) were of high importance in explaining almost all

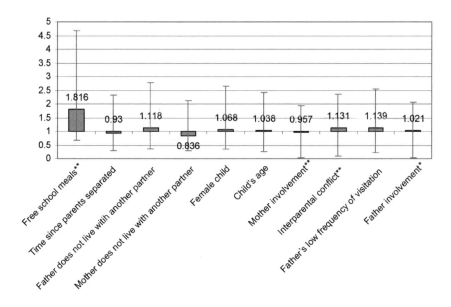

Figure 8.9 Odds ratios (OR) with 95% confidence intervals (95% CI) predicting children's severe peer problems from non-resident (biological or social) father's involvement and contact (children's reports)
Notes: *$p < 0.05$; **$p < 0.01$

emotional and behavioural outcomes, although their contribution to the explanation of cognitive outcomes was rather marginal. Although this study included measures such as mother and father involvement and interparental conflict which tap at least aspects of Ram and Hou's (2003) ineffective parenting and family disruption, it did not measure parental depression mainly because the children's rather than the parents' reports were used. Fourth, it should be remembered that time since parental separation varied widely in this study's children. Although for almost a third of children (31.3%) the parents were separated for 10 years or more, for 7.2% the parents never lived together, and for 8.8% the parents were separated for less than one year. In other words, this study considered together children who have presumably adjusted to their parents' separation, children with a very recent experience of parental separation, and children who may never have experienced family transitions. This variation is significant given that research suggests that children whose fathers never lived with them fare as well as children in two-parent families (MacCallum & Golombok, in press), and that separated families may stabilise by two (Hetherington & Kelly, 2002) or five (Ahrons & Tanner, 2003) years postdivorce, with several changes (such as remarriages, the introduction of step- and halfsiblings, changes in economic resources, geographical moves) occurring in most separated families within five years. This suggests that even if parents stabilise their personal, separation-related stress, the introduction of new relationships can result in imbalances that create new stresses with which children must cope. Finally, the quality of the relationship with the resident social father or stepfather for those children who reported that they live with their mother and her partner (46.8% of the sample) was not assessed. Although studies have shown that there is little association between the quality of the relationship children formed with their non-resident fathers and stepfathers (White & Gilbreth, 2001), more recent investigations have found that the associations between children's relationships with their non-resident fathers and their adjustment were stronger if the children were in single-mother families – that is, if the children had only one father figure, and no stepfather (Dunn et al., 2004). Related to this, and in contrast with previous research, this study did not find links between parents' presence of partnerships and children's adjustment. There is evidence, for instance, that although boys may benefit in the long run from the presence of a stepfather, girls show more problems in response to remarriage of the custodial mother (Hetherington et al., 1982). Conversely, boys have been found to be more prone to depressive symptoms when their non-resident father was remarried, and girls when their non-resident father was not remarried (Tulisalo & Aro, 2000). In this study neither the mother's nor the father's partnership status was related to children's emotional and behavioural well-being.

So what are the implications of this study's findings? The study showed that non-resident father's frequency of contact was negatively related only to children's conduct problems in the clinical range. What predicted emotional and behavioural well-being in school-aged children with non-resident fathers was the high level of mother involvement and the low level of interparental conflict. Taken together, these findings suggest that efforts should perhaps concentrate on reducing levels of conflict between the resident and the non-resident parent, rather than on encouraging non-resident fathers' contact, and on helping mothers to remain and be involved with their children. Encouraging non-resident fathers' contact, especially contact 'at all costs', has been criticised as putting pressure on mothers to concede too much 'for the sake of the children' to (in many cases) violent men (Radford, Hester, Humphries & Woodfield, 1997). Reviewing developments in the law's response to domestic violence in England, Radford et al. (1997) argued that within the family law, procedural and substantive changes have made it more difficult for women and children to break free from violent men: a contact presumption and focus upon agreements made 'for the sake of the children' through mediation/ conciliation frequently expose both women and children to 'intolerable risks' (p. 471). The consensus seems to be that the value of contact for children who have lived through domestic violence requires careful consideration.

CHAPTER 9

CONCLUSIONS

The task of this chapter is to bring together the main messages that have emerged from the preceding chapters. As research on fathering is usually motivated by concern for children's well-being, the obvious question is: Does 'good' fathering promote 'good' children's outcomes? The answer will have to be simply 'it depends'. It depends on what we mean by 'fathering' (and 'good' fathering, in particular), what children's outcomes we have in mind, and what groups of parents and children we look at.

'FATHERING' AND 'GOOD FATHERING'

Unlikely coalitions between feminist and fathers' rights interests have pushed during the last decade for more emphasis on fathering research. A key theoretical theme in the recent work with fathers is that fathering is undergoing a transition from 'ascribed' to 'achieved'. Ascribed fatherhood is a relationship rooted in the biological tie between father and child, and in the gendered division of labour between married parents, wherein fathers are breadwinners, disciplinarians and emotionally distanced, and mothers are nurturing carers. Slowly but increasingly, fathering is becoming an achieved social relationship, rooted in new expectations that fathers should engage with their children as physically and emotionally involved carers (Edwards, Bäck-Wiklund, Bak & Ribbens McCarthy, 2002). Others, however, have argued that even the belief that fathers should be involved (rather than just be 'present') often co-exists with the conviction that mothers are primarily responsible for the children. Families that claim to share childcare are often characterised by 'manager–helper' dynamics in which mothers are responsible for childcare and fathers simply help when asked, therefore also subscribing to the ideology of 'intensive motherhood' (Deutsch, 2001).

If we take the view that fathering is (among other things) the father's or the father figure's 'parenting', problems also lie with the definition of 'parenting'. For instance, many have challenged the construct validity of several operationalisations of aspects of parenting as parent-reported parenting *attitudes* – which are routinely used to infer quantity or (usually) quality of parenting – may not reflect actual parenting *behaviours* (Holden & Edwards, 1989). Furthermore, one might find it natural to conclude that, as 'maladaptive', 'inadequate', 'ineffective' or 'non-optimal' parenting is a risk factor for children's adverse psychological outcomes, so is 'bad' fathering. A problem with this, as explained in Chapter 1, is that terms like 'risk factors' or 'causal risk factors' are used liberally. A second problem lies with the much debated construct of 'bad', 'maladaptive', 'inadequate', 'ineffective' or 'non-optimal' parenting. Ever since Diana Baumrind's (1971) much cited work on parenting styles, numerous studies have shown, for instance, that children whose parents use authoritarian practices (e.g. value obedience, favour punitive and forceful measures, believe children should accept their parents' word for what is right, and do not encourage verbal give and take use) are more likely to have emotional and behavioural problems as this parenting style, for instance, impedes the development of autonomy and self-direction, by undermining autonomy and self-confidence and by contributing to feelings of personal distress and inadequacy (Barber, 1996). However, a recent line of work has shown that authoritarian childrearing attitudes are associated with family poverty or parental low socio-economic status (Furstenberg, Cook, Eccles, Elder & Sameroff, 1999), and so the link between authoritarian parenting and children's psychological maladjustment might be because low socio-economic status is associated with both. At the same time, questions have been raised about the ethnocentricity of the North American construct of authoritarian parenting as pertaining to minority ethnic groups (Wu et al., 2002) or to other cultures and countries, about the classicist assumption that parenting 'effects' findings from studies using middle-class suburban youths are generalisable to working-class (Hanson, McLanahan & Thomson, 1997) or upper-class (Luthar, 2003) children, and about the underlying right-wing ideology that parenting is another stick with which to beat the poor. Simons et al. (2002), for instance, exploring how the community context might influence the association between parenting and child outcomes, showed that although there was a positive relationship between caretaker corporal punishment and child conduct problems in communities where physical discipline was rare, there was no association between the two variables in communities where physical discipline was widely prevalent, suggesting that a particular parenting strategy may be more effective in some neighbourhood environments than others.

SUMMARISING THE RESEARCH

The studies presented in this book summarise the research I have carried out since 2000, both on father involvement and child outcomes, and on determinants of father involvement in Britain. Below is a summary of the main findings that were presented in Chapters 2 to 8.

Father involvement and children's mental health was explored in Chapter 3. The evidence presented there showed that father figure's involvement was negatively associated with adolescents' severe prosocial behaviour problems, and severe total difficulties (Study I), was positively related to adolescents' life satisfaction (Study V) and happiness (Study VI), and had more impact on decreasing emotional and behavioural problems in adolescence when the father figure was not the child's biological father than when he was (Study III). Study II, which explored links between retrospectively assessed father involvement and psychological distress in women, provided evidence for the protective role of father involvement in daughters' mental health problems: father involvement was negatively associated with adult daughters' psychological distress (Study II). Even when father involvement was measured prospectively and both sons' and daughters' adult psychological distress was assessed (Studies III and IV) the association between father involvement in adolescence and psychological distress in adult life was stronger for daughters than for sons (Study III), and the association between father involvement in childhood and psychological distress in adult life was significant only for daughters (Study IV).

Father involvement and children's academic achievement was explored in Chapter 4, which showed that, even after controlling for mother involvement, father involvement was significantly related to adolescents' academic motivation (Study II), but insignificantly related to adolescents' career maturity (Study III). Early father involvement predicted educational attainment in adult life in both genders (Study I) in the 1958 birth cohort but only in women (Study IV) in the 1970 birth cohort.

Father involvement and children's aggressive behaviour was explored in Chapter 5. Father involvement was negatively associated with trouble with the police in adolescence only in boys (Study I), but it was inversely related to peer aggression in both boys and girls (Study II). However, it was not associated with recovery from externalising behaviour problems (Study III).

Father involvement and children's family relationships was investigated in Chapter 6 which showed that although feelings of closeness to mother in adolescence were not related to levels of mother involvement in childhood, feelings of closeness to father were predicted from levels of earlier father involvement, especially for daughters, which suggests that feelings of closeness to fathers were 'earned', especially for girls.

Father involvement and children's social and economic outcomes was explored in Chapter 7. Early father involvement was not related to adult children's labour force participation, state benefits receipt, and subsidised housing, although it had a protective effect against an experience of homelessness in men from lower socio-economic groups (Study I). However, it was not related to either adolescent (Study II) or adult (Study III) children's survival (as opposed to self-expression) values.

Non-resident father's parenting and adolescent children's mental health outcomes was investigated in Chapter 8, which showed that neither father involvement nor level of contact was associated with children's global emotional and behavioural well-being. However, when children's emotional and behavioural problems were assessed as being in the clinical range or not, father's frequency of contact was negatively related to conduct disorder, and father involvement was negatively related to severe peer problems.

Factors associated with father involvement were explored in Chapters 2 and 8 which investigated the determinants of resident and non-resident father involvement, respectively. Father involvement in continuously intact two-parent biological families in the 1958 birth cohort was investigated in Study I, which showed that in all childhood sweeps (ages 7, 11 and 16) mother involvement was strongly and positively related to father involvement. In general, sons and psychologically adjusted children elicited higher levels of father involvement: fathers were more likely to both manage and 'be seen' with their sons than with their daughters, and with well-adjusted rather than 'difficult' children. Study II, which explored factors associated with father involvement in adolescents in 2001, also showed that children's self-esteem was positively associated with father involvement (although it is not clear if high self-esteem was the *cause* or the *result* (see Chapter 3) of high father involvement). Resident biological fathers were perceived by the children as the most involved and social fathers as the least involved. However, both child-reported and father-reported father involvement was not higher for boys than for girls. Chapter 8 showed that non-resident fathers' involvement with adolescent children was positively related to mother involvement and negatively related to interparental conflict. Time elapsed was the only factor that was (negatively) related to frequency of visitation at the multivariate level.

TOWARDS NEW DIRECTIONS

Coltrane (2001) argued that in the Unites States religious and free-market conservatives have successfully joined forces to promote public policies favouring married heterosexual parents over other household types by relying on specious comparisons between 'traditional' and 'non-traditional' families, and urged social scientists of all faiths to remember that they have a moral obligation to ensure that their research findings are not misinterpreted in the service of a narrow religious agenda, or inappropriately used to justify nostalgic exclusionary family policies. Despite this, neoconservative social scientists have claimed that fathers are essential to positive child development, and that responsible fathering is most likely to occur within the context of heterosexual marriage (Coltrane & Adams, 2003). Walker (2003) described how similar tensions in Britain have resulted in repeated calls in England and Wales for the reinstatement of traditional family values based on a two-biological-parent household, rather than for support for diverse household structures in which people can adapt to changes in postmodern family life. This position views the absence of fathers from postdivorce households as having particularly detrimental effects on child development, and children as the innocent victims of their parents' selfish behaviour. Both Coltrane and Adams (2003) and Walker (2003) showed how political debates about marriage and divorce are at their most intense when effects on children are discussed, with deeply held moral, religious and political views dominating the agenda. In contrast to the neo-conservative perspective, research on gay and lesbian couples has shown that neither a mother nor a father is essential (Golombok et al., 1997, 2003; Silverstein & Auerbach, 1999). Similarly, research with divorced (Rodgers & Rose, 2002), never-married (Biblarz & Raftery, 1999) and remarried parents (Dunn, Deater-Deckard, Pickering, O'Connor & Golding, 1998), as well as research with multigenerational households (DeLeire & Kalil, 2002), has found that a wide variety of family structures can support positive child outcomes. In an article that generated a long and heated debate, Silverstein and Auerbach (1999) argued that children need at least one responsible, caretaking adult who has a positive emotional connection to them, and with whom they have a consistent relationship. Because of the emotional and practical stress involved in childrearing, a family structure that includes more than one such adult is more likely to contribute to positive child outcomes. Silverstein and Auerbach (1999) showed that neither the sex of the adult(s) nor the biological relationship to the child has emerged as a significant variable in predicting positive development. One, none, or both of those adults could be a father [or mother]. Instead, it was the stability of the emotional connection and the predictability of the caretaking relationship that were the significant variables predicting positive child adjustment.

Others have taken the view that marriage is a panacea not only for children but for women as well, despite evidence showing that although the economic benefits of marriage may be especially strong among women from disadvantaged families, for women who marry but later divorce, poverty rates exceed those of never-married women (Lichter, Graefe &

Brown, 2003), or evidence showing that married stepfathers provide limited benefit for adolescents when contrasted with single-mother families (Manning & Lamb, 2003). Although there is emerging evidence that current family structure is not as important as family stability and fluidity (Hao & Xie, 2001) in determining child outcomes, and that it is not unreasonable to expect that the idea that a child might have three legal parents, possibly with different responsibilities, should not be rejected out of hand (Vonk, 2004), systematic efforts are being made to help to promote a moral view of the superiority of the two married heterosexual parent families (Coltrane & Adams, 2003).

At the other end, the importance of individual differences in parenting has been questioned by some (Harris, 1998) in recent years, and others have argued that, except for children who are raised in extreme circumstances (e.g. abuse, neglect), individual differences in caregiving contribute little to individual differences in children's development (Scarr, 1997). A more conservative line of research suggests that there is merit in examining the extent to which neighbourhood distress and residential mobility attenuate the apparent effects of family structure, and changes therein, on child outcomes. Crowder and Teachman (2004) in the United States showed that family composition and change helped to shape the risk of pregnancy and school dropout in adolescents, in part by affecting the frequency of residential mobility and the types of neighbourhoods to which young people are exposed, suggesting that, at the very least, the apparent direct link between adolescent outcomes and both childhood living arrangements and changes in these living arrangements may have been overstated in some past research. Along similar lines, a nationwide study of 2-year-old twins by Caspi, Taylor, Moffitt and Plomin (2000) in Britain showed that children in deprived neighbourhoods were at increased risk for emotional and behavioural problems over and above any genetic liability. In Caspi et al.'s (2000) study, environmental factors shared by members of a family accounted for 20% of the population variation in children's behaviour problems, and neighbourhood deprivation accounted for 5% of this family-wide environmental effect. Research with Dutch (Schneiders et al., 2003) and Canadian (Curtis, Dooley & Phipps, 2004) samples, for example, has also confirmed that neighbourhood disadvantage is associated with children's adjustment problems. Others have highlighted the importance of developing theoretical arguments that move beyond assumptions regarding differences in parenting practices and family socialisation process to place importance on peer groups (Criss, Pettit, Bates, Dodge & Lapp, 2002; Harris, 1998) and broader contextual conditions. For example, Sampson, Morenoff and Gannon-Rowley (2002), who assessed the importance of 'neighbourhood effects', moved beyond traditional characteristics such as concentrated poverty to evaluate the salience of social-interactional and institutional mechanisms (such as neighbourhood ties, social control, mutual trust, institutional resources, disorder and routine activity patterns) in explaining neighbourhood-level variations in several child outcomes. Alternative methodological strategies that distinguish between child-specific and family-wide effects, such as multilevel modelling, may offer important advantages over the methods customarily used in behavioural genetics. For example, O'Connor et al. (2001) found that a significant and sizeable amount of variation in children's adjustment could be attributed to family-level effects, and that the amount of family-level effects was greater in high-risk settings, such as lone-parent and complex stepfamilies.

On the other hand, research that continues to concentrate on the role of the family-level characteristics in children's outcomes warns that several empirical studies aggressively push ideologies and political agendas. Recently, MacCallum and Golombok (in press), who assessed the social and emotional development of children raised in fatherless (lesbian or single heterosexual mother) families, showed that the absence of a father in the home from the outset did not seem to have negative consequences for the children, and that the sexual orientation of the mother did not influence the parent–child interaction or the socio-emotional development of the child. Others have relatedly argued that one should not lose sight of the fact that claims about the necessity of non-resident father's contact and involvement at all costs echo fears, such as those voiced since the mid-1990s by the self-proclaimed 'fatherhood responsibility movement', that fathers are being marginalised. Gavanas (2004) argued that the 'fatherhood responsibility movement', broken into the 'pro-marriage' wing which sees marriage as the key to solving all social problems, and the 'fragile family' wing which worries about unemployment, racism and discrimination, seeks to re-establish the necessity of men in families by converging on three long-standing and overlapping arenas for masculinisation: heterosexuality, sport and religion.

What many increasingly recognise, however, is that there is considerable diversity of children's outcomes in two-parent families, as well as diversity of children's outcomes in lone-parent families (Amato, 2003), with studies informed by behavioural genetics actually reminding us that even children in the same family are sometimes very different in term of outcomes (Plomin, Asbury & Dunn, 2001). O'Connor, Caspi, DeFries and Plomin (2003) showed recently that the association between parental separation and children's psychological and emotional and social adjustment may not be entirely environmental in origin. Genetic vulnerability was accentuated by major psychosocial stresses, which may partly explain the wide individual differences in children's adjustment to family transitions. Several other investigations in this regard have demonstrated that family environments are not, by definition, shared. Children are treated differently by their parents – especially in stepfamilies (Mekos, Hetherington & Reiss, 1996) – or may experience their parents' behaviour differently (Turkheimer & Waldron, 2000), and differential parental treatment is related to children's problem behaviour (Reiss et al., 1995). Tamrouti-Makkink, Dubas, Gerris and Aken (in press), who explored the effect of both absolute levels of fathers' and mothers' warmth and coercive control and parents' differential treatment in Dutch adolescents' externalising and internalising problems, found that differential parental treatment was uniquely associated with child problem behaviour above the absolute level of parenting for girls and early-born children in mixed-gender sibling pairs, and suggested that any examination of the effects of differential treatment should not be undertaken without considering the gender and birth rank of the sibling pairs. In particular, Tamrouti-Makkink et al. (in press) showed that although father's warmth was related to both internalising and externalising problem behaviours for adolescents in same-gender sibling pairs, for adolescents in mixed-gender sibling pairs absolute levels of father's warmth were only related to the externalising problems of early-borns, whereas there was no association found between father's warmth and later-borns' problem behaviours. Tamrouti-Makkink et al. (in press) argued that studies that report a clear negative relation between both maternal and paternal warmth and adolescent problem behaviour have either combined mothers' and fathers' parenting behaviours or did not examine the role of gender of the child and/or the sibling, which suggests that even research on absolute levels of parenting has ignored the role of family members' gender. They also found differential treatment-adjustment links among mixed-gender pairs (although not among same-gender pairs): differential parental coercive control was linked to internalising problems in girls but not in boys in mixed-gender sibling pairs. Although 'parenting' studies increasingly differentiate between father's and mother's parenting in exploring children's outcomes, they still tend not to explore the role of differential parental treatment or the role of the sibship's gender composition. A lot more research has been carried out to explore if the parent–child relationship is child specific within families, which is consistent with theories regarding bi-directional parent and child effects in socialisation (see Deater-Deckard & Petrill, 2004, for a description of some of these studies).

Furthermore, although there has been a slow but steady move away from 'main effects' theorising about the role of parenting (in child-specific designs) in child outcomes towards documenting mechanisms of influence, empirical studies still do not adequately justify which parenting factors are specific to the development of which child outcomes, and how they exert their influence. A lot of the research in developmental psychopathology, in general, still tends to consider equifinality (different stressors lead to the same outcome) and multifinality (the same (or similar) stressors lead to multiple outcomes) rather than specificity (the particular parenting factor that is *uniquely* related to a specific child outcome) (McMahon, Grant, Compas, Thurm & Ey, 2003).

CONCLUSIONS

As mentioned in Chapter 1, recent studies on fathering and children's outcomes are starting to define not only the child outcomes and the fathering dimensions but also the child and father populations with greater precision. Recent studies, for instance, are starting to pay attention to groups of fathers such as poor fathers (Gavin et al., 2002), gay fathers (Anderssen, Amlie & Ytteroy, 2002), stepfathers (Dunn, 2002), social fathers (Jayakody & Kalil, 2002), single fathers (Leinonen et al., 2003b), teen fathers (Xie, Cairns & Cairns, 2001), ethnic minority fathers (Hofferth, 2003; King et al., 2004), fathers of children born to teenage mothers (Ekéus & Christensson, 2003), substance-abusing fathers (Fals-Stewart et al., 2004) and mentally ill fathers (Connell & Goodman, 2002). Studies are also starting to explore differences in fathers' behaviours between countries that differ not only in terms of vaguely described 'culture' but also in terms of state support to families (e.g. Bernhardt & Goldscheider, 2001; Clarke, Cooksey & Verropoulou, 1998; Edwards, Bäck-Wiklund, Bak & Ribbens McCarthy, 2002; Whitehouse, 2002). In terms of the empirical studies' analytic strategy, there has been a noticeable shift of focus from simply reporting the absence or presence of linear effects of 'fathering' to exploring mechanisms of influence or mediating processes, and effect moderators. The idea that particular factors (such as, for example, biological father involvement in two-parent continuously intact families) may be linked with particular child outcomes only in the presence of particular moderating and mediating processes fits with the concept of specificity in developmental psychology which, however, has not generally been taken on board (McMahon et al., 2003). In addition, researchers sometimes assume that father involvement effects in one child adjustment domain might be relevant across theoretically dissimilar child adjustment domains (see Luthar, Cicchetti & Becker, 2000, for a discussion).

The studies described in this book showed that father involvement was sometimes associated with 'good' children's outcomes (e.g. it was positively related to happiness and academic motivation) and sometimes unrelated to 'good' children's outcomes (e.g. early father involvement was not related to career maturity in adolescence, or to labour force participation, state benefits receipt and subsidised housing in adult life). But more importantly, they showed that certain aspects of father involvement in certain groups of fathers was associated with certain outcomes in certain groups of children – for example, father involvement was associated with low risk for delinquency (Chapter 5) in sons (but not in daughters); father's interest in the child's education was related to adult daughters' (but not adult sons') educational attainment in adult life (Chapter 4); and father involvement protected against an experience of homelessness in adult sons (but not in daughters) from low (but not high) socio-economic groups (Chapter 7). Perhaps this is the most important conclusion.

REFERENCES

Abidin, R.R. & Brunner, J.F. (1995). Development of a parenting alliance inventory. *Journal of Clinical Child Psychology*, 24, 31–40.

Abidin, R.R. (1990). *Parenting Stress Index: Short form manual.* Charlottesville: Pediatric Psychology Press.

Abu, H. & Maher, M. (2000). A structural model of attitudes towards school subjects, academic aspiration and achievement. *Educational Psychology*, 20, 75–84.

Accordino, D.B., Accordino, M.P. & Slaney, R.B. (2000). An investigation of perfectionism, mental health, achievement, and achievement motivation in adolescents. *Psychology in the Schools*, 37, 535–545.

Achenbach, T.M. (1995). Epidemiological applications of multiaxial empirically based assessment and taxonomy. In F.C. Verhulst & H.M. Koot (eds), *The epidemiology of child and adolescent psychopathology* (pp. 22–41). Oxford: Oxford University Press.

Ackerman, B.P., Brown, E.D. & Izard, C.E. (2004). The relations between persistent poverty and contextual risk and children's behavior in elementary school. *Developmental Psychology*, 40, 367–377.

Ackerman, B.P., Schoff, K., Levinson, K., Youngstrom, E. & Izard, C.E. (1999). The relations between cluster indexes of risk and promotion and the problem behaviours of 6- and 7-year-old children from economically disadvantaged families. *Developmental Psychopathology*, 6, 1355–1366.

Ahrons, C.R. & Tanner, J.L. (2003). Adult children and their fathers: Relationship changes 20 years after parental divorce. *Family Relations*, 52, 340–351.

Albrecht, S.L. (1979). Correlates of marital happiness among the remarried. *Journal of Marriage and Family*, 41, 857–867.

Aldous, J. & Mulligan, G.M. (2002). Fathers' child care and children's behavior problems. *Journal of Family Issues*, 23, 624–647.

Allen, S.F. (2003). Working parents with young children: Cross-national comparisons of policies and programmes in three countries. *International Journal of Social Welfare*, 12, 261–273.

Almeida, D.M. & Galambos, N.L. (1991). Examining father involvement and the quality of father–adolescent relations. *Journal of Research on Adolescence*, 1, 155–172.

Almeida, D.M., Wethington, E. & McDonald, D.A. (2001). Daily variation in paternal engagement and negative mood: Implications for emotionally supportive and conflictual interactions. *Journal of Marriage and Family*, 63, 417–429.

Amato, P.R. (1993). Children's adjustment to divorce: Theories, hypotheses, and empirical support. *Journal of Marriage and Family*, 55, 23–38.

Amato, P.R. (1994). Father–child relations, mother–child relations, and offspring psychological well-being in early adulthood. *Journal of Marriage and Family*, 56, 1031–1042.

Amato, P.R. (1999). Children of divorced parents as young adults. In E.M. Hetherington (ed.), *Coping with divorce, single parenting, and remarriage: A risk and resilience perspective* (pp. 147–164). Mahwah, NJ: Lawrence Erlbaum.

Amato, P.R. (2000). The consequences of divorce for adults and children. *Journal of Marriage and Family*, 62, 1269–1287.

Amato, P.R. (2003). Reconciling divergent perspectives: Judith Wallerstein, quantitative family research, and children of divorce. *Family Relations*, 52, 332–339.

Amato, P.R. & Gilbreth, J.G. (1999). Nonresident fathers and children's well-being: A meta-analysis. *Journal of Marriage and Family*, 61, 557–574.

Amato, P.R. & Keith, B. (1991). Parental divorce and the well-being of children: A meta-analysis. *Psychological Bulletin*, 100, 26–46.

Amato, P.R. & Rezac, S. (1994). Contact with nonresident parents, interparental conflict, and children's behaviour. *Journal of Family Issues*, 15, 191–207.

Amato, P.R. & Sobolewski, J.M. (2001). The effects of divorce and marital discord on adult children's psychological well-being. *American Sociological Review*, 66, 900–921.

American Psychiatric Association (1987). *Diagnostic and Statistical Manual of Mental Disorders, 3rd edition, revised (DSM-III-R)*. Washington, DC: American Psychiatric Association.

American Psychiatric Association (1994). *Diagnostic and Statistical Manual of Mental Disorders*, 4th edition. Washington, DC: American Psychiatric Association.

Anderssen, N., Amlie, C. & Ytteroy, E.A. (2002). Outcomes for children with lesbian or gay parents: A review of studies from 1978 to 2000. *Scandinavian Journal of Psychology*, 43, 335–351.

Andersson, G. & Woldemicael, G. (2001). Sex composition of children as a determinant of marriage disruption and marriage formation: Evidence from Swedish register data. *Journal of Population Research*, 18, 143–153.

Argys, L.M., Peters, H.E., Brooks-Gunn, J. & Smith, J.R. (1998). The impact of child support on cognitive outcomes of young children. *Demography*, 35, 159–173.

Arnold, F. (1997). *Gender preferences for children*. Demographic and Health Surveys Comparative Studies No. 23.

Atkinson, T., Cantillon, B., Marlier, E. & Nolan, B. (2002). *Social indicators: The EU and social inclusion*. Oxford: Oxford University Press.

Baer, J. (1999). The effects of family structure and SES on family processes in early adolescence. *Journal of Adolescence*, 22, 341–354.

Baldry, A.C. & Farrington, D.P. (2000). Bullies and delinquents: Personal characteristics and parental styles. *Journal of Community and Applied Social Psychology*, 10, 17–31.

Bandura, A. (2001). Social cognitive theory: An agentic perspective. *Annual Review of Psychology*, 52, 1–26.

Barber, B.K. (1996). Parental psychological control: Revisiting a neglected construct. *Child Development*, 67, 3296–3319.

Barnett, R.C., Marshall, N.L. & Pleck, J.H. (1992). Adult-son–parent relationships and their associations with son's psychological distress. *Journal of Family Issues*, 13, 505–525.

Bassuk, E.L., Buckner, J.C., Weinreb, L.F., Browne, A., Bassuk, S.S., Dawson, R. & Perloff, J.N. (1997). Homelessness in female-headed families: Childhood and adult risk and protective factors. *American Journal of Public Health*, 87, 241–248.

Baumrind, D. (1971). Current patterns of parental authority. *Developmental Psychology*, 4, 1–103.

Bebbington, P.E., Dunn, G., Jenkins, R., Lewis, G., Brugha, T., Farrell, M. & Meltzer, H. (1998). The influence of age and sex on the prevalence of depressive symptoms: Report from the national study of psychiatric morbidity. *Psychological Medicine*, 28, 9–19.

Belk, R.W. (1985). Materialism: Trait aspects of living in the material world. *Journal of Consumer Research*, 12, 265–280.

Bell, R.Q. & Harper, L.V. (1977). *Child effects on adults*. Lincoln: University of Nebraska Press.

Bellair, P.E. & Roscigno, V.J. (2000). Local labor-market opportunity and adolescent delinquency. *Social Forces*, 78, 1509–1538.

Belsky, J. (1984). The determinants of parenting: A process model. *Child Development*, 55, 83–96.

Belt, W. & Abidin, R.R. (1996). The relation of childhood abuse and early parenting experiences to current marital quality in a nonclinical sample. *Child Abuse and Neglect*, 20, 1019–1030.

Benzeval, M. (1998). The self-reported health status of lone parents. *Social Science and Medicine*, 46, 1337–1353.

Berdondini, L. & Smith, P.K. (1996). Cohesion and power in the families of children involved in bully/victim problems at school: An Italian replication. *Journal of Family Therapy*, 18, 99–102.

Bernhardt, E.M. & Goldscheider, F.K. (2001). Men, resources, and family living: The determinants of union and parental status in the United States and Sweden. *Journal of Marriage and Family*, 63, 793–803.

Biblarz, T.J. & Raftery, A.E. (1999). Family structure, educational attainment, and socio-economic success: Rethinking the 'pathology of matriarchy'. *American Journal of Sociology*, 105, 321–365.

Biller, H.B. & Lopez Kimpton, J. (1997). The father and the school-aged child. In M.E. Lamb (ed.), *The role of the father in child development* (pp. 143–161). New York: John Wiley & Sons.

Bjarnason, T., Andersson, B., Choquet, M., Elekes, Z., Morgan, M. & Rapinett, G. (2003). Alcohol culture, family structure and adolescent alcohol use: Multilevel modeling of frequency of heavy drinking among 15–16 year old students in 11 European countries. *Journal of Studies on Alcohol*, 64, 200–208.

Bjarnason, T., Davidaviciene, A.G., Miller, P., Nociar, A., Pavlakis, A. & Stergar, E. (2003). Family structure and adolescent cigarette smoking in eleven European countries. *Addiction*, 98, 815–824.

Bjoerkqvist, K., Lagerspetz, K.M. & Kaukiainen, A. (1992). Do girls manipulate and boys fight? Developmental trends in regard to direct and indirect aggression. *Aggressive Behavior*, 18, 117–127.

Björkqvist, K., Österman, K. & Kaukiainen, A. (1992) The development of direct and indirect aggressive strategies in males and females. In K. Björkqvist & P. Niemelä (eds), *Of mice and women: Aspects of female aggression* (pp. 51–64). San Diego, CA: Academic Press.

Black, M.M., Dubowitz, H. & Starr, R.H. (1999). American fathers in low income, urban families: Development, behavior, and home environment of their three-year-old children. *Child Development*, 70, 967–978.

Blackwell, A. & Dawe, F. (2003). *Non-resident parental contact*. London: Office for National Statistics.

Blackwell, L. (2003) Gender and ethnicity at work: Occupational segregation and disadvantage in the 1991 British Census. *Sociology*, 37, 713–731.

Blair, S.L., Wenk, D. & Hardesty, C. (1994). Marital quality and paternal involvement: Interconnections of men's spousal and paternal roles. *Journal of Men's Studies*, 2, 221–237.

Blankenhorn, D. (1995). *Fatherless America: Confronting our most urgent social problem*. New York: Basic Books.

Blascovich, J. & Tomaka, J. (1991). Measures of self-esteem. In J.P. Robinson, P.R. Shaver & L.S. Wrightman (eds), *Measures of personality and social psychological attitudes* (pp. 115–160). San Diego, CA: Academic Press.

Blau, P. & Duncan, O.D. (1967). *The American occupational structure*. New York: John Wiley & Sons.

Bond, R. & Saunders, P. (1999). Routes of success: Influences on the occupational attainment of young British males. *British Journal of Sociology*, 50, 217–249.

Bonney, J.F., Kelley, M.L. & Levant, R.F. (1999). A model of father's behavioral involvement in child care in dual-earner families. *Journal of Family Psychology*, 13, 401–415.

Bos, H.M.W., van Balen, F. & van den Boom, D.C. (2004). Experience of parenthood, couple relationship, social support, and child-rearing goals in planned lesbian mother families. *Journal of Child Psychology and Psychiatry*, 45, 755–764.

Bose, S. & South, S.J. (2003). Sex composition of children and marital disruption in India. *Journal of Marriage and Family*, 65, 996–1006.

Bowlby, J. (1982). Attachment and loss: Retrospect and prospect. *American Journal of Orthopsychiatry*, 52, 664–678.

Bradbury, T.N., Fincham, F.D. & Beach, S.R.H. (2000). Research on nature and determinants of marital satisfaction: A decade in review. *Journal of Marriage and Family*, 62, 964–980.

Bradshaw, J. & Finch, N. (2003). Overlaps in dimensions of poverty. *International Journal of Social Policy*, 32, 513–525.

Bradshaw, J. & Millar, J. (1991). *Lone parent families in the UK: DSS Report 6*. London: The Stationery Office.

Bradshaw, J., Stimson, C., Skinner, C. & Williams, J. (1999). *Absent fathers?* London: Routledge.

Bronfenbrenner, U. (1979). *The ecology of human development: Experiments by nature and design*. Cambridge, MA: Harvard University Press.

Brook, J.S. & Newcomb, M.D. (1995). Childhood aggression and unconventionality: Impact on later academic achievement, drug use, and workforce involvement. *Journal of Genetic Psychology*, 156, 393–410.

Brown, A. & Bassuk, S.S. (1997). Intimate violence in the lives of homeless and poor housed women: Prevalence and patterns in an ethnically diverse sample. *American Journal of Orthopsychiatry*, 67, 261–278.

Brunod, R. & Cook-Darzens, S. (2002). Men's roles and fatherhood in French Caribbean families: A multi-systemic 'resource' approach. *Clinical Child Psychology and Psychiatry*, 7, 559–569.

Buchanan, A. & Flouri, E. (2001). Recovery after age 7 from externalizing behavior problems: The role of risk and protective factors. *Children and Youth Services Review*, 23, 899–914.

Buchanan, A., Flouri, E. & Ten Brinke, J. (2002). Emotional and behavioral problems in childhood and distress in adult life: Risk and protective factors. *Australian and New Zealand Journal of Psychiatry*, 36, 521–527.

Buchanan, A., Hunt, J., Bretherton, H. & Bream, V. (2001). *Families in conflict: Perspectives of children and parents on the Family Court Welfare Service*. Bristol: Policy Press.

Buchanan, A., Ten Brinke, J. & Flouri, E. (2000). Parental background, social disadvantage, public 'care', and psychological problems in adolescence and adulthood. *Journal of the American Academy of Child and Adolescent Psychiatry*, 39, 1415–1423.

Bullock, H.E. (1995). Class acts: Middle-class responses to the poor. In B. Lott & D. Maluso (eds), *The social psychology of interpersonal discrimination* (pp. 118–159). New York: Guilford.

Bumpass L. & Lu, H.H. (2000). Trends in cohabitation and implications for children's family contexts in the United States. *Population Studies*, 54, 29–41.

Burghes, A., Clarke, L. & Cronin, N. (1997). *Fathers and fatherhood in Britain*. Occasional Paper 23. London: Family Policy Centre.

Burns, A. & Dunlop, R. (1998). Parental divorce, parent–child relations, and early adult relationships: A longitudinal Australian study. *Personal Relationships*, 5, 393–407.

Burroughs, J.E. & Rindfleisch, A. (2002). Materialism and well-being: A conflicting values perspective. *Journal of Consumer Research*, 29, 348–370.

Bussell, D.A., Neiderhiser, J.M., Pike, A., Plomin, R., Simmens, S., Howe, G.W., Hetherington, E.M., Carroll, E. & Reiss, D. (1999). Adolescents' relationships to siblings and mothers: A multivariate genetic analysis. *Developmental Psychology*, 35, 1248–1259.

Butler, N., Despotidou, S. & Shepherd, P. (1980). *1970 British Cohort Study: Ten-year follow-up.* London: Social Statistics Research Unit, City University.

Bynner, J. (1998). Education and family components of identity in the transition from school to work. *International Journal of Behavioral Development,* 22, 29–53.

Bynner, J. & Joshi, H. (2002). Equality and opportunity in education: Evidence from the 1958 and 1970 birth cohort studies. *Oxford Review of Education,* 28, 405–425.

Cabrera, N., Moore, K., Bronte-Tinkew, J., Halle, T., West, J., Brooks-Gunn, J., Reichman, N., Teitler, J., Ellingsen, K., Nord, C.W. & Boller, K. (2004). The DADS initiative: measuring father involvement in large-scale surveys. In R.D. Day & M.E. Lamb (eds), *Conceptualizing and measuring father involvement* (pp. 417–452). Mahwah, NJ: Lawrence Erlbaum.

Cabrera, N.J., Tamis-LeMonda, S., Bradley, R.H., Hofferth, S. & Lamb, M.E. (2000). Fatherhood in the twenty-first century. *Child Development,* 71, 127–136.

Caputo, R.K. (1997). Escaping poverty and becoming self-sufficient. *Journal of Sociology and Social Welfare,* 24, 5–23.

Carlson, M.J. & McLanahan, S.S. (2001). *Fragile families, father involvement, and public policy.* Working Paper #01-24-FF. Center for Research on Child Wellbeing.

Carson, J.L. & Parke, R.D. (1996). Reciprocal negative affect in parent–child interactions and children's peer competency. *Child Development,* 67, 2217–2226.

Caspi, A., Taylor, A., Moffitt, T.E. & Plomin, R. (2000). Neighborhood deprivation affects children's mental health: Environmental risks identified in a genetic design. *Psychological Science,* 11, 338–342.

Caspi, A., Wright, B.R.E., Moffitt, T.E. & Silva, P.A. (1998). Early failure in the labor market: Childhood and adolescent predictors of unemployment in the transition to adulthood. *American Sociological Review,* 63, 424–451.

Chang, L., Schwartz, D., Dodge, K.A. & McBride-Chang, C. (2003). Harsh parenting in relation to child emotion regulation and aggression. *Journal of Family Psychology,* 17, 598–606.

Chen, Z.Y. & Kaplan, H.B. (2003). School failure in early adolescence and status attainment in middle adulthood: A longitudinal study. *Sociology of Education,* 76, 110–127.

Christiansen, S.L. & Palkovitz, R. (2001). Why the 'good provider' role still matters: Providing as a form of paternal involvement. *Journal of Family Issues,* 22, 84–106.

Christophers, U., Stoney, S., Whetton, C., Lines, A. & Kendall, L. (1993). *Measure of Guidance Impact (MGI): User Manual.* London: National Foundation for Education Research.

Chung, Y.B., Baskin, M.L. & Case, A.B. (1999). Career development of Black males: Case studies. *Journal of Career Development,* 25, 161–171.

Churchill, G.A. Jr & Moschis, G.P. (1979). Television and interpersonal influences on adolescent consumer learning. *Journal of Consumer Research,* 6, 23–35.

Clarkberg, M. (1999). The price of partnering: The role of economic well-being in young adults' first union experiences. *Social Forces,* 77, 945–968.

Clarke, L., Cooksey, E.C. & Verropoulou, G. (1998). Fathers and absent fathers: Sociodemographic similarities in Britain and the United States. *Demography,* 35, 217–228.

Clarke, L. & O'Brien, M. (2004). British research and policy evidence. In R.D. Day & M.E. Lamb (eds), *Conceptualizing and measuring father involvement* (pp. 39–60). Mahwah, NJ: Lawrence Erlbaum.

Clarke-Stewart, K.A. & Hayward, C. (1996). Advantages of father custody and contact for the psychological well-being of school-aged children. *Journal of Applied Developmental Psychology,* 17, 239–270.

Clarke-Stewart, K.A., Vandell, D.L., McCartney, K., Owen, M.T. & Booth, C. (2000). Effects of parental separation and divorce on very young children. *Journal of Family Psychology,* 14, 304–326.

Cohen, P., Brook, J.S., Cohen, J., Velez, C. & Garcia, C. (1991). Common and uncommon pathways to adolescent. In L. Robins & M. Rutter (eds) *Straight and devious pathways from childhood to adulthood*. New York: Cambridge University Press.

Cohen, P. & Cohen, J. (1996). *Life values and adolescent mental health*. Mahwah, NJ: Lawrence Erlbaum.

Coiro, M.J. & Emery, R.E. (1998). Do marriage problems affect fathering more than mothering? A quantitative and qualitative review. *Clinical Child and Family Psychology Review*, 1, 23–40.

Coleman, J.S. (1988). Social capital in the creation of human capital. *American Journal of Sociology*, 94 (Suppl.), S95–120.

Coley, R.L. (2003). Daughter–father relationships and adolescent psychosocial functioning in low-income African American families. *Journal of Marriage and Family*, 65, 867–875.

Colhoun, H. & Prescott-Clarke, P. (eds) (1996). *Health Survey for England 1994*. London: The Stationery Office.

Coltrane, S. (1996). *Family man*. New York: Oxford University Press.

Coltrane, S. (2001). Marketing the marriage 'solution': Misplaced simplicity in the politics of fatherhood. *Sociological Perspectives*, 44, 387–418.

Coltrane, S. & Adams, M. (2003). The social construction of the divorce 'problem': Morality, child victims, and the politics of gender. *Family Relations*, 52, 363–372.

Coltrane, S., Parke, R.D. & Adams, M. (2004). Complexity of father involvement in low-income Mexican American families. *Family Relations*, 53, 179–189.

Conger, R.D., Cui, M., Bryant, C.M. & Elder, G.H., Jr (2000). Competence in early adult romantic relationships: A developmental perspective on family influences. *Journal of Personality and Social Psychology*, 79, 224–237.

Connell, A.M. & Goodman, S.H. (2002). The association between psychopathology in fathers versus mothers and children's internalizing and externalizing behavior problems: A meta-analysis. *Psychological Bulletin*, 128, 746–773.

Cooksey, E.C. & Craig, P.H. (1998). Parenting from a distance: The effects of paternal characteristics on contact between non-residential fathers and their children. *Demography*, 35, 187–200.

Corcoran, M. (1995). Rags to rags: Poverty and mobility in the United States. *Annual Review of Sociology*, 21, 237–267.

Cowan, P.A., Cowan, C.P. & Kerig, P.K. (1993). Mothers, fathers, sons, and daughters: Gender differences in family formation and parenting style. In P.A. Cowan & D. Field (eds), *Family, self, and society: Toward a new agenda for family research* (pp. 165–195). Hillsdale, NJ: Lawrence Erlbaum.

Creighton, C. (1999). The rise and decline of the 'male breadwinner family' in Britain. *Cambridge Journal of Economics*, 23, 519–541.

Crick, N.R., Wellman, N.E., Casas, J.F., O'Brien, K.M., Nelson, D.A., Grotpeter, J.K. & Markon, K. (1999). Childhood aggression and gender: A new look at an old problem. In D. Bernstein (ed.), *Nebraska Symposium on Motivation*, 45. Lincoln: University of Nebraska Press.

Criss, M.M., Pettit, G.S., Bates, J.E., Dodge, K.A. & Lapp, A.L. (2002). Family adversity, positive peer relationships, and children's externalizing behavior: A longitudinal perspective on risk and resilience. *Child Development*, 73, 1220–1237.

Crockenberg, S.C. & Leerkes, E.M. (2003). Parental acceptance, postpartum depression, and maternal sensitivity: Mediating and moderating processes. *Journal of Family Psychology*, 17, 80–93.

Crockett, L.J., Eggebeen, D.J. & Hawkins, A.J. (1993). Father's presence and young children's behavioral and cognitive adjustment. *Family Relations*, 14, 355–377.

Crowder, K. & Teachman, J. (2004). Do residential conditions explain the relationship between living arrangements and adolescent behavior? *Journal of Marriage and Family*, 66, 721–738.

Cummings, E.M. & Davies, P.T. (1999). Depressed parents and family functioning: Interpersonal effects and children's functioning and development. In T. Joiner & J.C. Coyne (eds), *The interactional nature of depression: Advances in interpersonal approaches* (pp. 299–327). Washington: American Psychological Association.

Curtis, L.J., Dooley, M.D. & Phipps, S.A. (2004). Child well-being and neighbourhood quality: Evidence from the Canadian National Longitudinal Survey of Children and Youth. *Social Science and Medicine*, 58, 1917–1927.

Cutrona, C.E., Hessling, R.M., Bacon, P.L. & Russell, D.W. (1998). Predictors and correlates of continuing involvement with the baby's father among adolescent mothers. *Journal of Family Psychology*, 12, 369–387.

Dadds, M.R., Atkinson, E., Turner, C., Blums, G.J. & Lendich, B. (1999). Family conflict and child adjustment: Evidence for a cognitive-contextual model of intergenerational transmission. *Journal of Family Psychology*, 13, 194–208.

Daly, M. & Wilson, M. (1998). *The truth about Cinderella: A Darwinian view of parental love*. London: Weidenfeld & Nicolson.

Davies, P.T. & Cummings, E.M. (1994). Marital conflict and child adjustment: An emotional security hypothesis. *Psychological Bulletin*, 116, 387–411.

Deater-Deckard, K. & Petrill, S.A. (2004). Parent–child dyadic mutuality and child behavior problems: An investigation of gene–environment processes. *Journal of Child Psychology and Psychiatry*, 45, 1171–1179.

DeKlyen, M., Speltz, M.L. & Greenberg, M.T. (1998). Fathering and early onset conduct problems: Positive and negative parenting, father–son attachment, and the marital context. *Clinical Child and Family Psychology Review*, 1, 3–21.

DeLeire, T. & Kalil, A. (2002). Good things come in threes: Single-parent multigenerational family structure and adolescent adjustment. *Demography*, 39, 393–413.

De Leo, D., Padoani, W., Lonnqvist, J., Kerkhof, A.J.F.M., Bille-Brahe, U., Michel, K., Salander-Renberg, E., Schmidtke, A., Wasserman, D., Caon, F. & Scocco, P. (2002). Repetition of suicidal behaviour in elderly Europeans: A prospective longitudinal study. *Journal of Affective Disorders*, 72, 291–295.

Demos, J. (1988). *Past, present, and personal: The family and the life course in American history*. New York: Oxford University Press.

Demuth, S. & Brown, S.L. (2004). Family structure, family processes, and adolescent delinquency: The significance of parental absence versus parental gender. *Journal of Research in Crime and Delinquency*, 41, 58–81.

Deutsch, F.M. (2001). Equally shared parenting. *Current Directions in Psychological Science*, 10, 25–28.

Deutsch, F.M., Servis, L.J. & Payne, J.D. (2001). Paternal participation in child care and its effects on children's self-esteem and attitudes toward gendered roles. *Journal of Family Issues*, 22, 1000–1024.

Diekmann, A. & Schmidheiny, K. (2004). Do parents of girls have a higher risk of divorce? An eighteen-country study. *Journal of Marriage and Family*, 66, 651–660.

Diener, E., Sapyta, J.J. & Suh, E. (1998). Subjective well-being is essential to well-being. *Psychological Inquiry*, 9, 33–37.

Diener, E., Suh, E.M., Lucas, R.E. & Smith, H.L. (1999). Subjective well-being: Three decades of progress. *Psychological Bulletin*, 125, 276–302.

Dixon, R.S., Gill, J.M.W. & Adair, V.A. (2003). Exploring paternal influences on the dieting behaviors of adolescent girls. *Eating Disorders*, 11, 39–50.

Doherty, W.J., Kouneski, E.F. & Erickson, M.F. (1998). Responsible fathering: An overview and conceptual framework. *Journal of Marriage and Family*, 60, 277–292.

Dornbusch, S., Carlsmith, J.M., Bushwall, S.J., Ritter, P.L., Leiderman, H., Hastorf, A.H. & Gross, R.T. (1985). Single parents, extended households, and the control of adolescents. *Child Development*, 56, 326–341.

Downey, D.B. (1995). When bigger is not better: Family size, parental resources, and children's educational performance. *American Sociological Review*, 60, 746–761.

Downey, G. & Coyne, J.C. (1990). Children of depressed parents: An integrative review. *Psychological Review*, 108, 50–76.

Dronkers, J. (1994). The changing effects of lone families on the educational attainment of their children in a European welfare state. *Sociology*, 28, 171–192.

Dubowitz, H., Black, M.M., Cox, C.E., Kerr, M.A., Litrownik, A.J., Radhakrishna, A., English, D.J., Wood Schneider, M. & Runyan, D.K. (2001). Father involvement and children's functioning at age 6 years: A multisite study. *Child Maltreatment*, 6, 300–309.

Dubowitz, H., Black, M.M., Kerr, M.A., Starr, R.H. & Harrington, D. (2000). Fathers and child neglect. *Archives of Pediatrics and Adolescent Medicine*, 154, 135–141.

Ducharme, J., Doyle, A.B. & Markiewicz, D. (2002). Attachment security with mother and father: Association with adolescents' reports of interpersonal behavior with parents and peers. *Journal of Social and Personal Relationships*, 19, 203–231.

Duncan, G.J. & Brooks-Gunn, J. (eds) (1997). *Consequences of growing up poor.* New York: Russell Sage.

Duncan, G.J., Brooks-Gunn, J., Yeung, W.J. & Smith, J.R. (1998). How much does childhood poverty affect the life chances of children? *American Sociological Review*, 63, 406–423.

Dunifon, R. & Kowaleski-Jones, L. (2002). Who's in the house? Race differences in cohabitation, single parenthood, and child development. *Child Development*, 73, 1249–1264.

Dunn, J. (2002). The adjustment of children in stepfamilies: Lessons from community studies. *Child and Adolescent Mental Health*, 7, 154–161.

Dunn, J. (2004). Annotation: Children's relationships with their nonresident fathers. *Journal of Child Psychology and Psychiatry*, 45, 659–671.

Dunn, J., Cheng, H., O'Connor, T.G. & Bridges, L. (2004). Children's perspectives on their relationships with their non-resident fathers: Influences, outcomes and implications. *Journal of Child Psychology and Psychiatry*, 45, 553–566.

Dunn, J., Davies, L.C., O'Connor, T.G. & Sturgess, W. (2000). Parents' and partners' life course and family experiences: Links with parent–child relationships in different family settings. *Journal of Child Psychology and Psychiatry*, 41, 955–968.

Dunn, J., Deater-Deckard, K., Pickering, K., O'Connor, T.G. & Golding, J. (1998). Children's adjustment and prosocial behaviour in step-, single-parent, and non-stepfamily settings: Findings from a community study. *Journal of Child Psychology and Psychiatry*, 39, 1083–1095.

Du Rocher Schudlich, T.D., Shamir, H. & Cummings, E.M. (2004). Marital conflict, children's representations of family relationships, and children's dispositions towards peer conflict strategies. *Social Development*, 13, 171–192.

Eaves, L.J., Silberg, J.L., Maes, H.H., Simonoff, E., Pickles, A., Rutter, M., Neale, M.C., Reynolds, C.A., Erickson, M.T., Heath, A.C., Loeber, R., Truett, K.R. & Hewitt, J.K. (1997). Genetics and developmental psychopathology: 2. The main effects of genes and environment on behavioral problems in the Virginia Twin Study of Adolescent Behavioral Development. *Journal of Child Psychology and Psychiatry*, 38, 965–980.

Eccles, J.S. & Harold, R.D. (1996). Family involvement in children's and adolescents' schooling. In A. Booth & J.F. Dunn (eds), *Family–school links: How do they affect educational outcomes?* (pp. 3–34). Hillsdale, NJ: Lawrence Erlbaum.

The Economist (2004). Swedish parental leave: Forced fatherhood. January 8th.

Edwards, R., Bäck-Wiklund, M., Bak, M. & Ribbens McCarthy, J. (2002). Policy and everyday experience in Britain and Sweden. *Sociological Research Online*, 7, U118–U135.

Ekéus, C. & Christensson, K. (2003). Socioeconomic characteristics of fathers of children born to teenage mothers in Stockholm, Sweden. *Scandinavian Journal of Public Health*, 31, 73–76.

Elliott, B.J. & Richards, M.P.M. (1991). Children and divorce: Educational performance and behaviour before and after parental separation. *International Journal of Law and the Family*, 5, 258–276.

Ellis, B.J., Bates, J.E., Dodge, K.A., Fergusson, D.M., Horwood, L.J., Pettit, G.S. & Woodward, L. (2003). Does father absence place daughters at special risk for early sexual activity and teenage pregnancy? *Child Development*, 74, 801–821.

Emery, R.E., Waldron, M., Kitzmann, K.M. & Aaron, J. (1999). Delinquent behavior, future divorce or nonmarital childbearing, and externalizing behavior among offspring: A 14-year prospective study. *Journal of Family Psychology*, 13, 568–579.

Engle, P.L. & Breaux, C. (1998). Fathers' involvement with children: Perspectives from developing countries. *Social Policy Report*, 7(1).

Eriksson, M. & Hester, M. (2001). Violent men as good-enough fathers? A look at England and Sweden. *Violence against Women*, 7, 779–798.

Eurostat Yearbook (2003). *People in Europe*. Eurostat.

Evans, G.W. (2004). The environment of childhood poverty. *American Psychologist*, 59, 77–92.

Fagan, J. & Iglesias, A. (1999). Father involvement program effects on fathers, father figures, and their Head Start children: A quasi-experimental study. *Early Childhood Research Quarterly*, 14, 243–269.

Fals-Stewart, W., Kelley, M.L., Fincham, F.D., Golden, J. & Logsdon, T. (2004). Emotional and behavioral problems of children living with drug-abusing fathers: Comparisons with children living with alcohol-abusing and non-substance-abusing fathers. *Journal of Family Psychology*, 18, 319–330.

Farrington, D.P. (1993). Understanding and preventing bullying. In M. Tonry (ed.), *Crime and justice: A review of research* (pp. 381–458). Chicago: University of Chicago Press.

Farrington, D.P. (1994). Early developmental prevention of juvenile delinquency. *Criminal Behaviour and Mental Health*, 4, 209–227.

Farrington, D.P. (1995). The development of offending and antisocial behaviour from childhood: Key findings from the Cambridge Study in Delinquent Development. *Journal of Child Psychology and Psychiatry*, 36, 929–964.

Farrington, D.P. (1996). *Understanding and preventing youth crime*. York: Joseph Rowntree Foundation.

Farrington, D.P., Barnes, G.C. & Lambert, S. (1996). The concentration of offending in families. *Legal and Criminological Psychology*, 1, 47–63.

Feinstein, L. & Symons, J. (1999). Attainment in secondary school. *Oxford Economic Papers*, 51, 300–321.

Feldman, R. (2000). Parents' convergence on sharing and marital satisfaction, father involvement, and parent–child relationship at the transition to parenthood. *Infant Mental Health Journal*, 21, 176–191.

Fergusson, D.M. & Horwood, L.J. (1999). Prospective childhood predictors of deviant peer affiliations in adolescence. *Journal of Child Psychology and Psychiatry*, 40, 581–592.

Fisher, P.A. Leve, L.D., O'Leary, C.C. & Leve, C. (2003). Parental monitoring of children's behavior: Variation across stepmother, stepfather, and two-parent biological families. *Family Relations*, 52, 45–52.

Flaks, D.K., Ficher, I., Masterpasqua, F. & Joseph, G. (1995). Lesbians choosing motherhood: A comparative study of lesbian and heterosexual parents and their children. *Developmental Psychology*, 31, 105–114.

Flouri, E. (1999). An integrated model of consumer materialism: Can economic socialization and maternal values predict materialistic attitudes in adolescents? *Journal of Socio-Economics*, 28, 707–724.

Flouri, E. (2003). Parental socialization in childhood and offspring materialist and postmaterialist values in adult life. *Journal of Applied Social Psychology*, 33, 2106–2122.

Flouri, E. (2004). Correlates of parents' involvement with their adolescent children in restructured and biological two-parent families: The role of child characteristics. *International Journal of Behavioural Development*, 28, 148–156.

Flouri, E. (in press). Exploring the relationship between mothers' and fathers' parenting practices and children's materialist values. *Journal of Economic Psychology*.

Flouri, E. (under review – a). Father involvement, mother involvement, and child adjustment in adolescence: The role of inter-parental conflict and parental mental health.

Flouri, E. (under review – b). Nonresident fathers' relationships with their secondary school age children in the UK: Determinants and children's mental health outcomes.

Flouri, E. (under review – c). Parental interest in children's education, children's self-esteem and locus of control, and later educational attainment. Twenty-six year follow up of the 1970 British birth cohort.

Flouri, E. & Buchanan, A. (2002a). Life satisfaction in teenage boys: The moderating role of father involvement and bullying. *Aggressive Behavior*, 28, 126–133.

Flouri, E. & Buchanan, A. (2002b). What predicts good relationships with parents in adolescence and partners in adult life: Findings from the 1958 British birth cohort. *Journal of Family Psychology*, 16, 186–198.

Flouri, E. & Buchanan, A. (2002c). The protective role of parental involvement in adolescent suicide. *Crisis*, 23, 17–22.

Flouri, E. & Buchanan, A. (2002d). The role of work-related skills and career role models in adolescent career maturity. *Career Development Quarterly*, 52, 36–43.

Flouri, E. & Buchanan, A. (2002e). Childhood predictors of labor force participation in adult life. *Journal of Family and Economic Issues*, 23, 101–120.

Flouri, E. & Buchanan, A. (2002f). Father involvement in childhood and trouble with the police in adolescence: Findings from the 1958 British birth cohort. *Journal of Interpersonal Violence*, 17, 689–701.

Flouri, E. & Buchanan, A. (2003a). The role of father involvement in children's later mental health. *Journal of Adolescence*, 26, 63–78.

Flouri, E. & Buchanan, A. (2003b). The role of father involvement and mother involvement in adolescents' psychological well-being. *British Journal of Social Work*, 33, 399–406.

Flouri, E. & Buchanan, A. (2003c). The role of mother involvement and father involvement in adolescent bullying behaviour. *Journal of Interpersonal Violence*, 18, 634–644.

Flouri, E. & Buchanan, A. (2003d). What predicts fathers' involvement with their children? A prospective study of intact families. *British Journal of Developmental Psychology*, 21, 81–97.

Flouri, E. & Buchanan, A. (2004a). Childhood families of homeless and poor adults in Britain: A prospective study. *Journal of Economic Psychology*, 25, 1–14.

Flouri, E. & Buchanan, A. (2004b). Early father's and mother's involvement and child's later educational outcomes. *British Journal of Educational Psychology*, 74, 141–153.

Flouri, E., Buchanan, A. & Bream, V. (2002). Adolescents' perceptions of their fathers' involvement: Significance to school attitudes. *Psychology in the Schools*, 39, 575–582.

Foley, D.L., Pickles, A., Rutter, M., Gardner, C.O., Maes, H.H., Silberg, J.L. & Eaves, L.J. (2004). Risks for conduct disorder symptoms associated with parental alcoholism in stepfather families versus intact families from a community sample. *Journal of Child Psychology and Psychiatry*, 45, 687–696.

Foley, D.L., Pickles, A., Simonoff, E., Maes, H.H., Silberg, J.L., Hewitt, J.K. & Eaves, L.J. (2001). Parental concordance and comorbidity for psychiatric disorder and associate risks for current psychiatric symptoms and disorders in a community sample of juvenile twins. *Journal of Child Psychology and Psychiatry*, 42, 381–394.

Fortier, M.S., Vallerand, R.J. & Quay, F. (1995). Academic motivation and school performance: Toward a structural model. *Contemporary Educational Psychology*, 20, 257–274.

Fox, G.L., Benson, M.L., DeMaris, A.A. & Van Wyk, J. (2002). Economic distress and intimate violence: Testing family stress and resources theories. *Journal of Marriage and Family*, 64, 793–807.

Franco, A. & Winqvist, K. (2002). *Women and men reconciling work and family life.* Statistics in Focus, Population and Social Conditions: Eurostat.

Franz, C.E., McClelland, D.C. & Weineberger, J. (1991). Childhood antecedents of conventional social accomplishments in mid-life adults: A 35-year prospective study. *Journal of Personality and Social Psychology*, 60, 586–595.

Freeston, M.H. & Plechaty, M. (1997). Reconsiderations of the Locke–Wallace Marital Adjustment Test: Is it still relevant for the 1990s? *Psychological Reports*, 81, 419–434.

Furstenberg, F.F., Cook, P.D., Eccles, J., Elder, G.H. & Sameroff, A. (1999). *Managing to make it: Urban families and adolescent success.* Chicago: University of Chicago Press.

Furstenberg, F.F., Morgan, S.P., Allison, P.D. (1987). Paternal participation and children's well-being. *American Sociological Review*, 52, 695–701.

Gadeyne, E., Ghesquiere, P. & Onghena, P. (2004). Longitudinal relations between parenting and child adjustment in young children. *Journal of Clinical Child and Adolescent Psychology*, 33, 347–358.

Gadsden, V.L., Fagan, J., Ray, A. & Davis, J.E. (2004). Fathering indicators for practice and evaluation: The fathering indicators framework. In R.D. Day & M.E. Lamb (eds), *Conceptualizing and measuring father involvement* (pp. 385–416). Mahwah, NJ: Lawrence Erlbaum.

Gagnon, M.D., Hersen, M., Kabacoff, R.I. & Van Hasselt, V.B. (1999). Interpersonal and psychological correlates of marital dissatisfaction in late life: A preliminary report. *Clinical Psychology Review*, 19, 359–378.

Galambos, N.L., Barker, E.T. & Almeida, D.M. (2003). Parents *do* matter: Trajectories of change in externalizing and internalizing problems in early adolescence. *Child Development*, 74, 578–594.

Garside, R.B. & Klimes-Dougan, B. (2002). Socialization of discrete negative emotions: Gender differences and links with psychological distress. *Sex Roles*, 47, 115–128.

Gartstein, M.A. & Fagot, K.I. (2003). Parental depression, parenting and family adjustment, and child effortful control: Explaining externalizing behaviors for preschool children. *Journal of Applied Developmental Psychology*, 24, 143–177.

Gavanas, A. (2004). Domesticating masculinity and masculinizing domesticity in contemporary U.S. fatherhood politics. *Social Politics*, 15, 247–266.

Gavin, L.E., Black, M.M., Minor, S., Abel, Y., Papas, M.A. & Bentley, M.E. (2002). Young, disadvantaged fathers' involvement with their infants: An ecological perspective. *Journal of Adolescent Health*, 31, 266–276.

Gee, C.B. & Rhodes, J.E. (2003). Adolescent mothers' relationship with their children's biological fathers: Social support, social strain, and relationship continuity. *Journal of Family Psychology*, 17, 370–383.

Georgiou, S. (1999). Parental attributions as predictors of involvement and influences on child achievement. *British Journal of Educational Psychology*, 69, 409–429.

Gerson, K. (1993). *No man's land: Men's changing commitments to family and work*. New York: Basic Books.

Goetting, A. (1994). The parenting–crime connection. *Journal of Primary Prevention*, 14, 169–186.

Goldberg, D.P. (1978). *Manual of the General Health Questionnaire*. Windsor: NFER–Nelson.

Goldberg, D.P. & Williams, P. (1988). *A user's guide to the General Health Questionnaire*. Windsor: NFER–Nelson.

Golombok, S., Perry, B., Burston, A., Murray, C., Mooney-Somers, J., Stevens, M. & Golding, J. (2003). Children with lesbian parents: A community study. *Developmental Psychology*, 39, 20–33.

Golombok, S., Tasker, F. & Murray, C. (1997). Children raised in fatherless families from infancy: Family relationships and the socioemotional development of children of lesbian and single heterosexual mothers. *Journal of Child Psychology and Psychiatry*, 38, 783–791.

Goodenough, F. (1926). *Measurement of intelligence by drawings*. New York: Harcourt, Brace & World.

Goodman, R. (1994). A modified version of the Rutter parent questionnaire including extra items on children's strengths: A research note. *Journal of Child Psychology and Psychiatry*, 35, 1483–1494.

Goodman, R. (1997). The Strengths and Difficulties Questionnaire: A research note. *Journal of Child Psychology and Psychiatry*, 38, 581–586.

Graham, C.W., Fischer, J.L., Fitzpatrick, J. & Bina, K. (2000). Parental status, social support, and marital adjustment. *Journal of Family Issues*, 21, 888–905.

Graham, H. & Blackburn, C. (1998). The socio-economic patterning of health and smoking behaviour among mothers with young children on income support. *Sociology of Health and Illness*, 20, 215–240.

Graham, J.W. & Beller, A.H. (2002). Nonresident fathers and their children: Child support and visitation from an economic perspective. In C.S. Tamis-LeMonda & N. Cabrera (eds), *Handbook of father involvement: Multidisciplinary perspectives* (pp. 431–453). Mahwah, NJ: Lawrence Erlbaum.

Gray, M.R. & Steinberg, L. (1999a). Unpacking authoritative parenting: Reassessing a multidimensional construct. *Journal of Marriage and Family*, 61, 574–587.

Gray, M.R. & Steinberg, L. (1999b). Adolescent romance and the parent–child relationship: A contextual perspective. In W. Furman, B.B. Brown & C. Feiring (eds), *The development of romantic relationships in adolescence* (pp. 235–265). New York: Cambridge University Press.

Gray, P.B., Kahlenberg, S.M., Barrett, E.S., Lipson, S.F. & Ellison, P.T. (2002). Marriage and fatherhood are associated with lower testosterone in males. *Evolution and Human Behavior*, 23, 193–201.

Griesbach, D., Amos, A. & Currie, C. (2003). Adolescent smoking and family structure in Europe. *Social Science and Medicine*, 56, 41–52.

Grolnick, W.S., Benjet, C., Kurowski, C.O. & Apostoleris, N.H. (1997). Predictors of parent involvement in children's schooling. *Journal of Educational Psychology*, 89, 538–548.

Grolnick, W.S. & Slowiaczek, M.L. (1994) Parents' involvement in children's schooling: A multidimensional conceptualization and motivational model. *Child Development*, 65, 237–252.

Grych, J.H. & Fincham, F.D. (1990). Marital conflict and children's adjustment: A cognitive-contextual framework. *Psychological Bulletin*, 108, 267–290.

Grych, J.H., Seid, M. & Fincham, F.D. (1992). Assessing marital conflict from the child's perspective. *Child Development*, 63, 558–572.

Guastello, D.D. & Peissig, R.M. (1998). Authoritarianism, environmentalism, and cynicism of college students and their parents. *Journal of Research in Personality*, 32, 397–410.

Guerra, A.L. & Braungart-Rieker, J.M. (1999). Predicting career indecision in college students: The roles of identity formation and parental relationship factors. *Career Development Quarterly*, 47, 255–266.

Gupta, S., Smock, P.J. & Manning, W.D. (2004). Moving out: Transition to nonresidence among resident fathers in the United States, 1968–1997. *Journal of Marriage and Family*, 66, 627–638.

Haas, L. (2003). Parental leave and gender equality: Lessons from the European Union. *Review of Policy Research*, 20, 89–114.

Hagan, J., Macmillan, R. & Wheaton, B. (1996). New kid in town: Social capital and the life course effects of family migration on children. *American Sociological Review*, 61, 368–385.

Hallqvist, J., Lynch, J., Bartley, M., Lang, T. & Blane, D. (2004). Can we disentangle life course processes of accumulation, critical period and social mobility? An analysis of disadvantaged socio-economic positions and myocardial infarction in the Stockholm Heart Epidemiology Program. *Social Science and Medicine*, 58, 1555–1562.

Hammen, C., Rudolph, K., Weisz, J., Rao, U. & Burge, D. (1999). The context of depression in clinic-referred youth: Neglected areas in treatment. *Journal of the American Academy of Child and Adolescent Psychiatry*, 28, 64–71.

Han, W.-J., Huang, C.-C. & Garfinkel, I. (2003). The importance of family structure and family income on family's educational expenditure and children's college attendance: Empirical evidence from Taiwan. *Journal of Family Issues*, 24, 753–786.

Hanson, T.L., McLanahan, S. & Thomson, E. (1997). Economic resources, parental practices, and children's well-being. In G.J. Duncan & J. Brooks-Gunn (eds), *Consequences of growing up poor* (pp. 190–238). New York: Russell Sage.

Hao, L. & Xie, G. (2001). The complexity and endogenity of family structure in explaining children's misbehavior. *Social Science Research*, 31, 1–28.

Harper, C.C. & McLanahan, S.S. (2004). Father absence and youth incarceration. *Journal of Research on Adolescence*, 14, 369–397.

Harris, D.B. (1963). *Children's drawings as measure of intellectual maturity*. New York: Harcourt, Brace & World.

Harris, J.R. (1998). *The nurture assumption: Why children turn out the way they do?* New York: Free Press.

Harris, K.H. & Morgan, S.P. (1991). Fathers, sons, and daughters: Differential paternal involvement in parenting. *Journal of Marriage and Family*, 53, 531–544.

Harris, K.M., Furstenberg, F.F. Jr & Marmer, J.K. (1998). Paternal involvement with adolescents in intact families: The influence of fathers over the life course. *Demography*, 35, 201–216.

Harris, K.M. & Marmer, J.K. (1996). Poverty, paternal involvement, and adolescent well-being. *Journal of Family Issues*, 17, 614–640.

Hart, E.J., Lahey, B.B., Loeber, R. & Hanson, K.S. (1994). Criterion validity of informants in the diagnosis of disruptive behavior disorders in children: A preliminary study. *Journal of Consulting and Clinical Psychology*, 62, 410–414.

Hartog, J. & Oosterbeek, H. (1998). Health, wealth and happiness: Why pursue a higher education. *Economics of Education Review*, 17, 245–256.

Hatten, W., Vinter, L. & Williams, R. (2002). *Dads on dads: Needs and expectations at home and at work*. Manchester: Equal Opportunities Commission.

Hawkins, A.J. & Belsky, J. (1989). The role of father involvement in personality change in men across the transition to parenthood. *Family Relations*, 38, 378–384.

Hawkins, A.J., Bradford, K.P., Palkovitz, R., Christiansen, S.L., Day, R.D. & Call, V.R.A. (2002). The inventory of father involvement: A pilot study of a new measure of father involvement. *Journal of Men's Studies*, 10, 183–196.

Healey, A., Knapp, M. & Farrington, D.P. (2004). Adult labour market implications of antisocial behaviour in childhood and adolescence: Findings from a UK longitudinal study. *Applied Economics*, 36, 93–105.

Heaven, P.C.L., Newbury, K. & Mak, A. (2004). The impact of adolescent and parental characteristics on adolescent levels of delinquency and depression. *Personality and Individual Differences*, 36, 173–185.

Henwood, K. & Procter, J. (2003). The 'good father': Reading men's accounts of paternal involvement during the transition to first-time fatherhood. *British Journal of Social Psychology*, 42, 337–355.

Herman, D.B., Susser, E.S., Struening, E.L. & Link, B.L. (1997a). Adverse childhood experiences: Are they risk factors for adult homelessness? *American Journal of Public Health*, 87, 249–255.

Herman, M.A. & McHale, S.M. (1993). Coping with parental negativity: Links with parental warmth and child adjustment. *Journal of Applied Developmental Psychology*, 14, 121–130.

Herman, M.R., Dornbusch, S.M., Herron, M.C. & Herting, J.R. (1997b). The influence of family regulation, connection, and psychological autonomy on six measures of adolescent functioning. *Journal of Adolescent Research*, 12, 34–67.

Hetherington, E.M. (2003). Intimate pathways: Changing patterns in close personal relationships across time. *Family Relations*, 52, 318–331.

Hetherington, E.M., Cox, M. & Cox, R. (1982). Effects of divorce on parents and children. In M.E. Lamb (ed.), *Nontraditional families* (pp. 233–288). Hillsdale, NJ: Lawrence Erlbaum.

Hetherington, E.M. & Kelly, J. (2002). *For better or for worse: Divorce reconsidered*. New York: Norton.

Hetherington, E.M. & Stanley-Hagan, M.M. (1997). The effects of divorce on fathers and their children. In M.E. Lamb (ed.), *The role of the father in child development* (pp. 191–210). New York: John Wiley & Sons.

Hetherington, E.M. & Stanley-Hagan, M. (1999). The adjustment of children with divorced parents: A risk and resiliency perspective. *Journal of Child Psychology and Psychiatry*, 40, 129–140.

Hewlett, B.S. (1987). Intimate fathers: Patterns of paternal holding among Aka pygmies. In M.E. Lamb (ed.), *The father's role: Cross-cultural perspectives* (pp. 295–330). Hillsdale, NJ: Lawrence Erlbaum.

Hiedeman, B., Joesch, J.M. & Rose, E. (2004). More daughters in child care? Child gender and the use of nonrelative child care arrangements. *Social Science Quarterly*, 85, 154–168.

Hill, J., Kondryn, H., Mackie, E., McNally, R. & Eden, T. (2003). Adult psychosocial functioning following childhood cancer: The different roles of sons' and daughters' relationships with their fathers and mothers. *Journal of Child Psychology and Psychiatry*, 44, 752–762.

Hill, J., Mackie, E., Banner, L., Kondryn, H. & Blair, V. (1999). Relationship with Family of Origin Scale (REFAMOS). Interrater reliability and associations with childhood experiences. *The British Journal of Psychiatry*, 175, 565–570.

Hines, A.M. (1997). Divorce-related transitions, adolescent development, and the role of the parent–child relationship: A review of the literature. *Journal of Marriage and Family*, 59, 375–388.

Hinshaw, S. (1992). Externalizing behaviour problems and academic under-achievement in childhood and adolescence: Causal relationships and underlying mechanisms. *Psychological Bulletin*, 111, 127–155.

Hofferth, S.L. (2003). Race/ethnic differences in father involvement in two-parent families: Culture, context, or economy? *Journal of Family Issues*, 24, 185–216.

Hofferth, S.L. & Anderson, K.G. (2003). Are all dads equal? Biology versus marriage as a basis for paternal investment. *Journal of Marriage and Family*, 65, 213–232.

Hofferth, S.L., Pleck, J., Stueve, J.L., Bianchi, S. & Sayer, L. (2002). The demography of fathers: What fathers do. In C.S. Tamis-LeMonda & N. Cabrera (eds), *Handbook of father involvement: Multidisciplinary perspectives* (pp. 63–90). Mahwah, NJ: Lawrence Erlbaum.

Hoffmann, J.P. (2002). The community context of family structure and adolescent drug use. *Journal of Marriage and Family*, 64, 314–330.

Holden, G.W. & Edwards, L.A. (1989). Parental attitudes towards child-rearing: Instruments, issues, and implications. *Psychological Bulletin*, 106, 29–58.

Home Office Statistical Bulletin (1987). *Criminal careers of those born in 1953*. London: Home Office.

Home Office Statistical Bulletin (1989). *Criminal and custodial careers of those born in 1953, 1958 and 1963*. London: Home Office.

Horn, W. (2001). Wedding bell blues: Marriage and welfare reform. *Brookings Review*, 19, 39–42.

Horrell, S., Humphries, J. & Voth, H.-J. (2001). Destined for deprivation: Human capital formation and intergenerational poverty in nineteenth-century England. *Explorations in Economic History*, 38, 339–365.

Hosley, C.A. & Montemayor, R. (1997). Fathers and adolescents. In M.E. Lamb (ed.), *The role of the father in child development* (pp. 162–178). New York: John Wiley & Sons.

Howes, P. & Markman, H. (1989). Marital quality and child functioning: A longitudinal investigation. *Child Development*, 60, 1044–1051.

Hunt, J. & Roberts, C. (2004). *Child contact with non-resident parents*. Oxford: Family Policy Briefing 3.

Hurd, K.P., Wooding, S. & Noller, P. (1999). Parent–adolescent relationships in families with depressed and self-harming adolescents. *Journal of Family Studies*, 5, 47–58.

Hwang, C.P. & Lamb, M.E. (1997). Father involvement in Sweden: A longitudinal study of its stability and correlates. *International Journal of Behavioral Development*, 21, 621–632.

Ihinger-Tallman, M., Pasley, K. & Buehler, C. (1993). Developing a middle-range theory of father involvement post-divorce. *Journal of Family Issues*, 14, 550–571.

Inglehart, R. (1990). *Culture shift in advanced industrial society*. Princeton: Princeton University Press.

Inglehart, R. (2000). Culture and democracy. In S. Huntington & L. Harrison (eds), *Culture Matters*. New York: Basic Books.

Inglehart, R. & Baker, W.E. (2000). Modernization, cultural change, and the persistence of traditional values. *American Sociological Review*, 65, 19–51.

Ishii-Kuntz, M. (1994). Paternal involvement and perception toward fathers' roles: A comparison between Japan and the United States. *Journal of Family Issues*, 15, 30–48.

Jaffee, S.R., Caspi, A., Moffitt, T.E., Taylor, A. & Dickson, N. (2001). Predicting early fatherhood and whether young fathers live with their children: Prospective findings and policy considerations. *Journal of Child Psychology and Psychiatry*, 42, 803–815.

Jaffee, S.R., Moffitt, T.E., Caspi, A. & Taylor, A. (2003). Life with (or without) father: The benefits of living with two biological parents depend on the father's antisocial behavior. *Child Development*, 74, 109–126.

Jayakody, R. & Kalil, A. (2002). Social fathering in low-income, African American families with preschool children. *Journal of Marriage and Family*, 64, 504–516.

Johnson, M.P. (2002). The implications of unfulfilled expectations and perceived pressure to attend the birth on men's stress levels following birth attendance: A longitudinal study. *Journal of Psychosomatic Obstetrics and Gynecology*, 23, 173–182.

Johnson, W.E. Jr (2001). Paternal involvement among unwed fathers. *Children and Youth Services Review*, 23, 513–536.

Jorm, A.F., Dear, K.B.G., Rodgers, B. & Christensen, H. (2003). Interaction between mother's and father's affection as a risk factor for anxiety and depression symptoms. Evidence for increased risk in adults who rate their father as having been more affectionate than their mother. *Social Psychiatry and Psychiatric Epidemiology*, 38, 173–179.

Josephson, S.C. (2002). Fathering as reproductive investment. In C.S. Tamis-LeMonda & N. Cabrera (eds), *Handbook of father involvement: Multidisciplinary perspectives* (pp. 359–381). Mahwah, NJ: Lawrence Erlbaum.

Kaplan, P.S., Dungan, J.K. & Zinser, M.C. (2004). Infants of chronically depressed mothers learn in response to male, but not female, infant-directed speech. *Developmental Psychology*, 40, 140–148.

Karras, J., Van Deventer, M.C. & Braungart-Rieker, J.M. (2003). Predicting shared parent–child book reading in infancy. *Journal of Family Psychology*, 17, 134–146.

Kasser, T. (2002). *The high price of materialism*. Cambridge, MA: MIT Press.

Kasser, T. & Ryan, R.M. (1993). A dark side of the American dream: Correlates of financial success as a central life aspiration. *Journal of Personality and Social Psychology*, 65, 410–422.

Kasser, T., Ryan, R.M., Zax, M. & Sameroff, A.J. (1995). The relations of maternal and social environments to late adolescents' materialistic and prosocial values. *Developmental Psychology*, 31, 907–914.

Keith, T.Z., Keith, P.B., Quirk, K.J., Sperduto, J., Santillo, S. & Killings, S. (1998). Longitudinal effects of parent involvement on high school grades: Similarities and differences across gender and ethnic groups. *Journal of School Psychology*, 36, 335–363.

Kelly, J. (2000). Children's adjustment in conflicted marriage and divorce: A decade review of research. *Journal of the American Academy of Child and Adolescent Psychiatry*, 39, 963–997.

Kelly, J.B. & Emery, R.E. (2003). Children's adjustment following divorce: Risk and resilience perspectives. *Family Relations*, 52, 352–362.

Kemppainen, L., Jokelainen, J., Isohanni, M., Jaervelin, M.R. & Raesaenen, P. (2002). Predictors of female criminality: Findings from the Northern Finland 1966 birth cohort. *Journal of the American Academy of Child and Adolescent Psychiatry*, 41, 854–859.

Kennedy, C. & Fitzpatrick, S. (2001). Begging, rough sleeping and social exclusion: Implications for social policy. *Urban Studies*, 38, 2001–2016.

Kerig, P.K., Cowan, P.A. & Cowan, C.P. (1993). Marital quality and gender differences in parent–child interaction. *Developmental Psychology*, 29, 931–939.

Khatri, P., Kupersmidt, J.B. & Patterson, C. (2000). Aggression and peer victimisation as predictors of self-reported behavioral and emotional adjustment. *Aggressive Behavior*, 26, 345–358.

Kiecolt-Glaser, J.K. & Newton, T. (2001). Marriage and health: His and hers. *Psychological Bulletin*, 127, 472–503.

Kiernan, K.E. (1992). The impact of family disruption in childhood on transition made in young adult life. *Population Studies*, 46, 213–234.

Kiernan, K.E. & Cherlin, A.J. (1999). Parental divorce and partnership dissolution in adulthood: Evidence from a British cohort study. *Population Studies*, 53, 39–48.

Kiernan, K.E. & Hobcraft, J. (1997). Parental divorce during childhood: Age at first intercourse, partnership and parenthood. *Population Studies*, 51, 41–55.

King, V. (1994). Variation in the consequences of non-resident fathers' involvement for children's well-being. *Journal of Marriage and Family*, 56, 963–972.

King, V. (2002). Parental divorce and interpersonal trust in adult offspring. *Journal of Marriage and Family*, 64, 642–656.

King, V. (2003). The influence of religion on fathers' relationships with their children. *Journal of Marriage and Family*, 65, 382–395.

King, V., Harris, K.M. & Heard, H.E. (2004). Racial and ethnic diversity in nonresident father involvement. *Journal of Marriage and Family*, 66, 1–21.

King, V. & Heard, H.E. (1999). Nonresident father visitation, parental conflict, and mother's satisfaction: What's best for child well-being? *Journal of Marriage and Family*, 61, 385–396.

Kingree, J.B., Stephens, T., Braithwaite, R. & Griffin, J. (1999). Predictors of homelessness among participants in a substance abuse treatment program. *American Journal of Orthopsychiatry*, 69, 261–266.

Kitamura, T., Sugawara, M., Toda, M.A. & Shima, S. (1998). Childhood adversities and depression: I. Effects of early parental loss on the rearing behaviour of the remaining parent. *Archives of Women's Mental Health*, 1, 131–136.

Kitamura, T., Sugawara, M., Shima, S. & Toda, M.A. (1999). Childhood adversities and depression: II. Parental loss, rearing, and symptom profile of antenatal depression. *Archives of Women's Mental Health*, 1, 175–182.

Kokko, K. & Pulkkinen, L. (2000). Aggression in childhood and long-term unemployment in adulthood: A cycle of maladaptation and some protective factors. *Developmental Psychology*, 36, 463–472.

Kokko, K., Pulkkinen, L. & Puustinen, M. (2000). Selection into long-term unemployment and its psychological consequences. *International Journal of Behavioural Development*, 24, 310–320.

Korpi, T. (2001). Accumulating disadvantage. Longitudinal analyses of unemployment and physical health in representative samples of the Swedish population. *European Sociological Review*, 17, 255–273.

Kosterman, R., Haggerty, K.P., Spoth, R. & Redmond, C. (2004). Unique influence of mothers and fathers on their children's antisocial behavior. *Journal of Marriage and Family*, 66, 762–778.

Kraemer, H.C., Stice, E., Kazdin, A., Offord, D. & Kupfer, D. (2001). How do risk factors work together? Mediators, moderators, and independent, overlapping, and proxy risk factors. *American Journal of Psychiatry*, 158, 848–856.

Krishnakumar, A. & Black, M.M. (2003). Family processes within three-generation households and adolescent mothers' satisfaction with father involvement. *Journal of Family Psychology*, 17, 488–498.

Kuh, D., Hardy, R., Rodgers, B. & Wadsworth, M.E.J. (2002). Lifetime risk factors for women's psychological distress in midlife. *Social Science and Medicine*, 55, 1957–1973.

Kuo, H.-H.D. & Hauser, R.M. (1997). How does size of sibship matter? Family configuration and family effects on educational attainment. *Social Science Research*, 26, 69–94.

Kwong, M.J., Bartholomew, K., Henderson, A.J.Z. & Trinke, S.J. (2003). The intergenerational transmission of relationship violence. *Journal of Family Psychology*, 17, 288–301.

Laakso, M.-L. (1995). Mothers' and fathers' communication clarity and teaching strategies with their school-aged children. *Journal of Applied Developmental Psychology*, 16, 445–461.

Lamb, M.E. (ed.) (1986). *The father's role: Applied perspectives*. New York: John Wiley & Sons.

Lamb, M.E. (ed.) (1997). *The role of the father in child development*. New York: John Wiley & Sons.

Lamb, M.E. (2002). Infant–father attachments and their impact on child development. In C.S. Tamis-LeMonda & N. Cabrera (eds), *Handbook of father involvement: Multidisciplinary perspectives* (pp. 93–117). Mahwah, NJ: Lawrence Erlbaum.

Lamb, M.E., Pleck, J.H., Charnov, E.L. & Levine, J.A. (1985). Paternal behavior in humans. *American Zoologist*, 25, 883–894.

Lamb, M.E., Pleck, J.H., Charnov, E.L. & Levine, J.A. (1987). A biosocial perspective on paternal behavior and involvement. In J.B. Lancaster, J. Altmann, A.S. Rossi & L.R. Sherrod (eds), *Parenting across the lifespan: Biosocial perspectives* (pp. 111–142). Hawthorne, NY: Aldine.

Laucht, M., Esser, G., Baving, L., Gerhold, M., Hoesch, I., Ihle, W., Steigleider, P., Stock, B., Stoehr, R.M., Weindrich, D. & Schmidt, M.H. (2000). Behavioral sequelae of perinatal insults and early family adversity at 8 years of age. *Journal of the American Academy of Child and Adolescent Psychiatry*, 39, 1229–1237.

Lee, M., Vernon-Feagans, L., Vazquez, A. & Kolak, A. (2003). The influence of family environment and child temperament on work/family role strain for mothers and fathers. *Infant and Child Development*, 12, 421–439.

Lefcourt, H.M. (1991). Locus of control. In J.P. Robinson, P.R. Shaver & L.S. Wrightman (eds), *Measures of personality and social psychological attitudes* (pp. 413–499). San Diego, CA: Academic Press.

Leinonen, J.A., Solantaus, T.S. & Punamäki, R.-L. (2002). The specific mediating paths between economic hardship and the quality of parenting. *International Journal of Behavioral Development*, 26, 423–435.

Leinonen, J.A., Solantaus, T.S. & Punamäki, R.-L. (2003a). Parental mental health and children's adjustment: The quality of marital interaction and parenting as mediating factors. *Journal of Child Psychology and Psychiatry*, 44, 227–241.

Leinonen, J.A., Solantaus, T.S. & Punamäki, R.-L. (2003b). Social support and the quality of parenting under economic pressure and workload in Finland: The role of family structure and parental gender. *Journal of Family Psychology*, 17, 409–418.

Leite, R.W. & McKenry, P.C. (2002). Aspects of father status and postdivorce father involvement with children. *Journal of Family Issues*, 23, 601–623.

Leve, L.D., Scaramella, L.V. & Fagot, B.I. (2001). Infant temperament, pleasure in parenting, and marital happiness in adoptive families. *Infant Mental Health Journal*, 22, 545–558.

Lewis, C. & Lamb, M.E. (2003). Fathers' influence on children's development: The evidence from two-parent families. *European Journal of Psychology of Education*, 18, 211–228.

Lewis, J. (2001a). Debates and issues regarding marriage and cohabitation in the British and American literature. *International Journal of Law, Policy and the Family*, 15, 159–184.

Lewis, J. (2001b). The problem of fathers: Policy and behaviour in Britain. In B. Hobson (ed.), *Making men into fathers*. Cambridge: Cambridge University Press.

Lichter, D.T., Graefe, D.R. & Brown, J.B. (2003). Is marriage a panacea? Union formation among economically disadvantaged unwed mothers. *Social Problems*, 50, 60–86.

Lin, I.-F., Schaeffer, N.C., Seltzer, J.A. & Tuschen, K.L. (2004). Divorced parents' qualitative and quantitative reports of children's living arrangements. *Journal of Marriage and Family*, 66, 385–397.

Lis, A., Zennaro, A., Mazzeschi, C. & Pinto, M. (2004). Parental styles in prospective fathers: A research carried out using a semistructured interview during pregnancy. *Infant Mental Health Journal*, 25, 149–162.

Liu, R.X. (2004). Parent–youth conflict and school delinquency/cigarette use: The moderating effects of gender and associations with achievement-oriented peers. *Sociological Inquiry*, 74, 271–297.

Locke, H.J. & Wallace, K.M. (1959). Short marital adjustment and prediction tests: Their reliability and validity. *Marriage and Family Living*, 21, 251–255.

Loeber, R. & Farrington, D.P. (1994). Problems and solutions in longitudinal and experimental treatment studies of child psychopathology and delinquency. *Journal of Child Psychology and Psychiatry*, 62, 887–900.

Loeber, R. & Hay, D. (1997). Key issues in the development of aggression and violence from childhood to early adulthood. *Annual Review of Psychology*, 48, 371–410.

Loeber, R. & Stouthamer-Loeber, M. (1987). Prediction. In H.C. Quay (ed.), *Handbook of juvenile delinquency* (pp. 325–382). New York: John Wiley & Sons.

Loesel, F. & Bliesener, T. (1994). Some high-risk adolescents do not develop conduct problems: A study of protective factors. *International Journal of Behavioral Development*, 17, 753–777.

Lundberg, S. & Rose, E. (2002). The effects of sons and daughters on men's labor supply and wages. *Review of Economics and Statistics*, 84, 251–268.

Lundberg, S. & Rose, E. (2003). Child gender and the transition to marriage. *Demography*, 40, 333–349.

Luoma, I., Puura, K., Tamminen, T., Kaukonen, P., Piha, J., Rasanen, E., Kumpulainen, K., Moilanen, I., Koivisto, A.M. & Almqvist, F. (1999). Emotional and behavioural symptoms in 8–9-year-old children in relation to family structure. *European Child and Adolescent Psychiatry*, 8 (Suppl. 4), S029–S040.

Luoma, I., Tamminen, T. & Koivisto, A.-M. (2004). Fathers' and mothers' perceptions of their child and maternal depressive symptoms. *Nordic Journal of Psychiatry*, 58, 205–211.

Luthar, S.S. (2003). The culture of affluence: Psychological costs of material wealth. *Child Development*, 74, 1581–1593.

Luthar, S.S., Cicchetti, D. & Becker, B. (2000). The construct of resilience: A critical evaluation and guidelines for future work. *Child Development*, 71, 543–562.

Lyons-Ruth, K. (1996). Attachment relationships among children with aggressive behavior problems: The role of disorganized attachment patterns. *Journal of Consulting Clinical Psychology*, 64, 64–73.

MacCallum, F. & Golombok, S. (in press). Children raised in fatherless families from infancy: A follow-up of children of lesbian and single heterosexual mothers at early adolescence. *Journal of Child Psychology and Psychiatry*.

Maccoby, E.E. (2000). Parenting and its effects on children: On reading and misreading behavior genetics. *Annual Review of Psychology*, 51, 1–27.

Macdonald, W.L. & DeMaris, A. (2002). Stepfather–stepchild relationship quality: The stepfather's demand for conformity and the biological father's involvement. *Journal of Family Issues*, 23, 121–137.

MacKinnon-Lewis, C., Castellino, D.R., Brody, G.H. & Fincham, F.D. (2001). A longitudinal examination of the associations between fathers' and children's attributions and negative interactions. *Social Development*, 10, 473–487.

Maclean, M. & Eekelaar, J. (1997). *The parental obligation: A study of parenthood across households*. Oxford: Hart.

Macmillan, R. & Hagan, J. (2004). Violence in the transition to adulthood: Adolescent victimization, education, and socioeconomic attainment in later life. *Journal of Research on Adolescence*, 14, 127–158.

Mahoney, A., Pargament, K.I., Jewell, T., Swank, A.B., Scott, E., Emery, E. & Rye, M. (1999). Marriage and the spiritual realm: The role of proximal and distal religious constructs in marital functioning. *Journal of Family Psychology*, 13, 321–338.

Mak, A.S. (1994). Parental neglect and overprotection as risk factors in delinquency. *Australian Journal of Psychology*, 46, 107–111.

Manlove, E.E. & Vernon-Feagans, L. (2002). Caring for infant daughters and sons in dual-earner households: Maternal reports of father involvement in weekday time and tasks. *Infant and Child Development*, 11, 305–320.

Manning, W.D. & Lamb, K.A. (2003). Adolescent well-being in cohabiting, married and single-parent families. *Journal of Marriage and Family*, 65, 876–893.

Manning, W.D. & Smock, P.J. (2000). 'Swapping' families: Serial parenting and economic support for children. *Journal of Marriage and Family, 62,*111–122.

Marks, G.N. (1997). The formation of materialist and postmaterialist values. *Social Science Research,* 26, 52–68.

Marsiglio, W., Amato, P., Day, R. & Lamb, M.E. (2000). Scholarship on fatherhood in the 1990s and beyond. *Journal of Marriage and Family,* 62, 1173–1191.

Matheson, J. & Summerfield, C. (eds) (2001). *Social focus on men.* London: The Stationery Office.

Mau, W.C., Domnick, M. & Ellsworth, R. (1995). Characteristics of female students who aspire to science and engineering or homemaking occupations. *Career Development Quarterly,* 43, 323–337.

Maughan, B., Collishaw, S. & Pickles, A. (1998). School achievement and adult qualifications among adoptees: A longitudinal study. *Journal of Child Psychology and Psychiatry,* 39, 669–685.

McBride, B.A. & Rane, T.R. (1998). Parenting alliance as a predictor of father involvement: An exploratory study. *Family Relations,* 47, 229–236.

McBride, B.A., Schoppe, S.J. & Rane, T.R. (2002). Child characteristics, parenting stress, and parental involvement: Fathers versus mothers. *Journal of Marriage and Family,* 64, 998–1011.

McClun, L.A. & Merrell, K.W. (1998). Relationship of perceived parenting styles, locus of control orientation, and self-concept among junior high age students. *Psychology in the Schools,* 35, 381–390.

McDonough, P., Duncan, G.J., Williams, D. & House, J. (1997). Income dynamics and adult mortality in the United States, 1972 through 1989. *American Journal of Public Health,* 87, 1476–1483.

McLanahan, S.S. (1999). Father absence and the welfare of children. In E.M. Hetherington (ed.), *Coping with divorce, single parenting, and remarriage.* Mahwah, NJ: Lawrence Erlbaum.

McLanahan, S.S. & Carlson, M.J. (2002). Welfare reform, fertility, and father involvement. *Future of Children,* 12, 147–165.

McLanahan, S.S. & Sandefur, G.D. (1994). *Uncertain childhood, uncertain future.* Cambridge: Harvard University Press.

McLoyd, V.C. (1998). Socioeconomic disadvantage and child development. *American Psychologist,* 53, 185–204.

McMahon, S.D., Grant, K.E., Compas, B.E., Thurm, A.E. & Ey, S. (2003). Stress and psychopathology in children and adolescents: Is there evidence of specificity? *Journal of Child and Psychiatry,* 44, 107–133.

McMunn, A.M., Nazroo, J.Y., Marmot, M.G., Boreham, R. & Goodman, R. (2001). Children's emotional and behavioural well-being and the family environment: Findings from the Health Survey for England. *Social Science and Medicine,* 53, 423–440.

McRae, S. (2000). *Changing Britain: Families and households in the 1990s.* Oxford: Oxford University Press.

Mekos, E., Hetherington, E.M. & Reiss, D. (1996). Sibling differences in problem behavior: The role of differential treatment in nondivorced and remarried families. *Child Development,* 67, 148–165.

Meltzer, H., Gill, B., Petticrew, M. & Hinds, K. (1995). *The prevalence of psychiatric morbidity among adults living in private households.* London: The Stationery Office.

Merikangas, K.R. & Angst, J. (1994). The challenge of depressive disorders in adolescence. In M. Rutter (ed.), *Psychosocial disturbances in young people: Challenges for prevention.* New York: Cambridge University Press.

Mick, D.F. (1996). Are studies of dark side variables confounded by socially desirable responding? *Journal of Consumer Research,* 23, 106–119.

Midgett, J., Ryan, B.A., Adams, G.R. & Corville-Smith, J. (2001). Complicating achievement and self-esteem: Considering the joint effects of child characteristics and parent–child relationships. *Contemporary Educational Psychology*, 27, 132–143.

Miedel, W.T. & Reynolds, A.J. (1999). Parent involvement in early intervention for disadvantaged children: Does it matter? *Journal of School Psychology*, 37, 379–402.

Milkie, M.A., Bianchi, S.M., Mattingly, M.J. & Robinson, J.P. (2002). Gendered division of childrearing: Ideals, realities, and the relationship to parental well-being. *Sex Roles*, 47, 21–38.

Möller, K. & Stattin, H. (2001). Are close relationships in adolescence linked with partner relationship in midlife? A longitudinal, prospective study. *International Journal of Behavioral Development*, 25, 69–77.

Mondell, S. & Tyler, F. (1981). Parental competence and styles of problem solving/play behavior with children. *Developmental Psychology*, 17, 73–78.

Moore, T. & Kotelchuck, M. (2004). Predictors of urban fathers' involvement in their child's health care. *Pediatrics*, 113, 574–580.

Morgan, S.P., Lye, D.N. & Condran, G.A. (1988). Sons, daughters, and the risk of marital disruptions. *American Journal of Sociology*, 94, 110–129.

Mori, M. (1999). The influence of father–daughter relationship and girls' sex roles on girls' self esteem. *Archives of Women's Mental Health*, 2, 45–47.

Mortimer, J.T. & Johnson, M.K. (1998). New perspectives on adolescent work and the transition to adulthood. In R. Jessor (ed.), *New perspectives on adolescent risk behavior* (pp. 425–496). New York: Cambridge University Press.

Moynihan, D.P. (1965). *The Negro family: The case for national action*. Washington, DC: US Department of Labor.

Mulatu, M.S. & Schooler, C. (2002). Causal connections between socio-economic status and health: Reciprocal effects and mediating mechanisms. *Journal of Health and Social Behavior*, 43, 22–41.

Mulkey, L.M., Crain, R.L. & Harrington, A.J.C. (1992). One-parent households and achievement: Economic and behavioral explanations of a small effect. *Sociology and Education*, 65, 48–65.

Murray, A. & Sandqvist, K. (1990). Father absence and children's achievement from age 13 to 21. *Scandinavian Journal of Educational Research*, 29, 89–102.

Murry, E. & Mosidi, R. (1993). Career development counseling for African Americans: An appraisal of the obstacles and intervention strategies. *Journal of Negro Education*, 62, 441–447.

Netemeyer, R.G., Burton, S. & Lichtenstein, D.R. (1995). Trait aspects of vanity: Measurement and relevance to consumer behavior. *Journal of Consumer Research*, 21, 612–626.

Ni Bhrolchain, M. (2001). 'Divorce effects' and causality in the social sciences. *European Sociological Review*, 17, 33–57.

Ni Bhrolchain, M., Chappell, R., Diamond, I. & Jameson, C. (2000). Parental divorce and outcomes for children: Evidence and interpretation. *European Sociological Review*, 16, 67–91.

NICHD Early Care Research Network (2000). Factors associated with fathers' caregiving activities and sensitivity with young children. *Journal of Family Psychology*, 14, 200–219.

Nord, C.D., Brimhall, D. & West, J. (1997). *Fathers' involvement in their children's schools*. Washington, DC: National Center for Educational Statistics.

O'Brien, M. & Shemilt, I. (2003). *Working fathers: Earning and caring*. London: Equal Opportunities Commission.

O'Connor, T.G., Caspi, A., DeFries, J.C. & Plomin, R. (2003). Genotype–environment interaction in children's adjustment to parental separation. *Journal of Child Psychology and Psychiatry*, 44, 849–856.

O'Connor, T.G., Dunn, J., Jenkins, J.M., Pickering, K. & Rasbash, J. (2001). Family settings and children's adjustment: Differential adjustment within and across families. *British Journal of Psychiatry*, 179, 110–115.

Office for National Statistics (1998). *Living in Britain: Results from the 1996 General Household Survey.* London: The Stationery Office.

Office for National Statistics (2003). *Social Trends.* London: The Stationery Office.

Ohannessian, C.M., Lerner, R.M., Lerner, J.V. & von Eye, A. (1998). Perceived parental acceptance and early adolescent self-competence. *American Journal of Orthopsychiatry*, 68, 621–629.

Olrick, J.T., Pianta, R.C., Marvin, R.S. (2002). Mothers' and fathers' responses to signals of children with cerebral palsy during feeding. *Journal of Developmental and Physical Disabilities*, 14, 1–17.

Olweus, D. (1993). *Bullying at school.* Cambridge: Blackwell.

Parke, R.D. (2000). Father involvement: A developmental psychological perspective. *Marriage and Family Review*, 29, 43–58.

Parke, R.D. & Beitel, A. (1988). Disappointment: When things go wrong in the transition to parenthood. *Marriage and Family Review*, 12, 221–265.

Pasley, K. & Brave, S.L. (2004). Measuring father involvement in divorced, nonresident fathers. In R.D. Day & M.E. Lamb (eds), *Conceptualizing and measuring father involvement* (pp. 217–240). Mahwah, NJ: Lawrence Erlbaum.

Patten, C.A., Gillin, C., Farkas, A.J., Gilpin, E.A., Berry, C.C. & Pierce, J.P. (1997). Depressive symptoms in California adolescents: Family structure and parental support. *Journal of Adolescent Health*, 20, 271–278.

Patterson, G.R., DeBaryshe, B.D. & Ramsey, E. (1989). A developmental perspective on antisocial behavior. *American Psychologist*, 44, 329–335.

Patton, G.C., Coffey, C., Posterino, M., Carlin, J.B. & Wolfe, R. (2001). Parental 'affectionless control' in adolescent depressive disorder. *Social Psychiatry and Psychiatric Epidemiology*, 36, 475–480.

Pedersen, W. (1994). Parental relations, mental health, and delinquency in adolescents. *Adolescence*, 29, 975–990.

Perloff, J.N. & Buckner, J.C. (1996). Fathers of children on welfare: Their impact on child well-being. *American Journal of Orthopsychiatry*, 66, 557–571.

Perry, D.G., Perry, L.C. & Boldizar, J.P. (1990). Learning of aggression. In M. Lewis & S.M. Miller (eds), *Handbook of Developmental Psychopathology.* New York: Plenum.

Peters, H.E. & Mullis, N. (1997). The role of family income and sources of income in adolescent achievement. In G.J. Duncan & J. Brooks-Gunn (eds), *Consequences of growing up poor* (pp. 340–382). New York: Russell Sage Foundation.

Peterson, R.R. & Gerson, K. (1992). Determinants of responsibility of child care arrangements among dual-earner couples. *Journal of Marriage and Family*, 54, 527–536.

Pfiffner, L.J., McBurnett, K. & Rathouz, P.J. (2001). Father absence and familial antisocial characteristics. *Journal of Abnormal Child Psychology*, 29, 357–367.

Phares, V. (1996). *Fathers and developmental psychopathology.* New York: John Wiley & Sons.

Phillips, E. & Garfinkel, I. (1993). Income growth among nonresident fathers: Evidence from Wisconsin. *Demography*, 30, 227–241.

Piacentini, J.C., Cohen, P. & Cohen, J. (1992). Combining discrepant diagnostic information from multiple sources: Are complex algorithms better than simple ones? *Journal of Abnormal Child Psychology*, 20, 51–63.

Pleck, J.H. (1997). Paternal involvement: Levels, sources, and consequences. In M.E. Lamb (ed.), *The role of the father in child development* (pp. 66–103). New York: John Wiley & Sons.

Pleck, J.H. & Stueve, J.L. (2001). Time and paternal involvement. In K. Daly (ed.), *Minding the time in family experience: Emerging perspectives and issues*. Stamford: JAI Press.

Plomin, R., Asbury, K. & Dunn, J. (2001). Why are children in the same family so different? Nonshared environment a decade later. *Canadian Journal of Psychiatry*, 46, 225–233.

Plomin, R. & Bergeman, C.S. (1991). The nature of nurture: Genetic influence on 'environmental' measures. *Behavioral and Brain Sciences*, 14, 373–427.

Plotnick, R.D., Garfinkel, I., McLanahan, S.S. & Ku, I.H. (2004). Better child support enforcement: Can it reduce teenage premarital childbearing? *Journal of Family Issues*, 25, 634–657.

Polatnik, M.R. (2000). Working parents. *National Forum*, 80, 1–4.

Pollard, E.L. & Lee, P.D. (2003). Child well-being: A systematic review of the literature. *Social Indicators Research*, 61, 59–78.

Pong, S.L., Dronkers, J. & Hampden-Thompson, G. (2004). Family policies and children's school achievement in single- versus two-parent families. *Journal of Marriage and Family*, 65, 681–699.

Pong, S.L. & Ju, D.-B. (2000). The effects of change in family structure and income on dropping out of middle and high school. *Journal of Family Issues*, 21, 147–169.

Popenoe, F. (1996). *Life without father: Compelling new evidence that fatherhood and marriage are indispensable for the good of children and society*. New York: Martin Kessler Books.

Power, C., Manor, O. & Matthews, S. (1999). The duration and timing of exposure: Effects of socio-economic environment on adult health. *American Journal of Public Health*, 89, 1059–1065.

Power, C., Matthews, S. & Manor, O. (1998). Inequalities in self-rated health: Explanations from different stages in life. *The Lancet*, 351, 1009–1014.

Previti, D. & Amato, P.R. (2003). Why stay married? Rewards, barriers, and marital stability. *Journal of Marriage and Family*, 65, 561–573.

Pringle, D.G. & Walsh, J. (1999). Poor people, poor places: An introduction. In D.G. Pringle, J. Walsh & M. Hennessy (eds), *Poor people, poor places: A geography of poverty and deprivation in Ireland*. Dublin: Oak Tree Press.

Procidano, M.E. & Heller, K. (1983). Measures of perceived social support from friends and from family: Three validation studies. *American Journal of Community Psychology*, 11, 1–24.

Pulkkinen, L., Nygren, H. & Kokko, K. (2002). Successful development: Childhood antecedents of adaptive psychosocial functioning in adulthood. *Journal of Adult Development*, 9, 251–265.

Quadagno, J. (1994). *The color of welfare: How racism undermined the war on poverty*. New York: Oxford University Press.

Quigley, J.M., Raphael, S. & Smolensky, E. (2001). Homeless in America, homeless in California. *Review of Economics and Statistics*, 83, 37–51.

Radford, L., Hester, M., Humphries, J. & Woodfield, K.-S. (1997). For the sake of the children: The law, domestic violence and child contact in England. *Women's Studies International Forum*, 20, 471–482.

Radin, N. (1976). The role of the father in cognitive, academic, and intellectual development. In M.E. Lamb (ed.), *The role of the father in child development* (pp. 237–276). New York: John Wiley & Sons.

Radin, N. (1981). The role of the father in cognitive, academic, and intellectual development. In M.E. Lamb (ed.), *The role of the father in child development* (pp. 379–427). New York: John Wiley & Sons.

Radin, N. (1982). *Paternal Involvement in Child Care Index*. Ann Arbor, MI: University of Michigan School of Social Work.

Radin, N., Williams, E. & Coggins, K. (1994). Paternal involvement in childbearing and the school performance of native American children: An exploratory study. *Family Perspectives*, 27, 375–391.

Ram, B. & Hou, F. (2003). Changes in family structure and child outcomes: Roles of economic and familial resources. *Policy Studies Journal*, 31, 309–330.

Rangarajan, A. & Gleason, P. (1998). Young unwed fathers of AFDC children: Do they provide support? *Demography*, 35, 175–186.

Reiss, D., Hetherington, M., Plomin, R., Howe, G.W., Simmens, S.J., Henderson, S.H., O'Connor, T.J., Bussell, D.A., Anderson, E.R. & Law, T. (1995). Genetic questions for environmental studies: Differential parenting and psychopathology in adolescence. *Archives of General Psychiatry*, 52, 925–936.

Renk, K., Roberts, R., Roddenberry, A., Luick, M., Hillhouse, S., Meehan, C., Oliveros, A. & Phares, V. (2003). Mothers, fathers, gender role, and time parents spend with children. *Sex Roles*, 48, 305–315.

Resnick, M.D., Bearman, P.S., Blum, R.W., Bauman, K.E., Harris, K.M., Jones, J., Tabor, J., Beuhring, T., Sieving, R.E. Shew, M., Ireland, M., Bearinger, L.H. & Udry, J.R. (1998). Protecting adolescents from harm: Findings from the National Longitudinal Study on Adolescent Health. In R.E. Muuss & H.D. Porton (eds), *Adolescent behavior and society: A book of readings* (pp. 376–395). New York: McGraw-Hill.

Reynolds, A.J. (1992). Comparing measures of parent involvement and their effects on academic achievement. *Early Childhood Research Quarterly*, 7, 441–462.

Rhee, S.H. & Waldman, I.D. (2002). Genetic and environmental influences on antisocial behavior: A meta-analysis of twin and adoption studies. *Psychological Bulletin*, 128, 490–529.

Rhein, L.M., Ginsburg, K.R., Schwarz, D.F., Pinto-Martin, K.A., Zhao, H., Morgan, A.P. & Slap, G.B. (1997). Teen father participation in child rearing: Family perspectives. *Journal of Adolescent Health*, 21, 244–252.

Richins, M.L. (1987). Media, materialism, and human happiness. *Advances in Consumer Research*, 11, 352–356.

Richins, M.L. & Dawson, S. (1992). A consumer values orientation for materialism and its measurement: Scale development and validation. *Journal of Consumer Research*, 19, 303–316.

Rigby, K. & Cox, I. (1996). The contribution of bullying at school and low self-esteem to acts of delinquency among Australian teenagers. *Personality and Individual Differences*, 21, 609–612.

Rindfleisch, A., Burroughs, J.E. & Denton, F. (1997). Family structure, materialism and compulsive consumption. *Journal of Consumer Research*, 23, 312–325.

Ringbäck Weitoft, G., Burström, B. & Rosén, M. (2004). Premature mortality among lone fathers and childless men. *Social Science and Medicine*, 59, 1449–1459.

Risch, S.C., Jodl, K.M. & Eccles, J.S. (2004). Role of the father–adolescent relationship in shaping adolescents' attitudes toward divorce. *Journal of Marriage and Family*, 66, 46–58.

Ritsher, J.E.B., Warner, V., Johnson, J.G. & Dohrenwend, B.P. (2001). Inter-generational longitudinal study of social class and depression: A test of social causation and social selection models. *British Journal of Psychiatry*, 178 (Suppl. 40), S84–90.

Roberts, G.C., Block, J.H. & Block, J. (1984). Continuity and change in parents' child-rearing practices. *Child Development*, 55, 586–597.

Rodgers, B. (1991). Socio-economic status, employment and neurosis. *Social Psychiatry and Psychiatric Epidemiology*, 26, 104–114.

Rodgers, K.B. & Rose, H.A. (2002). Risk and resiliency factors among adolescents who experience marital transitions. *Journal of Marriage and Family*, 64, 1024–1037.

Roisman, G.I., Madsen, S.D., Hennighausen, K.H., Sroufe, L.A. & Collins, W.A. (2001). The coherence of dyadic behavior across parent–child and romantic relationships as mediated by the internalized representation of experience. *Attachment and Human Development*, 3, 156–172.

Rönkä, A. & Pulkkinen, L. (1995). Accumulation of problems in social functioning in young adulthood: A developmental approach. *Journal of Personality and Social Psychology*, 69, 381–391.

Rosenberg, M. (1965). *Society and the adolescent self-image*. Princeton: Princeton University Press.

Ross, C.E. & Broh, B.A. (2000). The role of self-esteem and the sense of personal control in the academic achievement process. *Sociology of Education*, 73, 270–284.

Ross, C.E. & van Willigen, M. (1996). Gender, parenthood, and anger. *Journal of Marriage and Family*, 58, 572–584.

Rossi, P.H. (1989). *Down and out in America: the origins of homelessness*. Chicago: University of Chicago Press.

Rowe, M.L., Cocker, D. & Pan, B.A. (2004). A comparison of fathers' and mothers' talk to toddlers in low-income families. *Social Development*, 13, 278–291.

Russell, A. & Saebel, J. (1997). Mother–son, mother–daughter, father–son, and father–daughter: Are they distinct relationships? *Developmental Review*, 17, 111–147.

Rutter, M.J., Tizard, J. & Whitmore, K. (1970). *Education, health and behaviour*. London: Longman.

Sabatelli, R.M. & Bartle-Haring, S. (2003). Family-of-origin experiences and adjustment in married couples. *Journal of Marriage and Family*, 65, 159–169.

Sabatini, L. & Leaper, C. (2004). The relation between mothers' and fathers' parenting styles and their division of labor in the home: Young adults' retrospective reports. *Sex Roles*, 50, 217–225.

Sadowski, H., Ugarte, I., Kolvin, C., Kaplan, C. & Barnes, J. (1999). Early life family disadvantages and major depression in adulthood. *British Journal of Psychiatry*, 174, 112–120.

Sampson, R.J., Morenoff, J.D. & Gannon-Rowley, T. (2002). Assessing 'neighborhood effects': Social processes and new directions in research. *Annual Review of Sociology*, 28, 443–478.

Sandberg, J.F. & Hofferth, S.L. (2001). Changes in children's time with parents: United States, 1981–1997. *Demography*, 38, 423–436.

Sandefur, G.D. & Wells, T. (1999). Does family structure really influence educational attainment? *Social Science Research*, 28, 331–357.

Sanderson, S. & Thompson, V.L.S. (2002). Factors associated with perceived paternal involvement in childrearing. *Sex Roles*, 46, 99–111.

Sanford, M., Offord, D., McLeod, K., Boyle, M., Byrne, C. & Hall, B. (1994). Pathways into the work force: Antecedents of school and work force status. *Journal of the American Academy of Child and Adolescent Psychiatry*, 33, 1036–1046.

Sangster, R.L. & Reynolds, R.W. (1996). A test of Inglehart's socialization hypothesis for the acquisition of materialist/postmaterialist values: The influence of childhood poverty on adult values. *Political Psychology*, 17, 253–269.

Santos, P.J. & Coimbra, J.L. (2000). Psychological separation and dimensions of career indecision in secondary school students. *Journal of Vocational Behavior*, 56, 346–362.

Scarr, S. (1997). Why child care has little impact on most children's development. *Current Directions in Psychological Science*, 6, 143–148.

Schmitt-Rodermund, E. & Vondracek, F.W. (1999). Breadth of interests, exploration, and identity development in adolescence. *Journal of Vocational Behavior*, 55, 298–317.

Schneiders, J., Drukker, M., van der Ende, J., Verhulst, F.C., van Os, J. & Nicolson, N.A. (2003). Neighbourhood socioeconomic disadvantage and behavioural problems from late childhood into early adolescence. *Journal of Epidemiology and Community Health*, 57, 699–703.

Schoon, I., Bynner, J., Joshi, H., Parsons, S., Wiggins, R.D. & Sacker, A. (2002). The influence of context, timing, and duration of risk experiences for the passage from childhood to midadulthood. *Child Development*, 73, 1486–1504.

Schoon, I., Parsons, S. & Sacker, A. (2004). Socioeconomic adversity, educational resilience, and subsequent levels of adult adaptation. *Journal of Adolescent Research*, 19, 383–404.

Schoon, I., Sacker, A. & Bartley, M. (2003). Socio-economic adversity and psychosocial adjustment: A developmental-contextual perspective. *Social Science and Medicine*, 57, 1001–1015.

Schoppe-Sullivan, S.J., Mangelsdorf, S.C., Frosch, C.A. & McHale, J.L. (2004). Associations between coparenting and marital behavior from infancy to the preschool years. *Journal of Family Psychology*, 18, 194–207.

Schroeder, J.E. & Dugal, S.S. (1995). Psychological correlates of the materialism construct. *Journal of Social Behavior and Personality*, 10, 243–253.

Scoon-Rogers, L. (1999). *Child support for custodial mothers and fathers: 1995*. Current Population Reports P66-196. Washington, DC: US Bureau of the Census.

Scott, S. (1998). Aggressive behaviour in childhood. *British Medical Journal*, 316, 202–206.

Seginer, R. & Mahajna, S. (2004). How the future orientation of traditional Israeli Palestinian girls links beliefs about women's roles and academic achievement. *Psychology of Women Quarterly*, 28, 122–135.

Seltzer, J.A. (1991). Relationship between fathers and children who live apart: The father's role after separation. *Journal of Marriage and Family*, 53, 79–101.

Seltzer, J.A. (1994). Consequences of marital dissolution for children. *Annual Review of Sociology*, 20, 235–266.

Sheeber, L., Hops, H., Andrews, J., Alpert, T. & Davis, B. (1998). Interactional processes in families with depressed and non-depressed adolescents: Reinforcement of depressive behavior. *Behaviour Research and Therapy*, 36, 417–427.

Sheeber, L.B. & Johnson, J.H. (1992). Child temperament, maternal adjustment, and changes in family lifestyle. *American Journal of Orthopsychiatry*, 62, 178–185.

Shek, D.T.L. (1999). Parenting characteristics and adolescent psychological well-being: A longitudinal study in Chinese context. *Genetic, Social and General Psychology Monographs*, 125, 27–45.

Shepherd, P. (1993). Appendix I: Analysis of response bias. In E. Ferri (ed.), *Life at 33: The fifth follow-up of the National Child Development Study* (pp. 184–188). London: National Children's Bureau.

Sidanius, J. & Pena, Y. (2003). The gendered nature of family structure and group-based anti-egalitarianism: A cross-national analysis. *Journal of Social Psychology*, 143, 243–251.

Silbereisen, R.K., Robins, L. & Rutter, M. (1995). Secular trends in substance use: Concepts and data on the impact of social change on alcohol and drug abuse. In M. Rutter & D.J. Smith (eds), *Psychosocial disorders in young people: Time trends and their causes* (pp. 490–543). Chichester: John Wiley & Sons.

Silberg, J., Rutter, M., Meyer, J., Maes, H., Hewitt, J., Simonoff, E., Pickles, A., Loeber, R. & Eaves, L. (1996). Genetic and environmental influences on the covariation between hyperactivity and conduct problems in juvenile twins. *Journal of Child Psychology and Psychiatry*, 37, 803–816.

Silver, B.D. & Dowley, K.M. (2000). Measuring political culture in multiethnic societies: Reaggregating the world values survey. *Comparative Political Studies*, 33, 517–550.

Silverstein, L.B. & Auerbach, C.F. (1999). Deconstructing the essential father. *American Psychologist*, 54, 397–407.

Simmerman, S., Blacher, J. & Baker, B.L. (2001). Fathers' and mothers' perceptions of father involvement in families with young children with a disability. *Journal of Intellectual and Developmental Disability*, 25, 325–338.

Simons, R.L., Lin, K.H., Gordon, L.C., Brody, G.H., Murry, V. & Conger, R.D. (2002). Community differences in the association between parenting practices and child conduct problems. *Journal of Marriage and Family*, 64, 331–345.

Simons, R.L., Lin, K.H., Gordon, L.C., Conger, R.D. & Lorenz, F.O. (1999). Explaining the higher incidence of adjustment problems among children of divorce compared with those in two-parent families. *Journal of Marriage and Family*, 61, 1020–1033.

Simons, R.L., Whitbeck, L.B., Beaman, J. & Conger, R.D. (1994). The impact of mothers' parenting, involvement by non-residential fathers, and parental conflict on the adjustment of adolescent children. *Journal of Marriage and Family*, 56, 356–374.

Sloper, P. (1996). Needs and responses of parents following the diagnosis of childhood cancer. *Child: Care, Health and Development*, 22, 187–202.

Smith, C.A. & Farrington, D.P. (2004). Continuities in antisocial behavior and parenting across three generations. *Journal of Child Psychology and Psychiatry*, 45, 230–247.

Smith, D.J. (1995). Youth crime and conduct disorders: Trends, patterns, and causal explanations. In M. Rutter & D.J. Smith (eds), *Psychosocial disorders in young people: Time trends and their causes* (pp. 389–489). Chichester: John Wiley & Sons.

Smith, P.K. (2000). Bullying and harassment in schools and the rights of children. *Children and Society*, 14, 294–303.

Snarey, J. (1993). *How fathers care for the next generation: A four-decade study*. Cambridge, MA: Harvard University Press.

Statistics of Education (1998). *Schools in England*. Department for Education and Employment, London: The Stationery Office.

Steelman, L.C., Powell, B., Werum, R. & Carter, S. (2002). Reconsidering the effects of sibling configuration: Recent advances and challenges. *Annual Review of Sociology*, 28, 243–269.

Steinberg, L., Mounts, N.S., Lamborn, S.D. & Dornbusch, S.M. (1991). Authoritative parenting and adolescent adjustment across varied ecological niches. *Journal of Research on Adolescence*, 1, 19–36.

Stewart, A., Copeland, A., Chester, N., Malley, J. & Barenbaum, N. (1997). *Separating together: How divorce transforms families*. New York: Guilford.

Stewart, S.D. (2003). Nonresident parenting and adolescent adjustment: The quality of nonresident father–child interaction. *Journal of Family Issues*, 24, 217–244.

Stocker, C.M. (1995). Differences in mothers' and fathers' relationships with siblings: Links with children's behavior problems. *Development and Psychopathology*, 7, 499–513.

Stocker, C.M., Richmond, M.K., Low, S.M., Alexander, E.K. & Elias, N.M. (2003). Marital conflict and children's adjustment: Parental hostility and children's interpretations as mediators. *Social Development*, 12, 149–161.

Stocker, C.M. & Youngblade, L. (1999). Marital conflict and parental hostility: Links with children's sibling and peer relationships. *Journal of Family Psychology*, 13, 598–609.

Sturgess, W., Dunn, J. & Davies, L. (2001). Young children's perceptions of their relationships with family members: Links with family setting, friendships, and adjustment. *International Journal of Behavioral Development*, 25, 521–529.

Sun, Y.M. & Li, Y.Z. (2001). Marital disruption, parental investment, and children's academic achievement: A prospective analysis. *Journal of Family Issues*, 22, 27–62.

Sweeting, H. & West, P. (1995). Family life and health in adolescence: A role for culture in the health inequalities debate? *Social Science and Medicine*, 40, 163–175.

Swinford, S.P., DeMaris, A., Cernkovich, S.A. & Giordano, P.C. (2000). Harsh physical discipline in childhood and violence in later romantic involvements: The mediating role of problem behaviors. *Journal of Marriage and Family*, 62, 508–519.

Tamrouti-Makkink, I.D., Dubas, J.S., Gerris, J.R.M. & Aken, M.A.G. (in press). The relation between the absolute level of parenting and differential parental treatment with adolescent siblings' adjustment. *Journal of Child Psychology and Psychiatry*.

Taylor, J., McGue, M. & Iacono, W.G. (2000). Sex differences, assortative mating, and cultural transmission effects on adolescent delinquency: A twin family study. *Journal of Child Psychology and Psychiatry*, 41, 433–440.

Teachman, J. (2003). Childhood living arrangements and the formation of coresidential unions. *Journal of Marriage and Family*, 65, 507–524.

Teachman, J.D. (2004). The childhood living arrangements of children and the characteristics of their marriages. *Journal of Family Issues*, 25, 86–111.

Thomas, G., Farrell, M.P. & Barnes, G.M. (1996). The effects of single-mother families and nonresident fathers on delinquency and substance abuse in black and white adolescents. *Journal of Marriage and Family*, 58, 884–894.

Townsend, N. (2002). Cultural contexts of father involvement. In C.S. Tamis-LeMonda & N. Cabrera (eds), *Handbook of father involvement: Multidisciplinary perspectives* (pp. 249–277). Mahwah, NJ: Lawrence Erlbaum.

Tulisalo, U.K. & Aro, H.M. (2000). Paternal remarriage as a modifier of proneness to depression in young adulthood. *Journal of Affective Disorders*, 57, 179–184.

Turkheimer, E. & Waldron, M. (2000). Nonshared environment: A methodological and quantitative review. *Psychological Bulletin*, 126, 78–108.

Turner, C.M. & Barrett, P.M. (1998). Adolescent adjustment to perceived marital conflict. *Journal of Child and Family Studies*, 7, 499–513.

Uhlendorff, H. (2004). After the Wall: Parental attitudes to child rearing in East and West Germany. *International Journal of Behavioral Development*, 28, 71–82.

United Nations (2000). *The world's women 2000: Trends and statistics*. New York: United Nations.

Updegraff, K.A., McHale, S.M. & Crouter, A.C. (1996). Gender roles in marriage: What do they mean for girls' and boys' school achievement? *Journal of Youth and Adolescence*, 25, 73–88.

Updegraff, K.A., McHale, S.M., Crouter, A.C. & Kupanoff, K. (2001). Parents' involvement in adolescents' peer relationships: A comparison of mothers' and fathers' roles. *Journal of Marriage and Family*, 63, 655–668.

US Bureau of the Census (1998). *Statistical abstract of the United States 1998*. Washington, DC: US Government Printing Office.

Van der Broucke, S., Vandereycken, W. & Vertommen, H. (1995). Marital intimacy: Conceptualization and assessment. *Clinical Psychology Review*, 15, 217–233.

Van Egeren, L.A. (2003). Prebirth predictors of coparenting experiences in early infancy. *Infant Mental Health Journal*, 24, 278–295.

van de Mheen, H., Stronks, K., Schrijvers, C.T.M. & Mackenbach, J.P. (1999). The influence of adult ill health on occupational class mobility and mobility out of and into employment in The Netherlands. *Social Science and Medicine*, 49, 509–518.

Ventura, S.J. & Bachrach, C.A. (2000). *Nonmarital childbearing in the United States, 1940–99. National Vital Statistics Report, 48(16)*. Hyattsville, MD: National Center for Health Statistics.

Vonk, M. (2004). One, two or three parents? Lesbian co-mothers and a known donor with 'family life' under Dutch law. *International Journal of Law, Policy and the Family*, 18, 103–117.

Walby, S. (1997). *Gender transformations*. London and New York: Routledge.

Walker, J. (2003). Radiating messages: An international perspective. *Family Relations*, 52, 406–417.

Wardle, J., Robb, K. & Johnson, F. (2002). Assessing socioeconomic status in adolescents: The validity of a home affluence scale. *Journal of Epidemiology and Community Health*, 56, 595–599.

Watson, G.S. & Gross, A.M. (2000). Familial determinants. In M. Hersen & R.T. Ammerman (eds), *Advanced abnormal child psychology* (pp. 81–99). Mahwah, NJ: Lawrence Erlbaum.

Waynforth, D. (2002). Evolutionary theory and reproductive responses to father absence: Implications of kin selection and the reproductive returns to mating and parenting effort. In C.S. Tamis-LeMonda & N. Cabrera (eds), *Handbook of father involvement: Multidisciplinary perspectives* (pp. 337–357). Mahwah, NJ: Lawrence Erlbaum.

Webster, P., Orbuch, T. & House, J. (1995). Effects of childhood family background on adult marital quality and perceived stability. *American Journal of Sociology*, 101, 404–432.

Weissman, M. & Jensen, P. (2002). What research suggests for depressed women with children. *Journal of Clinical Psychiatry*, 63, 641–647.

Welsh, E., Buchanan, A., Flouri, E. & Lewis, J. (2004). *'Involved' fathering and child well-being: Fathers' involvement with secondary school age children.* London: National Children's Bureau.

Wentzel, K.R. (1994). Family functioning and academic achievement in middle school: A socio-emotional perspective. *Journal of Early Adolescence*, 14, 268–291.

White, L.K. & Booth, A. (1991). Divorce over the life course: The role of marital happiness. *Journal of Family Issues*, 12, 5–12.

White, L. & Gilbreth, J. (2001). When children have two fathers: Effects of relationships with stepfathers and noncustodial fathers on adolescent outcomes. *Journal of Marriage and Family*, 63, 155–167.

Whitehouse, G. (2002). Parenthood and pay in Australia and the UK: Evidence from workplace surveys. *Journal of Sociology*, 38, 381–397.

Whiteside, M.F. & Becker, B.J. (2000). Parental factors and the young child's post divorce adjustment: A meta-analysis with implications for parenting arrangements. *Journal of Family Psychology*, 14, 5–26.

Whitney, I. & Smith, P.K. (1993). A survey of the nature and extent of bullying in junior middle and secondary-schools. *Educational Research*, 35, 3–25.

Wiesner, M., Vondracek, F. W., Capaldi, D.M. & Porfeli, E. (2003). Childhood and adolescent predictors of early adult career pathways. *Journal of Vocational Behavior*, 63, 305–328.

Wigfield, A. & Eccles, J.S. (2000). Expectancy-value theory of achievement motivation. *Contemporary Educational Psychology*, 25, 68–81.

Wiggins, R.D. & Bynner, J. (1993). Social attitudes. In E. Ferri (ed.), *Life at 33: The fifth follow-up of the National Child Development Study* (pp. 162–183). London: National Children's Bureau.

Williams, E. & Radin, N. (1999). Effect of father participation in child rearing: Twenty-year follow-up. *American Journal of Orthopsychiatry*, 69, 328–336.

Wilson, W.J. (1987). *The truly disadvantaged*. Chicago: University of Chicago Press.

Wolfinger, N.H. (2003). Parental divorce and offspring marriage: Early or late? *Social Forces*, 82, 337–353.

Wolke, D., Woods, S., Bloomfield, L. & Karstadt, L. (2000). The association between direct and relational bullying and behaviour problems among primary school children. *Journal of Child Psychology and Psychiatry*, 41, 989–1002.

Woodward, L.J. & Fergusson, D.M. (2000). Childhood peer relationship problems and later risks of educational under-achievement and unemployment. *Journal of Child Psychology and Psychiatry*, 41, 191–201.

World Health Organization (2000). *Violence against women*. Geneva: WHO.

Wu, P., Robinson, C.C., Yang, C., Hart, C.H., Olsen, S.F., Porter, C.L., Jin, S., Wo, J. & Wu, X. (2002). Similarities and differences in mothers' parenting of preschoolers in China and the United States. *International Journal of Behavioral Development*, 26, 481–491.

Xie, H.L., Cairns, B.D. & Cairns, R.B. (2001). Predicting teen motherhood and teen fatherhood: Individual characteristics and peer affiliations. *Social Development*, 10, 488–511.

Yeung, W.J., Sandberg, J.F., Davis-Kean, P.E. & Hofferth, S.L. (2003). Children's time with fathers in intact families. *Journal of Marriage and Family*, 63, 136–154.

Yongman, M.W., Kindlon, D. & Earls, F. (1995). Father involvement and cognitive/behavioral outcomes of preterm infants. *Journal of the American Academy of Child and Adolescent Psychiatry*, 34, 58–66.

Zimmermann, P. (2004). Attachment representations and characteristics of friendship relations during adolescence. *Journal of Experimental Child Psychology*, 88, 83–101.

INDEX